THE FAYRE FORMEZ OF THE PEARL POET

Medieval Texts and Studies
General Editor: John A. Alford

---

1. *The Soul's Address to the Body: The Worcester Fragments*
   Edited by Douglas Moffat
2. *A Concordance to Eddic Poetry*
   By Robert Kellogg
3. *An Annotated Bibliography of North American Doctoral Dissertations on Old English Language and Literature*
   By Philip Pulsiano
4. *Poema de Fernan Gonzalez*
   Edited by John Lihani
5. *John Gower. Mirour de l'Omme*
   Translated by William Burton Wilson
6. *The Teaching of Grammar in Late Medieval England*
   Cynthia Renée Bland
7. *The Latin Verses in the Confessio Amantis*
   Translated by Siân Echard and Claire Fanger
8. *Scorn for the World: Bernard of Cluny's De Contemptu Mundi*
   Translated by Ronald E. Pepin
9. *The Chester Mystery Cycle*
   Edited by David Mills
10. *Silence: A Thirteenth-Century French Romance*
    Translated by Sarah Roche-Mahdi
11. *Popular and Practical Science of Medieval England*
    Edited by Lister M. Matheson
12. *Old English Poetry and the Genealogy of Events*
    By Richard J. Schrader
13. *Eustache Deschamps. L'Art de Dictier*
    Translated by Deborah Sinnreich-Levi
14. *Studies in Troilus: Chaucer's Text, Meter, and Diction*
    By Stephen A. Barney
15. *Suche Werkis to Werche: Essays on Piers Plowman in Honor of David C. Fowler*
    Edited by Míceál F. Vaughan
16. *Chaucer's Legend of Good Women*
    Edited by Janet Cowen and George Kane
17. *A Complete Concordance to the French Poetry and Prose of John Gower*
    By Robert F. Yeager and Mark West
18. *The Fayre Formez of the Pearl Poet*
    By Sandra Pierson Prior

The Fayre Formez of the Pearl Poet

SANDRA PIERSON PRIOR

MICHIGAN STATE UNIVERSITY PRESS
EAST LANSING

All Michigan State University Press books are produced on paper which meets the requirements of American National Standard of Information Sciences—Permanence of paper for printed materials ANSI Z39.48-1984.

Michigan State University Press
East Lansing, Michigan 48823-5202

03 02 01 00 99 98 97 96 1 2 3 4 5 6 7 8 9

ISBN 0-87013-460-4

A Colleagues Book

In memoriam

STEPHEN JOHN PRIOR

He gef vus to be His homly hyne
Ande precious perlez vnto His pay.

CONTENTS

ILLUSTRATIONS

ABBREVIATIONS

EETS	Early English Text Society
Lewis and Short	*A Latin Dictionary*, ed. Charlton T. Lewis and Charles Short
MED	*Middle English Dictionary*
OED	*Oxford English Dictionary*
PL	*Patrologiae Cursus Completus . . . Series Latina*, ed. J.-P. Migne

PREFACE

My study of the Pearl poet owes much to the mentors, colleagues, and students who have read this poet's works with me over the course of many years. In particular, I am indebted to Robert W. Hanning, who first introduced me to *Sir Gawain and the Green Knight* when I was just embarking on my graduate study, and who subsequently guided my dissertation on the Pearl poet. My study of the poet has taken many turns since then, but several of my best insights go back to Robert Hanning's inspiring teaching and critical acumen; for the present form of my work, I owe him as well, since he read individual chapters at various stages and gave valuable advice for improving them. To others, too, who have responded to various portions of the book, I am grateful: to Sarah Spence, who willingly read several chapters of a study largely outside her field and who urged me to take a less plodding approach to incorporating the iconography and art; to Robert M. Stein, who was especially helpful with the discussion of the lyric features of *Pearl* in chapter four and pointed me towards the most relevant troubadour lyrics; to Edward W. Tayler, who not only read and commented upon chapter three with much care, but who, for the last several years, has been an unfailing source of support in all my scholarly and professional endeavors; and finally, to George Economou, who read the entire manuscript and caught a number of errors and offered other suggestions for general improvement. Any mistakes in fact, lapses in interpretative judgment, or infelicities of rhetoric that still remain are solely my own doing.

I am grateful to the Department of English and Comparative Literature of Columbia University for support for the publication of this study. I am grateful also to the University of Chicago Press for permission to reprint portions of my article

"*Patience*—Beyond Apocalypse," which I have used in chapters two and three. The article appeared in *Modern Philology* 83 (1986): 337–48. (Copyright 1986 by the University of Chicago Press. All rights reserved. Reprinted by permission of the University of Chicago Press.) In addition, some portions of my discussion of all four poems appear in the study of the Pearl Poet that I wrote for the Twayne English Authors series (*The Pearl Poet Revisited* [New York, 1994]). Although the Twayne volume was written after this one, it appeared in print some months earlier, so, in fact, the borrowings on my own work have been from this study, not to it. In any event, the overlaps are few, since the Twayne book takes a different approach and is aimed at a different audience.

Finally, I wish to thank my children, Elizabeth, Michael, and Sarah, for their encouragement, support, and love. And, in gratitude for the love and joy of his short life, this book, like the dissertation that was its precursor, is dedicated to the memory of my son Stephen.

INTRODUCTION

Fayre Formez in a Medieval Christian Poet

IN THIS study I aim to define and describe the poetics of a major medieval poet, a poet who is a skilled and careful craftsman, who writes primarily about biblical subjects, and who explicitly concerns himself with the truth of Christianity and the problems of fulfilling God's will. Because I am primarily interested in the Pearl poet's art and its forms, I do not draw on social, political, or economic contexts, although there are places in his poetry when such might be valid, and there are aspects of his work that have been successfully explored in such terms.[1] I often make use of, or at least work in the context of, formalism and new criticism, critical approaches belonging to earlier generations of this century. More recent work, especially in narrative, has contributed somewhat to my study of the poet, although for the most part his own texts and sources have provided the inferences I make about his narrative art. The poet's sources are particularly important and revealing, since three of his four poems draw heavily on biblical texts, not just for their subjects and stories, but for their assumptions about history and narrative and about signs and patterns and how to interpret them.

[1]Nor do I subject the poetry to a feminist reading, which has proved fruitful for *Sir Gawain and the Green Knight* especially. For a good feminist reading of *Gawain*, see Sheila Fisher's article, better and certainly earlier than the recent one by Geraldine Heng. Muscatine's book, *Poetry and Crisis in the Age of Chaucer*, provides a cultural context, rather than the social, political, or economic backgrounds so favored by the new historicists, but this I feel is particularly appropriate with a poet as traditional, literary, and biblical as the Pearl poet. There are, of course, many articles, too numerous to name, that provide historical backgrounds for particular aspects or passages in the four poems. Some of these are more useful than others and will be mentioned where relevant in my discussion.

I do go outside the texts and their immediate sources to adduce evidence from the poet's culture, particularly from art and biblical exegesis, as well as from other medieval poetry, both English and continental vernacular. The Pearl poet is a learned poet, with an impressive grasp of biblical studies, but he is also a poet writing in a native vernacular tradition that is, at least fictionally, an oral tradition.[2] At the same time, he is a courtly poet, in the sense that he presumably writes for a courtly audience, for he often includes matters of interest to courts, like feasts and hunting, and he uses the literary forms and conventions found in poets, such as Chaucer and Gower, whom we know to be affiliated with, or writing for, courts. In *Sir Gawain and the Green Knight*, for example, the poet shows a detailed knowledge of such late medieval courtly pastimes as hunting and heraldry, practices that were still more French (or Norman) than English, as is clear from their Anglo-Norman vocabulary; and, in *Pearl*, on the other hand, the narrator employs the language and conventions of courtly love lyrics.[3] In both *Gawain* and *Pearl*, the poet exploits the respective genres of romance and

[2]The discussion of orality and oral formulaic verse does not really concern me here, since for one thing I think the dichotomy of oral versus literary a false one for the late Middle Ages (if it's ever valid). What I do think important are the places (in *Gawain* especially) when the poem assumes that there is a present audience listening to a reciting narrator. For a very smart discussion of this aspect of orality in the Ricardian poets, see Burrow (*Ricardian Poetry* 13–14). On the issue of oral formulaic, see, for example, Waldron, "Oral-Formulaic Technique"; and, for an argument against the oral character of even Old English verse, L. D. Benson, "Anglo-Saxon Formulaic Poetry." The question as to whether the practice of alliterative verse was revived in the fourteenth century or had developed in an uninterrupted line from Old English poetry is still debated; Turville-Petre takes the middle position (perhaps leaning more towards revival), that the late medieval alliterative poets "consciously—and by gradual stages—remodelled a written tradition of alliterative composition [including prose as well as verse] that led back only by rather tortuous routes to Old English verse" (17).

[3]I am using "courtly" as an adjective to modify "love poetry," not "courtly love" as a term for a certain kind of poetry. There is little point in my engaging here in the controversy over the efficacy of the term "courtly love." For the record, I take a middle-of-the-road position, somewhere between those who

dream vision and engages in the kinds of virtuosity found only in courtly poets in medieval England—demanding versification, sophisticated language games, and in general, a self-conscious, attention-getting craft.

These features of the Pearl poet's work are obvious and have been noted by most readers, although the questions raised when they are considered together are seldom addressed. In some respects, the poet's skills and his choices for his poetry—of subject, genre, and verse forms, even his dialect—fit together and are consistent with Muscatine's view of him as "a man for whom the perfection of his art has become a kind of defense against crisis" (69).[4] Yet, while the Pearl poet does seem aggressively, if only implicitly, old-fashioned, there is at least a potential contradiction in the several different traditions he works with: one, the learned and the biblical; another, the courtly and predominantly French or continental; and finally, the native and oral English tradition. Most especially there is an implicit contradiction between, on the one hand, the poet's impressive skill as a *makere* of poetry and his playfulness with language, and, on the

---

eschew the term "courtly love" altogether and those who follow C. S. Lewis in seeing a complete mindset and worldview that can be called "courtly love." Certainly, the best defense of the term is provided by the collection of essays in *In Pursuit of Perfection*. For my purposes, it is enough to grant the existence of courtly poetry—self-conscious, conventional, crafted poetry, in which the persona of the poet is strongly present, whether or not her or his actual identity is known. I further assume that this kind of poetry was created for an audience that was either literally a court or could be addressed as one, an audience familiar with the conventions of literature and art, an audience that presumably had wealth, position, and leisure, or that at least was close to those who did.

[4]This is essentially the conclusion of Muscatine's chapter on the Pearl poet. Compare Shoaf, for example, in his Preface to *The Poem as Green Girdle*, where he states that his study of *Gawain* combines two critical approaches, one "historical and unashamedly so" and the other, which "might be called 'poststructuralist' " (vii). Shoaf explains: "The two methods combined are a questioning of mind in its historical context" (viii). One of the quarrels I have with Shoaf's reading of *Gawain*, and with studies like his, stems from his failure to put the poem in its literary and manuscript context, as well as in its historical context. Without the former, I don't think we can begin to "question mind."

other hand, his looking to the Bible as virtually the only text and the only story worth reading or retelling.

It should by now be clear that in this study I work on the assumption that a real individual poet, with a single poetic consciousness, has carefully crafted these poems. This is an unpopular position today, since twentieth-century criticism more and more has moved away from a consideration of the author's role in producing a text, even for those texts that are connected to a known and named historical personage. It would appear even more tenuous to speak of a "poet" and his consciousness when there is no such creature, when in fact only through surmise and consensus can we attribute all four poems of the manuscript Cotton Nero A.x. to a single author.[5] However, the "poet" I am writing about is not the historical person who composed those texts (although I believe there was such a person), but the poetic consciousness that I firmly believe lies behind the corpus. We lack a name for this poet, but there are places in his poetry where we get some sense of an identity and a personality (albeit of a generalized, not individualized, type). This poetic personality is strongest in *Pearl*, and that is why I have chosen to use "Pearl poet" rather than "Gawain poet" as the title by which to refer to him—*Sir Gawain and the Green Knight* is the better known and more popular poem, but "pearl" has a

[5]The arguments for and against common authorship have produced many articles. A good summary in favor is Vantuono's "the case for common authorship." As for *St. Erkenwald*, a poem not in the same manuscript (nor even the same dialect), I concur in the scholarly consensus that this poem is not by the same poet who produced the texts in Cotton Nero A.x. (see L. D. Benson, "*St. Erkenwald*"; and Spearing, *Gawain-Poet* 33). There continue to be a few dissenters from the assumption of common authorship of even the four poems in Cotton Nero A.x., Tajima, for one. The contemporary critical challenge to the role of the author and the corollary focus on the reader's response is probably best summed up by Barthes: "the birth of the reader must be at the cost of the death of the author" (148).

more direct and specific connection to him as a poet than "Gawain" does.[6]

In fact, the recent discussion about the role of the author poses interesting problems when applied to medieval literature. The issue is surely more complicated than some would have it. While Barthes, for example, traces the concern with the "person" of the author to post-medieval culture (142–43), Minnis claims that the idea of a named author was important to the medieval reader. "To be 'authentic,'" in the Middle Ages, Minnis claims, "a saying or a piece of writing had to be the genuine production of a named *auctor*" (11).[7] In addition, a number of medieval authors, especially of vernacular courtly lyrics and romances, betray in their prologues and commentaries a concern with individual fame. Marie de France, Chrétien de Troyes, and Chaucer, for example, maintain a possessiveness towards their own poems that belies the often-held view that medieval poets were anonymous and their identities not a matter of concern for them or their readers.[8]

As recent work tends to show, the conflicting evidence, of anonymity versus self-promotion, is probably owing to the complexities of a manuscript culture, in which literacy and orality are mixed in ways we are only beginning to understand. This is then made even harder to sort out in England, where so

[6]Spearing points to the importance of the pearl imagery for the poet—not just in *Pearl*, but in *Gawain* and *Cleanness* as well (*Gawain-Poet* 33–34). It seems all the odder therefore that Spearing has opted not to use the label "the Pearl poet."

[7]Carruthers points out, however, that *auctores* were, "first of all, texts, not people" (190). She has since said that these texts could be represented as "embodied voices," like Vergil in the *Divine Comedy* (this in response to a question at a lecture she delivered at the Medieval Club, CUNY Graduate Center, October 4, 1991). One way to resolve Minnis and Carruthers (and maybe even Barthes) with my view of the Pearl poet would probably be to say I am studying the "embodied voice" of the Pearl poems.

[8]Marie de France's Prologue to the *Lais*, Chrétien de Troyes's closing lines to *Yvain*, and Chaucer's famous stanza, beginning "Go, litel bok," near the end of *Troilus*, are three of the better-known statements by medieval poets about their fame and their concern for the proper preservation and interpretation of their poems.

much that was written down was lost during the sixteenth century.[9] Although the issue of the poet's role and identity is thus more complex than we used to think, everything indicates that the Middle Ages had entered upon the process of understanding the term "*auctor*" in the sense of an individual authority and a self-conscious creator. In late medieval England we find but the beginning of the process, not to be completed for hundreds of years, of joining *auctor* as authority, with poet as *makere* or craftsman, with artist as *artifex* or creator.[10] In this, as in much else, the Pearl poet seems to lag behind his age, no doubt in part because he writes mostly about biblical subjects and is therefore often ceding the role of *auctor* to the writer of the original biblical text. Even so, his extreme care for the craft of his versification marks him as a *makere*, if not quite an *artifex*, and only partially an *auctor*. This concern with "making" poetry does distinguish my critical approach to the Pearl poet from much current criticism that focuses on the reader, since I will be looking closely at the poet's craft, specifically on how he fashions his poetry, and I will be assuming that his intentions and goals are relevant.

It may be that the Pearl poet's contemporaries knew very well who he was, or it may be that the poems in the British Library manuscript are not by one poet, but were placed together by some poet(s) or scribe(s) or reader(s), or, to use the current

[9]Some of the peculiarities of orality and authorship that are involved in the manuscript culture are discussed in the *New Philology* issue of *Speculum*, edited by Nichols (see esp. Fleischman 33–35 and Nichols 4–9). For earlier discussions, focusing on English literature, see R. Wilson and Chaytor.

[10]See Olson's discussion on *faiseur* in Deschamps and *makere* in Chaucer's poetry, where he discusses the " 'maker's' view of poetry" (721), in this case one that concentrates on forms that please, rather than on the subject matter. This is a view that Olson argues was not uncommon, although we still tend to think that medieval poets separated form and content in the mechanical way recommended by the rhetoricians, who "assert that 'poesis' is used to 'vestire' one's 'materiam' " (Olson 718). For the problems of humans adapting the role of *artifex*, see Prior, "Parodying Typology"; and Hanning, "Ye Have Begun a Parlous Playe"—however, both of these focus on the author/producer/director of plays, rather than on writers of narratives or lyrics, where the dangers of mimesis are less acute for human creators.

favorite term, compiler. Whatever the actual historical situation that produced the manuscript as we have it now (which it is unlikely we will ever know), the four poems, *Pearl*, *Cleanness*, *Patience*, and *Sir Gawain and the Green Knight*, are a reality as a group. It is precisely because the relevance of the actual historical identity of a poet has been questioned by recent critical theorists that we are free to stop worrying about who (and if) the Pearl poet was. Instead, we can concentrate on these four brilliant poems of Cotton Nero A.x. and come to them with the kinds of questions about them as poems and as a body of poetry that I feel we can better ask of a significant oeuvre, in this case within a single codex, than of a single text.[11] It is time we begin considering what these poems have in common as poems, what worldview and poetic forms they share, and what literary traditions they draw upon. A firm grasp of the poetics in these four works can enlarge and complicate our sense of English poetry, and I believe, since theirs was a society that did not banish poets, to understand more of medieval English poetry is to understand more of medieval English culture. My hope is that my study will help us answer two larger, more historical questions: What do the poems tell us about the culture, especially the courtly literary culture, of medieval England, more particularly of late fourteenth-century England in the country outside of London; and how is this poetic world like and how different from Chaucer's and Langland's?[12]

To define and describe the Pearl poet's art is then the project of this book. To do that I believe we should concentrate on what

[11]It has now been well over a decade since Davenport first called for us to examine the works of this poet in ways possible only if we assume single authorship and treat the four poems as a unified body of poetry (1).

[12]Admittedly these are slightly different questions (and may yield different answers) from the kinds of questions asked by recent scholars using a more "new historicist" approach. One of the problems with much of this group's work is that they often read poetry as though it were a set of historical documents—see, for example, Harwood's recent study of the gift of the girdle in *Gawain*, an essay which doesn't once consider the humor, irony, or style of the farcical bedroom scenes.

the poems tell us and to induce from them their poetics. Often we need to draw inferences when the poet is not explicit about the standards and goals of his art. I will begin, however, with an explicit statement from the opening lines of that much neglected poem, *Cleanness*, a passage that uses the phrase *fayre formez*, which I have adopted as the central term for this poet's poetics:

> Clannesse whoso kyndly cowþe comende
> And rekken vp alle þe resounȝ þat ho by riȝt askeȝ
> *Fayre formeȝ* myȝt he fynde in forering his speche,
> And in þe contrare kark and combraunce huge
> (For wonder wroth is þe Wyȝ þat wroȝt alle þinges
> Wyth þe frek þat in fylþe folȝes hym after),
> As renkeȝ of relygioun þat reden and syngen,
> And aprochen to hys presens, and presteȝ arn called,
> Thay teen vnto his temmple and temen to hym seluen;
> Reken, wyth reuerence, þay rechen his auter.
> Þay hondel þer his aune body and vsen hit boþe.
> If þay in clannes be clos, þay cleche gret mede,
> Bot if þay conterfete crafte, and cortaysye wont,
> As be honest vtwyth, and inwith all fylþeȝ,
> Þen ar þay synful hemself, and sulped altogeder,
> Loþe God and his gere, and hym to greme cachen.
> He is so clene in his courte, þe Kyng þat al weldeȝ,
> And honeste in his housholde, and hagherlych serued
> With angeleȝ enourled in alle þat is clene,
> Boþe wythinnne and wythouten, in wedeȝ ful bryȝt;
> And ȝif he nere scoymus and skyg, and non scaþe louied,
> Hit were a meruayl to much; hit moȝt not falle.
> (Vantuono ed., 1–16; emphasis and punctuation mine)[13]

[13]Although I usually (unless otherwise noted) cite from Andrew and Waldron's edition, I have used Vantuono here, mostly because I am adopting his retention of the manuscript's *forering* and not emending, as many do, to *forþering*. I think Vantuono is correct in translating *forering* as "fashioning" and

It is clear from the Prologue to *Cleanness* that *fayre formez* are tools for a writer or speaker, more precisely for a poet since this passage introduces a poem. Although *fayre formez* here is usually glossed as "examples," this is far too narrow a definition, and the kind of reductive reading that has so crippled our critical appreciation of this poet. The Middle English word for "examples" is not *formez*, but *ensamples* or *samples*, these latter words used by many writers, especially writers like Chaucer and the Pearl poet himself, when speaking of exemplary tales. In *Cleanness*, for example, the poet speaks of the prophet Daniel's use of "samples" to teach Nebuchadnezzar that "alle goudes com of God" (1326).

Formez, on the other hand, is a much bigger term than *samples*. The primary meanings of the Middle English *forme*, which are almost identical to those of the Latin *forma*, are: 1) "shape," "outline," "pattern," and 2) "image," "likeness" (*MED*). The term *forma* is particularly used by rhetoricians to refer to the rhetorical "form" or structure of a sermon or a letter, roughly equivalent to "outline" as we might use it in a modern rhetoric or composition text.[14] The Middle English word also seems to be used, as the Latin word certainly is, to mean "beauty" (*MED*; cf. Lewis and Short); the Pearl poet brings out this connotation with the adjective "fayre." *Formez* thus indicates poetic tools that are at once more structural, more conceptual,

---

seeing this as consistent with the poet's use of clothing imagery and symbolism in the Parable of the Wedding Feast (see esp. p. 289, note to line 3). As I have indicated, the punctuation is my own—adapted because I feel it yields a much sounder reading of this critical passage.

[14]See, for example, Alanus de Insulis who writes: "The form preaching [*forma predaecandis*] ought to take is this: let it be based on a text from Scripture . . ." (Miller 232); see Murphy's discussion of this treatise (303–10, esp. 307 and 310). Murphy's selection of texts also indicates that *formae* can be used in other ways: 1) in the smallest sense as "samples" (not "examples")—since that would be my understanding of the forty-five short paragraphs—called "*formae*"—provided by Bernold of Kaisersheim in his *Summa prosaici dictaminis* for use by clerics; and 2) in the largest sense of rhetorical form, as in the title to Albert of Morra's treatise on letter-writing: *Forma dictandi* (250).

more visual, and more aesthetic than *(en)samples*. *Fayre formez* are, in short, the narrative and structural patterns, along with the visual and verbal images, that the poet uses to *forere* his *speche*. Specifically, *fayre formez* then are assumed to be the poetic tools of choice; a poet setting about making a poem on a subject would naturally reach for *fayre formez*, if any were suited to his project.

Much of what the poet goes on to tell us about *fayre formez* is particular to the subject of *Cleanness*, but even so it has implications, I believe, for all of his poems. We learn, for example, that, although many *fayre formez* are available to a poet who chooses to praise *clanness*, they are not however ready at hand for a poet embarked on the *contraré*, that is, the condemning of uncleanness (this is the only possible reading here—obviously no Christian poet in his right mind would attempt to praise uncleanness or to condemn cleanness).[15] Condemning uncleanness is a "kark and a combraunce huge," because it involves dealing with the wrath of the Creator, the King who is surrounded by beauty, brightness, purity, and perfection—all definitions of *clanness* and included in the phrase "He is so clene in his courte." Praising the King, picturing his court in all its glory, is obviously a much less onerous task than condemning uncleanness and indeed is done at some length by the Pearl Maiden in *Pearl*. Moreover, that image of the King in his court, the *Maestas Domini* so popular in medieval art, stands behind all of the Pearl poet's work, along with other images of the celebration of God by his "homly hyne" (*Pearl* 1211), who look to be restored to his kingdom in the end.

Secondly, we learn that *fayre formez* are like the *formez* available

[15]Both Menner and Moorman assume that the difficulty lay in praising uncleanness, while Andrew and Waldron, as well as Anderson before them, believe the *contraré* that causes trouble is the denigration of cleanness. Vantuono thinks neither to be the case, but that "the poet means that *kark* and *combraunce* are to be found in themes about uncleanness" (p. 289, note to line 4). In this I am closest to Vantuono, for I am certain that it is precisely the task the Pearl poet does undertake in *Cleanness* that is a *kark*, although I would not use the term "themes."

to priests, for the extended simile introduced in line seven (and made clearer by my new punctuation) draws an analogy between poets and priests, and between liturgy and poetry.[16] A writer or poet can find *fayre formez* in discourse, as priests find them in the sacraments. Priests have the Word of God, the words of humanity celebrating God's kingdom, and the visual symbols of bread and wine, Christ's *aune body*, which can give them *gret mede* provided they use it worthily. Poetry is thus likened to liturgy, which involves words, song, movement, and visual images. This last is especially important, for, as critics of *Gawain and the Green Knight* have long recognized, the Pearl poet is a very visual poet, a master of *pointing*, that is, of tour-de-force, detailed descriptions.[17] The difference between poetry and liturgy is critical, however, since the latter is made up of divinely inspired words (mostly from the Bible) and divinely instituted sacraments, especially the eucharist, which is God's

[16]By separating lines 5 and 6 with parentheses (since I believe they form a parenthetical aside), I have tried to clarify the analogy the poet is making between the one who wishes to praise *clannesse* (the "whoso" of line 1 and "he" and "his" in line 3) and the "renkeȝ of relygioun" (7). Having established the analogy, the poet goes on to focus on his vehicle, the priests, as a way of indirectly commenting on his tenor, the poet. Other editors punctuate these lines in various ways. Andrew and Waldron, for example, put a period after the fourth line and begin a new sentence with "For wonder wroth . . ." and then place a dash after line six, so that the analogy to priests stands as an aside to the comment on the Creator's anger. I find this totally unacceptable, since it shifts the emphasis away from what I believe to be the dominant figure of the passage—the analogy between priests and poets. Although Vantuono's punctuation is not so drastic, his facing-page translation makes it clear that he too reads the "renkeȝ of relygioun" as examples of those who make the Creator angry (82–83).

[17]Burrow was the first critic to label this craft of visual description "pointing," taking the term from Chaucer and the Pearl poet (*Ricardian Poetry* 69–73). See Renoir, "Descriptive Techniques" and "Progressive Manifestation," for superb analyses of this aspect of the Pearl poet's craft. Hanning, "Red Herring," also examines the poet's uses and manipulations of description. For an important study of this aspect of the poet's art, one that draws on recent work with vision and perception, see Stanbury.

aune body, all of which constitute a reality and a presence not available to a poet.

Implicit in the passage from *Cleanness* is that the fairest are the holiest and the closest to God, for indeed the fairest *formez* are God's *gere*. Furthermore, as the poet's choice of subject matter in *Cleanness* suggests, God's *gere* includes not just the sacraments, but also the scriptures, for it is the Bible that provides the Pearl poet with the principal *formez* of his poetry.

It has been, of course, impossible to ignore the importance of the Bible as a source for this poet, but few have noticed that the Pearl poet's use of biblical material hardly stops with the adaptation of Old Testament narratives or with verse renderings of passages from the New. It is, in fact, from the Bible that the Pearl poet takes not just stories, but many of his poetic patterns and images. Moreover, even though certain of his poetic techniques are secular in origin—his rhetorical figures, for example, owe something to classical rhetoric (or the medieval version thereof), and his versification is decidedly medieval and English—the Pearl poet turns to the Bible and biblical exegesis for models of narrative structure. Indeed, medieval rhetoricians do not really discuss narrative patterns (they are primarily interested in description and in rhetorical structures and figures), but exegetes definitely do concern themselves with the pattern of the story of God and his people. This exegesis (like allegorization and other kinds of interpretation) begins in the Old Testament, where prophets explicate Israel's history and discuss its patterns, and it is from this biblical analysis that the Pearl poet draws his narrative patterns, which are primarily biblical. The poet's structures and narrative patterns either follow those of the Bible very closely, as in *Cleanness* and *Patience*, or are best read in the light of biblical narratives and their exegesis. Even the *formez* from courtly romances, dream poems, and lyric, which figure importantly in *Sir Gawain and the Green Knight* and *Pearl*, are, I believe, informed and influenced by those derived from the Bible, and, as such, they do not constitute an exception to the priority of biblical patterning.

Like the narrative patterns, the central images in the Pearl poet's works are also biblical, sometimes taken directly from the Bible and sometimes derived through the media of iconography and exegesis. Most of these images, both visual and verbal, are not just biblical, but more precisely apocalyptic. Drawn either directly from the Bible or from biblical iconography, they include images of judgment and ending, of separation, loss, and despair, and of joyous restoration and reunion—especially those of God in his court, or the Lamb with his followers, or the New Jerusalem, all images of the blessed enjoying the beatific vision. These images were unusually abundant at the time of the poet, owing to the prolific production of illustrated apocalyptic manuscripts during the centuries immediately preceding, in both England and France. Apocalyptic imagery also dominated church tympana in France and could be seen in stained glass programs and in the famous tapestry series of Angers.[18] That the popularity had not dimmed even by the end of the fourteenth century, when the Pearl poet was writing, is evident from the full illustration of St. John's Apocalypse in the East Window of York Minster, a window that can be dated fairly accurately to the first decade of the fifteenth century.[19]

The poet's fairest images are signs of God and his kingdom.

[18]For a complete edition reproducing the tapestry series at Angers, see Planchenault. The tapestry series, and similar stained glass series (such as the fifteenth-century window at York Minster), were part of the enormous number of artistic representations of John's Apocalypse that appeared in the late Middle Ages, primarily in England and France. Mâle argues that the iconographic development of the Apocalypse was essentially based on manuscript illustrations, which were in turn linked to the great interest in Apocalypse commentaries and their wide reproduction and dissemination after the eleventh century (*Religious Art* 5–8). For a general survey of the Apocalypse in art, see van der Meer; for a discussion that focuses on the Pearl poet's use of the Apocalypse, see Prior, "Poet of the Word" (esp. Chapter One).

[19]On the dating of the York window, see Harrison. York Minster, built on the site of a much earlier church, underwent several major stages of construction, staggered between 1220 and 1470. The second-to-last stage, the construction of the apse, was done in the latter half of the fourteenth century, with the glazing done at the same time or immediately after; Harrison quotes from BL Harley 6971, which details the duties and pay for John Thornton, "between the years 1405 and 1408," to work on the window (13).

The signs can point to Christ himself (as does the Lamb in *Pearl*), or to the joys of the otherworld (as does the New Jerusalem), or to the Last Days, during which God will demonstrate his might and establish his kingdom (which is what the images in *Cleanness* do). The signs can be explicit images, carefully pointed and fully developed visual pictures, as is the New Jerusalem, but they also can be primarily verbal, not visual, and implicit or only briefly alluded to—this is the way the signs of God and his kingdom generally work in *Patience*, where Jonah grouchily and ironically refers to that popular medieval image of God, the *Maestas Domini*, "Oure Syre [who] syttes . . . on sege so hyȝe, / In his glowande glorye" (93) and where the *heuen-ryche* is internalized as a quality.

Also predominantly apocalyptic is the basic narrative pattern that lies behind all four poems, but is clearest in *Cleanness*. This apocalyptic pattern is one of beginning at the end, then turning back to a beginning, and progressively working through until the end is reached again. Put more precisely, the structure consists of: first, as an introduction, a vision of the End; next the narrative, which begins at the beginning of the history of a society or even of the entire human race; and eventually a narrative that progresses through history towards the eschaton and thus towards, or back to, the reminder of the end that begins the text. Such a pattern is, like salvation history in general, eschatological and ostensibly linear. However, it uses the eschaton, not just for a conclusion, but for a focal point and an introduction, much like the apocalyptic scenes that greeted congregations at the entrance of churches or dominated the East or West wall of their interior, as in York.[20] This apocalyptic pattern thus has elements of repetitiveness and circularity, which un-

[20]Compare Kermode's theory that "[W]e project ourselves—a small, humble elect, perhaps—past the End, so as to see the structure whole, a thing we cannot do from our spot of time in the middle" (8). Kermode's fascinating and influential study, which I read only after first noting the Pearl poet's interest in the apocalyptic mode, has subsequently had a great effect on my reading of this poet. I would caution, however, that, as in so many other ways, what Kermode uses mostly figuratively, as even do Spenser and Shakespeare perhaps, the

dercut the presumed linearity of eschatological perspectives. Furthermore, because the promises included in the apocalyptic visions of life beyond this world are often thought of as a return to God and a restoration of his kingdom, the ultimate pattern of Providence, the one that takes in all of history from the beginning of time until its end, is a circular one. This narrative pattern I call the "pattern of conversion"; the fairest narrative *forme* in the Bible, it is alluded to in *Cleanness* and *Pearl*, exemplified in *Patience*, and I think stands behind the medieval genres of the dream vision and the romance, which the Pearl poet uses for his two most popular poems.

The basic pattern and variations of providential history can arguably be found underlying most or all of late medieval narrative, but they are exploited and made central in the Pearl poet's work in ways that do not characterize his contemporaries, Chaucer, or Gower, or even Langland.[21] The manuscript itself enables us to see this. First, the order of the poems in the manuscript (whether so because of the author, or a perceptive compiler) follows the basic pattern I outlined above. In the beginning we have a vision of the End (*Pearl*); next we proceed to stories from the beginning of history (the Genesis accounts of Adam, Noah, and Abraham in *Cleanness*); then we move on through later biblical history (Daniel in *Cleanness* and then Jonah in *Patience*); and finally we end with a fictional account of a "modern" Christian and his society (*Gawain*). Since *Pearl*, like *Gawain*, is in a medieval genre and concerns medieval charac-

medieval Christian poet tends to take much more literally. The predilection to literalize the most figurative of images and signs is a late medieval characteristic (some would say an annoyance, if not a vice) and is part, I believe, of the conviction that all *signa* and *res* in God's creation are part of a meaningful, coherent whole.

[21]Bloomfield argues quite convincingly in a book-length study that *Piers Plowman* is a "fourteenth century apocalypse." Granting Bloomfield's thesis, although I would quarrel with it in part, Langland does not really seem to be grappling with the implications and dangers of an apocalyptic mode or perspective in the self-conscious way that the Pearl poet does.

ters, at least for its narrative frame, *Sir Gawain and the Green Knight*'s place as last in the manuscript represents a return to the world and time and literary context of the first poem. Furthermore, within both of these poems, *Gawain* and *Pearl*, the poet stresses the particular genre's inherent circularity and potential pattern of return.

However, the circularity of *Pearl* and *Gawain* does not qualify them as conversion narratives. The dream vision and the romance are only partly *fayre formez*, for they are not genres of restoration and return, except potentially, and only in fallen human versions. The ironic and often humorous ambiguity surrounding Gawain's adventure and the sudden, heartbreaking end to the dreamer's dream in *Pearl* both emphasize how little the quests of these poems' two protagonists are like the ultimate return to God's kingdom promised in the pattern of providential history. In addition, within the manuscript as a whole, the return to the world and culture of the poet that comes when we move from *Cleanness* and *Patience* to *Sir Gawain and the Green Knight* is not really progress, but a falling off, since this return brings the poet and his audience back to a corrupt world where God's voice is no longer heard or followed. We are thus shown that the fairest *formez* are not humanity's, but God's, and are more available in sacrament and sacred history than in anything medieval poets can create.

The *heuen-ryche* of *Patience* and the *frelych feste* of *Cleanness*, which are, respectively, the promise of God's kingdom in the world to come and the eschatological banquet humanity hopes to enjoy in that kingdom, remain for the poet and his late medieval audience just that—promises. The full presence of God, known to the Old Testament patriarchs in his voice and words, and to the New Testament disciples in Jesus's earthly person, is apparently no longer available to God's people in this life, although in *Patience* the poet undertakes to internalize the *heuen-ryche*, so that it can be present now. To other medieval Christians, mystical or visionary experiences come close to this presence, at least for those Christians privileged to have them, but the Pearl poet's one record of a vision, *Pearl*, is, as the narrator repeatedly reminds us, decidedly secondhand—all taken from John's Apocalypse, and as John saw it, and with the words John used to describe it.

The closest the medieval Christian can come to finding God fully present, as the Pearl poet explicitly tells us at the end of *Pearl*, and as he implies in *Cleanness*, is in the eucharist. Otherwise, God is hard to find and harder to see and hear. The longing that comes from this absence is very like the desire described by Derrida and his followers. But there is an important exception. Although we might conclude, as deconstructionists usually do, that there is never anything but absence in our words, that there is no present voice since presence is a myth and writing comes before speaking, the Pearl poet clearly believes in that myth and in the primacy of voice.[22] Although he himself cannot know God's full, real presence, at least not in this world, the Pearl poet obviously writes under the assumption that some did once, and all could eventually. Interestingly enough, when Derrida (whose quarrel with logocentrism tends to concentrate on, or at least start from, Plato) directly addresses the issue of biblical texts, he focuses on apocalyptic writing. In "Of an Apocalyptic Tone recently adopted in Philosophy," Derrida points to the desire to predict and to unveil (using the first-person singular of the Greek—*apokalupto* [64]), which underlies apocalyptic writing. But most of the Bible is not apocalyptic. Most prophets are not apocalyptic seers—they do not *see* hidden things, but rather they *speak* God's words in God's voice.

As the Pearl poet traces in *Cleanness*, apocalyptic writing is a falling-off, from those better days when God did not use arcane written messages or symbolic dreams that require interpreta-

[22]See, for example, Schneidau (10–11) and Derrida (*Of Grammatology* 52–53), although one could give numerous other references, since so much of Derrida's work deals with the question of writing and speaking; as Barbara Johnson puts it, "Derrida's critique of Western metaphysics focuses on its privileging of the spoken word over the written word" (viii). In fact, the Pearl poet is just one more proof of this "privileging," although, at least in what I have read of Derrida, Plato (and Socrates) are the focus of his critique.

tion, but spoke "in comly comfort ful close and cortays wordez" as he does to Noah in *Cleanness* (512). It is after the diaspora, in that godless city of Babylon, that the Lord sends the Writing on the Wall, which can only be read and understood by Daniel. Except for this secret message, and the dreams God formerly sent to Nebuchadnezzar, the voice of the divine is absent in Babylon. Significantly, Belshazzar tries to communicate with "falce goddes" (1522), made of "stokkes and stones" (1523; cf. 1343), but, of course, these "gods" are "stille euermore — / Neuer steuen hem astel, so stoken is hor tonge" (1523–24). We, as twentieth-century readers, whether deconstructionists or not, may harbor our suspicions as to whether any god has ever been anything but "stille euermore," but, in order to appreciate the Pearl poet's work, we need to set aside that suspicion for a while. We need to enter into the fiction that God has been present, in voice for the faithful Israelites, and in person for Jesus's disciples, that he can be "present," at least in a non-indicative mode in the eucharist, and that he will be fully present in that *frelych feste* of the *heuen-ryche* to come. In the meantime, we have a secondhand vision, "so swete a sange," that may or may not be a "ueray and soth sermoun" (*Pearl* 19 and 1185), or "ferlyes on þis folde" (*Gawain* 23), magical wonders that are not from God but rather fairy tales of this world, and may even come from the devil.

The poet's variations in the patterns of sacred history are paralleled by his modifications of basic apocalyptic and eschatological images. Probably the most central, and also the most elusive, of these modifications is the poet's transformation of a word from a sign — often one with a basic visual image behind it, like the pearl — into a thing itself, a word endowed with its own reality. This aspect of the Pearl poet's art, in many ways his most modern feature (it has much in common with Renaissance wit and concords well with recent sign theory) though oddly enough the most neglected,[23] reflects the complex relationship

[23]It has, however, received some attention by critics of a decade or so ago. See, for example, Brewer's article on the word and concept "*cortaysye*" in all four

between divine signs that are verbal and those that are visual. While the complexity and sometimes the slipperiness of signs have most often been noted in the poet's secular words and terms, they can be found in biblical and iconographic images as well, in traditional signs that one would expect to be more certain in form and meaning than merely human creations.

To appreciate the Pearl poet's witty use of language, it is therefore useful (indeed I believe essential) to examine the way he uses biblical signs and images of the divine and particularly how he at once is attracted to the highly visual imagery of the Apocalypse and at the same time fully aware that, with the notable exception of Christ's earthly life and person, the divine is most fully present and realized in voice and words, not in visual images.

In every respect, the Pearl poet gives precedence to the *fayre formez* of the Bible and the sacraments over any human artistic creations, while for us as modern readers of poetry, and I suspect for his contemporaries as well, it is impossible to ignore the sheer brilliance of this poet's own craft. He never explicitly writes of himself as a poet (although I am certain the persona of the jeweller in *Pearl* points to him as an artist); he is clearly interested in the truth of Christianity and its sacred text (an interest which, despite Dante and Milton, we still tend to assume precludes art); and he has been damned with faint praise for his "verse homilies."[24] Yet all this in no way prevents his

---

poems; and also the final chapter, "The Poet and His Art," in Davenport's book, in which he draws attention to the "poet's combination, or his attempt at combination, of different levels of meaning" (195) and the poet's "liking for 'university wit' " (216). Very recently there has been some useful development and application of sign theory to medieval literature, most of it taking Augustine as a starting point. See, for example (to mention only a few among many): Nichols, (*Romanesque Signs*), Vance, and, for a focus on *Sir Gawain and the Green Knight*, Shoaf (*The Poem as Green Girdle*).

[24]"Verse homilies," or "literary homily" as Andrew and Waldron have it (17), is the term commonly applied to *Patience* and *Cleanness* by most critics. For extensive explications of the homiletic aspects of, respectively, *Cleanness* and *Patience*, see Means, and Vantuono ("Structure and Sources"). Some of the

being a very self-conscious, gifted and skilled, poetic genius. In a way not really possible in the modern world, the Pearl poet has taken from sacred texts and traditions some of its most central stories, its most sublime visions, and its most evocative signs, and both used them and transformed them—these, God's *fayre formez*, are recreated in the dazzling forms of a human artist's poetry, and while he himself would no doubt point to the inadequacy of his recreation, I hope in this study to help us see just how remarkable and nearly perfect is his very human art.

---

structural analyses of these and similar articles are helpful, and I have no doubt that the Pearl poet was influenced by the rhetorical treatises that set forth the structural patterns for sermons. But, to call these poems "sermons" is insulting to the poet's craft, implying as it does that a sermon has merely been transcribed into some kind of verse or even "ryme doggerel." Although certain critics have insisted, as Ordelle Hill puts it, that " '*Patience* is first of all a poem' " (quoted in Vantuono, "Structure and Sources," 401), the focus on the poems as homilies leads to a flat-footed and reductive kind of criticism, and even to some silly contradictions. Means, for example, opens his article by telling us that "the most obvious characteristic of the Middle English *Cleanness* is that it is a homily" (165) and then later admits that it does not begin the way a sermon does "doubtless because [it] is a poem rather than a sermon" (166).

ONE

The Lombe and *His Meyny Schene*: Signs of God in *Pearl* and the Apocalypse

IN THE Pearl poet's works the actual images of God Himself are rare—like the Bible, the poems of Cotton Nero A.x. avoid direct theophany, although *Pearl* and *Cleanness* offer images of the experience of theophany (not theophany itself) and promise the beatific vision as a reward awaiting us in the world beyond. On the other hand, images of God's kingdom, his *cort* or the *Lombe's meyny*, to use two of the Pearl poet's terms, are central to the poems *Pearl* and *Cleanness* and stand behind the assumptions in the other two, *Patience* and *Sir Gawain and the Green Knight*. Less frequent, but scarcely less important are the *contraré*, that is, the images of judgment, punishment, and cosmic catastrophe: flood, fire, dungeon, and axe, which historically are to precede the final establishment of the kingdom and our full enjoyment of it.

These visions and images of God and his Kingdom, of the End, of punishment and reward, of separation or reunion with God in *His cort*, as well as the human understanding and experience of those visions, are best understood in light of medieval apocalyptic tradition. There have been a number of varying (and often conflicting) definitions of "apocalyptic" by scholars, but for our purposes John's text and the iconography and commentary it inspired serve as the best models. Technically, "apocalypse" is but another term, one of Greek derivation (*apokalypsis*), for "revelation," but it was also used in the narrower sense, as Klaus Koch puts it, for "the title of literary compositions that resemble the Book of Revelation, i.e. secret divine disclosures about the end of the world and the heavenly state" (16). Koch further provides a list of the most common distinguishing features of apocalypses: "great discourse cycles" that include a "long dialogue between the apocalyptic seer and his heavenly counterpart" (21), as well as visions filled with "mythical images rich in symbolism" (23), and a mood of "spiritual turmoil" as a "result of the unexpected experience of vision and audition" (22). In addition, Koch points to pseudonymity as a common feature of many apocalypses (23), while other scholars remark on the tendency of apocalyptic texts to focus on the scribal mode of transmission.[1] Behind all the specific features of the apocalyptic mode and of apocalypses usually stands an eschatological perspective, a perspective minimized or denied by a few scholars, but otherwise considered central to the revelation of divine secrets that, one way or another, constitutes apocalypse.[2]

For many today and certainly for the Middle Ages, John's Apocalypse is the archetypal apocalyptic text, the one that defines and sets the model for all others. While it is not pseudonymous since the author identifies himself as John,[3] John's text contains all of the remaining features we associate with apocalyptic writing: it refers repeatedly to the seer's "spiritual turmoil"; it takes the form of a "great discourse cycle," a series of visions punctuated by dialogue with the interpreting angel; the visions are imbued with highly popular and influential "mythical images," many of them derived from Old Testatment apocalyptic visions, especially Ezekiel's; the events and images and

[1]Koch does not mention this "scribal" feature, but most other scholars do. See esp. Russell (118–22) and McGinn (*Visions* 5).

[2]Collins makes the clearest statement about the eschatology of apocalypse, pointing out that, while some rightly object to the equation of eschatology with apocalypticism, which is valid only for the "historical" type of apocalypse (like the Book of Daniel), all apocalypses "involve a transcendent eschatology that looks for retribution beyond the bounds of history" (9). See also Emmerson, who says: "Apocalypticism includes more than the last things. It sets eschatology in a historical context" (14).

[3]Traditionally, of course, this John was identified with the apostle John (who in turn was assumed to be the author of the fourth gospel), although since the third century many have questioned such an identification, usually while objecting to the canonicity of the Apocalypse (D'Aragon 468–69).

vision are all concerned with the Last Days and the world beyond; and finally, John's Apocalypse emphasizes the scribal mode of transmission—repeatedly the angel directs John to write down his visions, and books and written characters play important roles in the visions themselves.

For most of us, and for the Middle Ages, the "mythical images," generally eschatological and always "rich in symbolism," are probably the characteristics that first come to mind when we think of apocalypticism. Because of this, because I believe apocalyptic signs so important in all the poems of Cotton Nero A.x., and because the Pearl poet is such a visual poet, I shall begin this study of his poetics and his *fayre formez* with his apocalyptic imagery, with first of all the images in *Pearl* and their biblical and iconographic background. For it is *Pearl* that provides the reader with the visual and visionary introduction to the other three poems, in much the same way that an apocalyptic vision of God Enthroned stands over the west doorway of so many late medieval churches.[4] [Figure 1]

The dream in *Pearl* gives a glimpse of the future kingdom, which is visualized as the New Jerusalem, the new world where the saved celebrate their joyous love of God with the *canticum novum*, a celebration symbolized by the Wedding of the Lamb to his "meyny schene" (1145), his "homly hyne" (1211). God himself is symbolized by the Lamb, and his power by the Throne and by the light of the Lamb. Because all of these signs of God and his kingdom are drawn from John's Apocalypse—either directly, as word-for-word translations of the Vulgate text, or indirectly, through the traditions that developed in exegesis and iconography, close examination of each of these important signs in *Pearl*, along with their textual and iconographic sources, will help us understand their function in *Pearl* and their impact on the other poems.

[4]The twelfth- and thirteenth-century churches in France provide the best examples of this use of the apocalyptic vision of God Enthroned. In addition to the one at Moissac, which is shown in Figure 1, there are two more, at Autun and Conques, that I will be discussing in this chapter [Figures 3 and 4].

FIGURE 1. The Tympanum of the Church of St. Pierre, Moissac, France (1100–1115). (Photo: James Austin.)

Signs of God: The Throne and the Lamb

The sign that evokes God in *Pearl* is the Lamb. Before we can understand the force of this symbol in the Pearl poet's writing, we need first to examine its context in the Apocalypse and in the art based on John's text. First of all, the Lamb is not the preeminent symbol either in John's text or even in much of the artistic tradition. In the Apocalypse the dominant sign of God is the Throne, on which the Lamb, is sometimes, but not always, seated. The vision of God Enthroned occurs several times in John's text and was the most reproduced of his visions in the late Middle Ages. There is, however, an important difference between the biblical text and the later representations in art. Whereas the art of the high Middle Ages revels in glorious representations of God Enthroned, John's text seems to avoid actual visualization of this scene, an avoidance also prevalent in early Christian art. Because I think this difference, between the early reluctance toward full theophany and the later tendency to visualize God on his throne is important to the Pearl poet, I want to look more closely at the actual words of John's major visions and then compare the text to a few of the representations of the Throne in art.

The first of the several visions of the Throne occurs directly after John writes the letters to the seven churches. With his scribal and apostolic tasks accomplished, John then returns to the visionary mode, with which his text begins:

> Statim fui in spiritu,
> et ecce sedis posita erat in caelo,
> et supra sedem sedens.
> Et qui sedebat similis erat aspectui
> lapidis iaspidis et sardini.
> Et iris erat in circuitu sedis similis visioni zmaragdinae.
> (4.2–3)[5]

[5]I am using the Württembergische text of the Vulgate. Translations are my own, but with frequent use of modern English versions, especially the *New*

[At once I was in divine ectasy.
And behold a throne was standing there in heaven,
And on the throne (was) a Sitting (One).
And the One who was sitting was like the appearance
Of a jewel, of jasper and carnelian,
And around the throne was a rainbow like the
    appearance of emeralds.]

John suddenly finds himself *in spiritu*, a state in which perceptions are of a special nature, but even in this special state he does not claim he saw God, nor does he say that God or Christ was seated upon the throne. There is only a hint of visualization of the One on the Throne, when we are told what the Enthroned One's appearance was like (*similis erat aspectui*), a strange circumlocution that denies visual actuality. Furthermore, there is an unmistakable distancing in the omission of God's name. Indeed, in the passage above, no noun or pronoun of any kind is used for God, only a participle used substantively. The line, *et super sedem sedens*, does not introduce a substantive word or clause, but as the independent clause that follows makes clear, stands alone—in other words, what is sitting on the Throne is what is sitting on the Throne. God, here, is act and being, not visual reality. In this respect, John's vision of the Throne is close to the divine presence in the Old Testament, which is rarely visual, almost always verbal. However, unlike the God of the prophets and patriarchs, the Enthroned (One) of John's vision is not voice or words, even though in the vision of the first chapter of John's text, it was a voice he first experienced and a voice he wanted to see: "audivi post me vocem magnam. . . . et conversus sum ut viderem vocem quae loquebatur mecum" (1.10, 12). [I heard behind me a loud voice . . . and I turned around to see the voice that had spoken to

American Bible and the *New English Bible*. When I think it especially relevant for the Pearl poet, I give some very literal, and often stylistically awkward, translations of the Latin.

me.] The Lamb, as a sign of the divine presence, especially of the Son, soon appears in the middle of the Throne. Actually, the image of the Lamb is a separate vision, or at least a subsequent stage of envisioning, since it is first introduced with the phrase, "et vidi et ecce . . ." [and then I saw/envisioned, and behold there was. . .].

Throughout most of the rest of John's text the images of the Lamb and the Throne dominate as visual signs of God. In the final vision they are combined with the Voice, which has been heard throughout the book, but has never before been connected to the visual symbols. Coming as it does at the end of John's visions and as the climax of the revelation of the new creation, this manifestation of the divine as voice and words represents John's ultimate experience of God:

> Et audivi vocem magnam de throno . . .
> . . . .
> Et dixit qui sedebat in throno,
> "Ecce nova facio omnia."
> Et dicit, "Scribe quia haec verba fidelissima sunt et vera."
> Et dixit mihi, "Factum est.
> Ego sum A et Ω initium et finis." (21.3, 5–6)
>
> [And I heard a loud voice from the throne . . .
> . . . .
> And (the One) who sat on the throne said
> "Behold I make all things new!"
> And he said "Write (this) down, for the words are
> trustworthy and true!"
> And he said to me, "It (these words) is accomplished.
> I am Alpha and Omega, the Beginning and the End."[6]

It is significant that this final and climactic vision, though it places the divine voice on the Throne, still does not really con-

[6]See D'Aragon's commentary on this passage, where he points out that this is the only place in the Apocalypse where "God himself speaks" (491).

stitute a theophany, at least not a fully embodied visual one. Throughout his text, by using the visual symbols of the Lamb and the Throne, or the oral sign of the Voice, John avoids giving a record of the beatific vision (which he never claims to have experienced). Rather than recreating theophany itself, what the visions of the Throne and the Lamb do is to reveal the experience of theophany for those beyond the time and space of this world. This experience, for those who have it, can be divided into two phases: the act of judgment by the enthroned Christ, and the celebration of God's majesty by the saved. The former is an event within time, although at its outer edge; the latter is an eternal act.

The act of divine judgment, for many the most typically apocalyptic moment, is strangely almost a minor event in John's text. Coming just before the passage quoted above that places the Voice upon the Throne, the traditional scene of the Last Judgment is described in a brief passage:

> Et vidi thronum magnum candidum,
> et sedentem super eum
> a cuius aspectu fugit terra et caelum,
> et locus non est inventus ab eis.
> Et vidi mortuos magnos et pusillos stantes in conspectu
> throni.
> Et libri aperti sunt,
> et alius liber apertus est qui est vitae.
> Et iudicati sunt mortui ex his quae scripta erant in libris,
> secundum opera ipsorum.
> Et dedit mare mortuos qui in eo erant,
> et mors et inferus dederunt mortuos qui in ipsis erant,
> et iudicatum est de singulis secundum opera ipsorum.
> (20.11–13)

> [And I saw a large white throne,
> And (One) sitting on it,
> From whose appearance the earth and sky fled,
> And they could find no place to go.

And I saw the dead, the great and the lowly, standing
before the throne.
And the books were opened.
And another book was opened, which is the book of the
living,
And the dead were judged from the things which were
written in the books,
According to their deeds.
And the sea gave up the dead which were in it,
And death and the underworld gave up the dead which
were in them.
And each person was judged separately according to his
deeds.]

Yet, although John's vision of the Last Judgment seems of minor importance when compared to most of the other scenes in the Apocalypse, it is but one detail in a full dramatization of God as judge. In John's visions the Last Judgment comes as a conclusion and a culmination of the mythic and allegorical battles that occupy the bulk of the Apocalypse, since all of the text's monsters and devils function as figures of evil, and since their final defeat illustrates the power of God's judgment.[7] From the beginning, Christian exegesis and iconography have made this connection, and it has become so imbedded in tradition that few seem aware of how little basis John's Apocalypse gives for the popular Last Judgment scene.

The act of final judgment is historically the first of humanity's experiences of the theophany that will come at the end of time. For the saved, Christ's second coming will be heralded and celebrated by the *canticum novum*, a new song sung in the new world. It is this act of celebration, not the image of God

[7]See Augustine's discussion of "little judgments" as distinct from but anticipatory of the "last judgment" (*City of God* 20.1; pp. 710–11); see also McGinn's discussion of the various analyses of the Apocalypse's structure, including the view of "most modern scholars" that the text is a "cyclical presentation of visions repeating, or recapitulating, the same basic message of present persecution, imminent destruction of the wicked and reward of the just" ("Revelation" 525).

Himself, that is the focus of most of John's visions of the Lamb and the Throne, and as such those visions are best thought of as scenes of God adored. The first of the visions of the Throne, for example, provides a full description of those worshipping the enthroned one—the twenty-four elders (4.4) and the living beasts (*animalia*; 4.6–8)—and also repeats their words of praise:

> Sanctus, sanctus, sanctus, Dominus Deus omnipotens,
> Qui erat et qui est et qui venturus est.
> . . . .
> Dignus es Domine et Deus noster accipere gloriam et
> honorem et virtutem,
> Quia tu creasti omnia,
> Et propter voluntatem tuam erant et creata sunt.
> (4.8, 11)

> [Holy, holy, holy, Lord God almighty,
> Who was, who is, and who is to come.
> . . . .
> Worthy art thou, Lord, our God, to receive glory and
> honor and power,
> Because thou didst create all things,
> And by thy will they were and are created.]

In chapter seven, John witnesses another scene of adoration, this time by a great crowd:

> Post haec vidi turbam agnam quam dinumerare nemo
> poterat,
> ex omnibus gentibus et tribubus et populis et linguis,
> stantes ante thronum et in conspectu agni,
> amicti stolas albas,
> et palmae in manibus eorum.
> Et clamabant voce magna dicentes,
> "Salus Deo nostro qui sedet super thronum et agno."
> (7.9–10)

[After this I saw a huge crowd, which no one could
count,
From every nation and tribe and people and tongue,
Standing before the throne and in sight of the Lamb,
Dressed in white robes,
And with palm branches in their hands,
And they cried out in a loud voice, saying,
"Salvation is from our God, who is seated on the throne
and from the Lamb!"]

In a similar vision of the Lamb adored, in chapter fourteen, the Lamb stands on Mount Sion and is worshipped by 144,000 virgins (actually men, because they have not "been defiled by women"—14.4).

The climax of all these visions of the Lamb and the Throne is not a visual description of either, but the act of adoration by those witnessing the vision. In the vision recorded in chapter fourteen, the 144,000, like the twenty-four elders (*seniores*) and the four living beasts (*animalia*) of the earlier vision, celebrate God's reign with songs of praise. In this later vision John elaborates on the uniqueness of the song:

Et cantabant quasi canticum novum ante sedem et ante
quattor animalia et seniores.
Et nemo poterat discere canticum nisi illa centum
quadraginta quattuor milia qui empti sunt de terra.
(14.3)

[And they were singing a kind of new hymn,
Before the throne and before the four living creatures and
the elders,
And no one could learn this hymn, except the 144,000 who
had been ransomed from the world.]

This idea of a *canticum novum*, worthy to glorify God's unique power, goes back to the Old Testament, especially to the Psalms (see, for example, Pss. 32/33, 149/150, 150/151). In the

Psalms, however, the *canticum novum* celebrates the glory of a victorious Israel within human history. The psalmists expect, even demand, the community to join them in praising the Lord. The call to a new song that opens Ps. 32/33 is typical:

> Exultate iusti Domino; rectos decet laudatio.
> Confitemini Domino in cithara; in psalterio decem
> cordarum psallite illi.
> Cantate ei canticum novum; bene psallite in
> vociferatione.
>
> (Ps. 32/33.1–3)

> [Exult you just ones in the Lord; praise from the upright
> is fitting.
> Give thanks to the Lord on the harp; with the
> ten-stringed lyre chant his praises,
> Sing to him a new song;
> Chant skillfully, with loud voices.]

Glorious as this song of praise is to be, it is still to be performed with earthly instruments, by righteous, but fully mortal, singers.

The new song of John's Apocalypse, on the other hand, is sung only by those redeemed from the world and removed from human history. In John's text, even when the words of the worshippers are given, as in the vision of the adoring elders and beasts in chapter four, and even when those words are familiar ones from the prophets (the *Sanctus* hymn, for example, is taken from Isaiah's vision of the altar—Is. 6.3), even then John's context implies a *canticum novum* that is possible only beyond the eschaton.

When we turn from John's text to the images of God Enthroned in art, we find some interesting developments in the representation of theophany, both in general and in its particular manifestation as God Enthroned. In keeping with the spirit of John's text, the earliest use of the Apocalypse in art demonstrates a reluctance to present a vision of God *per se*. During the first centuries, the symbols of *alpha* and *omega* were more often used, sometimes together with Christ's initials, to represent the apocalyptic divinity. Later, the Throne appears in mosaics, occasionally with Christ, but more often either empty or with a cross or lamb. In the later Middle Ages the throne continued to be depicted empty, especially in the illustrated Apocalypses. [Figure 2] However, at the same time monumental representations of the enthroned deity also began to appear on tympana. Since the complex tradition of the enthroned Christ, or Christ in Majesty, owes much to the adaptation of imperial iconography, most of these tympana cannot really be considered as visual versions or interpretations of John's Apocalypse. This is particularly true since, as full theophany, these sculptures represent a substantial deviation from John's text. However, certain of the tympana in twelfth-century France offer fairly close visual representations of scenes in John's text, even while drawing on the separate development of the Christ in Majesty. I would like to take a brief, and highly selective, look at a few of these, in particular those of the churches in Autun, Conques, and Moissac and also of a few illustrated Apocalypses, since I think they are both typical and influential; typical, because they show us the medieval traditions of the end of time and the apocalyptic vision of Christ enthroned, and influential, because they appeared in important churches along the well-travelled pilgrimage routes to Santiago de Compostella and in widely disseminated and frequently copied manuscripts.

The tympanum on the west facade of the Church of St. Lazare at Autun, dating from after 1125 (Hearn 183), shows Christ returning at the end of time to judge humanity. [Figure 3] The patrons and artist(s) responsible for this magnificent sculpture, who were probably not thinking of any particular text, not even John's scene of Last Judgment, have included both the transcendent Christ, here seated (or rather barely seated, more floating in a spaceless, timeless dimension) on a scarcely visible throne, and also the historical event of the act of judging from John's description of the Last Judgment (20.4). To this scene have been added Enoch and Elias, the martyred

FIGURE 2. The Throne of God and the Lamb on Mt. Sion. Trinity Apocalypse, Trinity College Library, R. 16.2, fol. 16r (1230–50). By permission of the Master and Fellows of Trinity College Cambridge. (Photo: Trinity College Library.)

witnesses mentioned, but not named, in an earlier passage from the Apocalypse (11.3–13), and also the Virgin Mary enthroned, a detail certainly not in John's text.[8] At Autun there is a formal separation of the motionless, centered Christ from the flurry of activity surrounding him. This separation signals the radical differences between, on the one hand, eternal theophany beyond time and space and the beatific vision promised to all the saved, and, on the other hand, the moment at the end of history that will decide whether we are to participate in that vision. Everything about the fully frontal and almost two-dimensional Christ and his throne and his encompassing mandorla is still and static; everything and every creature outside is in motion—souls are being weighed (on the right), dressed in their new robes (on the left), pushed into hellmouth, or elevated into the company of angels. One small, naked creature among the souls just awakened from the dead is in the very process of being lifted up by a pair of grasping hands that has broken through the lower horizontal band separating this world from the next.[9] The tympanum at Autun is an eloquent representation of the medieval sense of the apocalyptic: the revelation of the transcendent otherworld shown in conjunction with the depiction of the crisis at the end of time that is epitomized in the Last Judgment.

The tympanum at Conques, ca. 1130–1140 (Hearn 182), above the west portal of the church of Ste. Foy, is a much more literal-minded version of the Last Judgment. [Figure 4] Lacking the sublimity of vision and craft that Autun boasts, the

[8]Although John does not name the two witnesses, earliest tradition identifies them as Enoch and Elias (Emmerson 41, 136–40), while modern scholarship believes that the descriptions in John "obviously fit Moses and Elijah" (D'Aragon 481). Including Mary in various theophanies was a late development in medieval art.

[9]See Nichols's discussion of this detail (*Romanesque Signs* 45), which is part of his general analysis of the "distribution of figures on a Romanesque tympanum, where the humans tend to be set in horizontal registers, while the theophanic Christ figure—as at Moissac, Vézelay, Autun, Beaulieu, Saint Denis, and others—cuts vertically across these bands at the center of the image field" (43).

FIGURE 3. The Tympanum of the Church of St. Lazare, Autun, France (after 1125). (Photo: James Austin.)

FIGURE 4. The Tympanum of the Church of Ste. Foy at Conques, France (ca. 1130–1140). (Photo: James Austin.)

tympanum at Conques provides us, nevertheless, with a typical, even archetypal, representation of the Last Judgment, as that event developed in iconography. Within a mandorla is Christ seated on a throne, a throne more visible than the one in Autun but hardly at the center of the vision, as it is in the passages from the Apocalypse. Specific references to John's text—the symbols *Alpha* and *Omega*, which are inscribed in Christ's nimbus, and the four Evangelists—are included, although they come not from the vision of the Last Judgment, but from the earlier visions in John's Apocalypse. The enthroned Christ at Ste. Foy displays his wounds, while above the entire drama angels are holding signs of the crucifixion—the cross, the lance, and the nails. These references to Christ's passion appear increasingly in later representations of the Last Judgment, an iconographic development that marks the tendency to associate Christ's final act of judging with his saving sacrifice and that corresponds to the symbolic wounds on the Lamb in John's Apocalypse (see esp. 4.6, 12).[10] The business of judgment, given in much greater detail in Conques than it is in the Apocalypse, is taking place around the enthroned Christ, while an angel holds the *liber vitae* from John's Last Judgment scene.

The Conques tympanum is justly famous for the contemporaneous details of the damned: the bad knight still in armor tumbling into hell as though he has just fallen off his horse; the adulterous couple standing before Satan in all their naked (and somewhat erotic) shame, while a leering devil whispers in Satan's ear (thereby depicting the scandal and loss of honor associated in courtly romances with adultery made known); the poacher being roasted on a spit, like the hares he presumably had been stealing from his lord (maybe even from the church's hunting preserves). This kind of specificity is lacking on the left

[10]The cross as an element of the Last Judgment scene is a characteristic of western iconographic tradition and can be found in Carolingian representations; these used the detail of the cross to interpret the passage in Matthew that says the "sign of the Son of Man" will appear at the Last Judgment (24.30). The other signs of Christ's actual suffering are new to the twelfth century, first appearing in Beaulieu (Mâle, *Religious Art* 407–408).

side, the realm of the saved, although the blessed do bear certain attributes to identify them, either as specific saints (St. Peter with his keys, for example), or as representational types (like the allegorized virtues around Abraham). The blessed are less tied to the time and place of the artists and patrons than are the damned—the latter could easily be someone the artists and viewers knew. The effect of this tympanum is quite different from the one at Autun, for Conques particularly marks the division between the saved and the damned, rather than between the otherworld and this. Furthermore, although the Conques Christ is still a transcendent Christ enthroned in majesty, the symbols of his saving passion and the clearer association of him with the act of judging help to place him more firmly in a moment in time, although a moment at the very end of time.

An important feature of the Conques tympanum—the contrast between the particularized, active damned and the more generalized, peaceful saved—can also be found in many manuscript illustrations of the Last Judgment. In the Trinity Apocalypse, executed in England in the mid-thirteenth century, heaven and hell are distinguished both by their contrasting moods and their different levels (Cambridge, Trinity MS. R.16.2, fol. 24v).[11] [Figure 5] Those in hell, on the bottom level, are in chaotic, constant motion, their unnaturally twisted bodies being flung around; while those in heaven above are calm and arranged in orderly rows. Even the color scheme participates in this separation: primarily monochromatic in hell, touches of color and gold in heaven.

Of the three tympana I have chosen to look at, the one above the west portal of the Church of St. Pierre at Moissac provides the closest representation of John's text. [Figure 1] In fact, one scholar, Emile Mâle, has argued that a double-paged illustration from the St. Sever Apocalypse, fols. 121v-122, was the

[11]For the dating and provenance of the Trinity Apocalypse, see James, Trinity (24–26); Brieger (14); and Henderson (127)—James and Brieger are the respective editors of the two facsimiles of the manuscript, the first published in 1909, the second in 1967.

FIGURE 5. The Last Judgment. The Trinity Apocalypse, Trinity College Library, R.16.2, fol. 24v (1230–1250). By permission of the Master and Fellows of Trinity College Cambridge. (Photo: Trinity College Library.)

direct source for the Moissac tympanum (*Religious Art* 4). Although later scholars have since questioned or modified Moissac's connection to the St. Sever manuscript, there is no doubt that the Moissac tympanum is essentially a rendering of John's vision of the throne in the fourth and fifth chapters of the Apocalypse.[12] While the artists and planners of this tympanum have gone beyond John's description by placing a visualized Christ on the throne, they have otherwise stayed close to the biblical text and brilliantly captured in sculpture the exact words of the passage, especially the joyous celebration of God and His reign in eternity. The energy of this celebration is at the point of ecstasy. The elders are in almost frenzied motion as they turn, harps in hand, to gaze at Christ; the elongated angels and the sharply twisting beasts seem to dance, while Christ himself remains still and frontal in the center, with only a slight suggestion of motion in his lower drapery (Schapiro, "Moissac" 203; Hearn 171–72). The separation, which in the depictions of the Last Judgment is either between the saved and the damned or between the judge and the judgment, is in this rendering between the envisioned and the visionaries. The visualized Christ at Moissac is the eternal essence of reality, the Creator who makes all things new, the beginning and the end; those privileged to see him are actively engaged in worship and celebration. The Moissac tympanum is thus more than a rendering of the vision of the throne or even than a visualization of God; it is also a representation of the joyous response to theophany—it is the *canticum novum* carved in stone.

In this brief survey of the visions of John's Apocalypse and their later artistic representations, the Throne emerges as the dominant image. In John's text the visions are of the Throne itself (and the Voice from the Throne), while in later medieval

[12]The sources for the iconography of the twelfth-century tympana have been extensively discussed and argued. Mâle's original thesis regarding the source for Moissac's tympanum was subsequently questioned or modified by several scholars, including Schapiro (306–27, esp. 317). More recently, Christe, in a study of all the Romanesque portals, has maintained that the tympana do not illustrate specific episodes from the Apocalypse or any other biblical text, but that each is presented as "une image synthetique" (143); earlier Schapiro had said of Moissac's tympanum that it "does not render a specific line" from the Apocalypse, but rather a "characteristic and impressive moment of the vision" (202).

art, especially monumental sculpture, the image is closer to full theophany, for it depicts Christ in Majesty upon the throne. There can be little doubt that the Pearl poet, as well as most of his audience, was familiar with the medieval image of God Enthroned as a primary symbol of the divine presence, for it is referred to in several places in his poetry. For example, Jonah in *Patience* speaks of "Oure Syre" who "syttes . . . on sege so hyȝe / In His glowande glorye" (93–94); and the narrator in *Cleanness* refers to "þe Kyng þat al weldez" (17). However, these references are just that—references—not actual visualizations or poetic ekphrases. This lack of visualization is a remarkable omission in a poet at once so visual and so concerned with *fayre formez*; such an omission provides strong evidence that the poet recognized and embraced the reluctance to visualize a full theophany, a reluctance found both in the Old Testament and in the Apocalypse. In *Pearl*, which contains the most visual signs of the divine, the *forme* most used for God's presence is the Lamb, which is a symbol not a visualization, and the preferred symbol of the deity in early Christian art (though not, as we have seen, later), and which in John's text either joins with the Throne or sometimes replaces the Throne in visions of the worship of God by the saved beyond this world and time.

In *Pearl*, which refers so often to the joyous celebration of the Lamb's *meyny*, it is natural that the Lamb as sign would dominate over the Throne. The Lamb is a more physical living reality than the Throne and essential to the very personal relationship the Pearl Maiden describes as her life in eternity. Additionally, I suspect that the Pearl poet relies on the Lamb as the visualization of the deity, because the Lamb is at once a more direct sign of God as living being (unlike the Throne which is a sign of divine power) and yet still only a sign of the deity, a symbol, not the image of the deity himself. Once John's words are translated into visual images, it is not surprising that the less-visual God Enthroned would give way to the highly visual sign of the Lamb, especially where there is a reluctance to depart from John's text and actually visualize God on the throne. In this respect, as in others, the rearrangements and various changes in detail that the Pearl poet makes of John's visionary recordings reflect not only traditional readings and artistic treatments of John's text, but the original perspective and spirit of John's text itself.

Like John, moreover, the Pearl poet conflates visions and signs, merging Throne, Lamb, the Lamb adored by his *meyny*, the Throne surrounded in majesty, and the heavenly city. The most important passage in *Pearl* for this conflation comes in the midst of the climactic vision of the New Jerusalem granted to the dreamer at the end of his dream. For this *forme* of the beatific vision and the kingdom, the Pearl poet makes particular use of the passage near the end of the Apocalypse in which John merges the Lamb with the visions of the heavenly city and God Enthroned (21.1–22.5). In this vision, John tells us:

> Et civitas non eget sole neque luna, ut luceant in ea; nam claritas Dei inluminavit eam, et lucerna eius est agnus.
>
> (21.23)

> [And the city needs neither sun nor moon to light it; for the splendor of God illumines it and that lamp is the Lamb.]

John then goes on to describe the Throne of God, the Lamb, and the river of the water of life (*fluvius aquae vitae*), all at the center of the heavenly city. The first stanza of section eighteen in *Pearl* uses the same transition, the Lamb as the city's light, to move from the vision of the city to a vision of the Lamb and of the Lamb adored:

> Such lyȝt þer lemed in alle þe stratez
> Hem nedde nawþer sunne ne mone.
>
> Of sunne ne mone had þay no nede;
> Þe Self God watz her lombe-lyȝt,
> Þe Lombe her lantyrne, withouten drede;

> Þurȝ Hym blysned þe borȝ al bryȝt.
> Þurȝ woȝe and won my lokyng ȝede;
> For sotyle cler noȝt lette no syȝt.
> Þe hyȝe trone þer moȝt ȝe hede
> With alle þe apparaylmente vmbepyȝte,
> As John þe appostel in termez tyȝte.
> Þe hyȝe Godez Self hit set vpone.
> A reuer of þe trone þer ran outryȝte
> Watz bryȝter þen boþe þe sunne and mone. (1043–56)

In this passage, the poet, like John, includes the river and the Throne and even two references to God, placing "Godez Self" on the Throne, without, however, giving any visual description of the enthroned deity. Although admittedly "Godez Self" is less circumlocutory than the *supra sedem sedens* of chapter four in John's Apocalypse, it still lacks the direct simplicity of the name "God" and seems to insist on not being a visual image of God, but rather a reference to the divine presence.

More importantly, the focus in the above passage in *Pearl*, and throughout the entire section, is upon the Lamb, not the Throne. Through elaborate wordplay, including the pun available in English upon "Lamb" and "Lamp," the poet is developing the motif of the Lamb as divine light, in contrast to earthly light from sun or moon.[13] The latter, the weaker and more flawed source of light ("to spotty ho is, of body to grym" [1070]), is particularly contrasted to the brilliant light of the Lamb. But the poet has done more than just make use of a pun available to him in English. He has obviously noted the Vulga-

[13]Andrew and Waldron point out this pun (103, note to 1046) and liken it to the wordplay on *mote* in line 947; they also add, concerning the latter, that "[t]here would have been no impropriety for a contemporary audience, despite the solemnity of the subject" (99, note to 947). Such a comment is odd not only in its patronizing tone, but also in its implication that punning is inappropriate for sacred subjects, when in fact exegesis includes much fanciful wordplay, usually under the guise of etymology. As Smalley puts it: "Philo, who probably knew little, if any, Hebrew, could apply the principle [of etymology] also to Greek words, since he held the Septuagint to be verbally inspired. It gave a rich

te's emphasis on *lucerna* (used as noun and in the previous clause as the verb *lucer*) and also more subtly the semantic and syntactical connection between *claritas* and *lucerna*: both are subjects of their respective clauses and one substitutes for the other (*lucerna* for *claritas*); also because the first belongs to God ("claritas Dei") and the second equals the Lamb, there is a distinction being made, between God (perhaps God the Father) and the Lamb.

In *Pearl* the appearance of the Lamb in the climax of the dream—notably still more a verbal reality than a visual one, a source of li3ht, not the object lighted—prepares the way for the vision of the Lamb adored by the 144,000, the subject of the second-to-last section of the poem. The Lamb himself is envisioned as he appears in the visions of the earlier chapters of the Apocalypse:

> With gret delyt þay glod in fere
> On golden gatez þat glent as glasse;
> Hundreth þowsandez I wot þer were,
> And alle in sute her liurëz wasse.
> Tor to knaw þe gladdest chere.
> Þe Lombe byfore con proudly passe
> Wyth hornez seuen of red golde cler;
> As praysed perlez His wedez wasse.
> Towarde þe throne þay trone a tras.
> Þaȝ þay wern fele, no pres in plyt,
> Bot mylde as maydenez seme at mas,
> So droȝ þay forth with gret delyt. (1105–16)

This stanza, taken from the vision of the seventh chapter of the Apocalypse, is followed by a paraphrase of John's vision of the adoration of the Lamb in chapter five:

---

scope to his fantasy: one cannot always say where etymology ends and the play upon words begins" (6). Paranomasia, in fact, characterizes much biblical language, as well as its exegesis (Alter and Kermode 105–06, 631–32, and passim).

Delyt þat Hys come encroched
To much hit were of for to melle.
Þise alderman, quen He aproched,
Grouelyng to His fete þay felle.
Legyounes of aungelez togeder uoched
Þer kesten ensens of swete smelle.
(1117–22; cf. Apoc. 4.7–11)

The vision of the Lamb adored then climaxes in *Pearl* in section nineteen with a *canticum novum*, which provides the final ecstatic moments of the dream:

Al songe to loue þat gay Juelle.
Þe steuen moȝt stryke þurȝ þe vrþe to helle
Þat þe vertues of heuen of joye endyte.
To loue þe Lombe His meyny inmelle
Iwysse I laȝt a gret delyt. (1124–28)

The verse in the first three stanzas of section nineteen achieves a tour-de-force comparable to that of the Moissac tympanum, one a verbal, the other a visual, mimesis of otherworldly joy and the ecstasy of those participating in eternal love. However, the dreamer's glimpse of divine love, the wholly transcendent love that the Pearl Maiden has been trying to explain to him since the beginning of the dream, is only a vision of heavenly joy, not the joy itself. The last line of the stanza quoted above suddenly and radically shifts the perspective from the heavenly response back to the earthly one of the dreamer. The "gret delyt," the linking phrase of this section, which is at first applied to the 144,000, is only later, in the stanza quoted above, applied to the dreamer, who "catches" the joy from the blessed. The dreamer's subsequent rash behavior, when he attempts to cross the river, reveals that he does not understand that the heavenly joy, the *gret delyt* verbalized in the *canticum novum*, cannot be his, any more than the Pearl's love can be his.

Even so, this vision towards the end of the poem, of the Lamb adored in the New Jerusalem, does attain a directness over the earlier part of the dream, where we are given more indirect versions in the Pearl Maiden's descriptions. In sections fourteen and fifteen, she begins to tell the dreamer in greater visual detail about her Lamb and his heavenly kingdom:

> "Lest les þou leue my talle farande,
> In Appocalyppece is wryten in wro:
> 'I seghe,' says John, 'þe Loumbe hym stande
> On þe mount of Syon, ful þryuen and þro:
> And wyth Hym maydennez, an hundreþe þowsande,
> And fowre and forty þowsande mo.
> On alle her forhedez wryten I fande
> Þe Lombez nome, hys Faderez also.
> A hue fro heuen I herde þoo,
> Lyk flodez fele laden runnen on resse;
> And as þunder þrowez in torrez blo—
> Þat lote, I leue, watz neuer þe les.
> . . . .
> A note ful nwe I herde hem warpe,
> To lysten þat watz ful lufly dere.
> As harporez harpen in her harpe,
> Þat nwe songe þay songen ful cler,
> In sounande notez, a gentyl carpe.' " (865–76, 879–83)

This earlier description of the *Lombe* and *His meyny* is basically third-hand, for the Pearl Maiden is telling the dreamer about John's description of the vision. She repeatedly cites John's Apocalypse as her authority, even quoting him directly for the climactic vision. John's text thereby is granted the privileged position of the first and best and most orthodox visualization of the Lamb adored—most orthodox because it, unlike the dreamer's version, does not end with a rash and unauthorized response.

Signs of God's Kingdom: The New Jerusalem and the Wedding Feast

In addition to the visions of the Throne and the Lamb adored, two other images of God's kingdom that are used in the Apocalypse proved especially popular in the later Middle Ages: the vision of the New Jerusalem and the reference to the Wedding Feast of the Lamb. Both of these figure importantly in the Pearl poet's work, especially in *Pearl.* The New Jerusalem, as it appears in late medieval art and literature, remains very close to John's text, in which the description of the New Jerusalem is the final and most sublime of his visions. It not only brings together several details of the earlier visions, along with various allusions in other New Testament texts, but also draws upon the many passages in the Old Testament that look forward to a return to the promised land and a restoration of the city of God's people.

The Voice from the Throne, in John's climactic vision, finally speaks, promising the comforts traditionally evoked by the prophets when they held out hope to the scattered remnant:

> Ecce tabernaculum Dei cum hominibus et habitabit cum eis.
> Et ipsi populus eius erunt,
> et ipse Deus cum eis erit eorum Deus.
> Et absterget Deus omnem lacrimam ab oculis eorum,
> et mors ultra non erit neque luctus neque clamor neque dolor erit ultra,
> quae prima abierunt. (21.3–4)

> [Behold the tabernacle (dwelling) of God is among men, and he shall dwell among them.
> And they will be his people,
> And he himself, "God-with-them," will be their god.[14]

[14]"God-with-them," following the *New English Bible*, transliterates the Hebrew *Emmanuel*, as does the Latin ("*Deus cum eis*").

And God will wipe every tear from their eyes,
And there will be no more death, neither will there be
any more mourning or crying or grief,
For the former things have passed away.]

While very close to the similar promises of the prophets, the words in John's text are less direct than they are, for example, in Ezekiel, where God speaks in the first person:

Et erit tabernaculum *meum* in eis,
et *ero* eis Deus et ipsi erunt *mihi* populus.
(Ezek. 37.27; emphasis mine)

[And *my* dwelling shall be with them.
And *I* will be their God, and they shall be *my* people.]

In contrast, the effect in the Apocalypse of having the Voice from the Throne speak of God in the third person is to distance the promise, to make it less immediate. The emphasis in John's vision is on the radical newness of the heavenly city and on its distance from this world and time. Unlike the restored or rebuilt Jerusalem promised by the prophets, John's Jerusalem comes from heaven and is a wholly new creation set beyond history.[15]

Paradoxically, while John's Jerusalem is less of this world than that of the prophets, it is nonetheless described in minute physical detail, most of it drawn from Old Testament passages.[16] This combination of otherworldliness and detailed visualization was no doubt one of the reasons that the New Jerusa-

[15] The distinction between the earthly Jerusalem and the heavenly one, the major theme of Augustine's *City of God*, is an important development in early Christian theology, one which has its basis not only in the Apocalypse, but also in Jesus's assurance in John's gospel that his kingdom "is not of this world" (18.36).

[16] The specific and direct source for the description of the New Jerusalem is Ezekiel, chapters 40–48 (D'Aragon 491), which in turn draws on other images of the restoration in the prophetic books.

lem exerted such appeal for late medieval artists and poets. In art the New Jerusalem sometimes appears as a recognizable medieval city, either in the background or as a main subject. [Figure 6] Elsewhere, especially in the Beatus manuscripts, the New Jerusalem is an abstract, colorful diagram, not a three-dimensional place;[17] the Trinity Apocalypse, although not a Beatus manuscript, partakes of that tradition in its full-page, two-dimensional map of the heavenly city, bejewelled and sparkling with its lavish use of goldleaf. [Figure 7] The Trinity's New Jerusalem is a perfect evocation of John's vision, especially of the verse that describes the city's jewel-like light:

> Habentem claritatem Dei,
> lumen eius simile lapidi pretioso tamquam lapidi iaspidis sicut cristallum. (21.11)

> [Having the splendor of God,
> And its light like that of a precious jewel, such as jasper or crystal.]

Pearl's description of the New Jerusalem contains the most extensive and the most direct use of John's actual words to be found in all of the poet's writings. Like the vision of the Lamb adored that I discussed earlier, the New Jerusalem is actually described twice in the poem, once by the Pearl Maiden, and later by the dreamer himself when he describes his own vision of the New Jerusalem. In both of these descriptions, the poet reminds us of how indebted he is to John. When the Pearl Maiden is describing the New Jerusalem, she cites John's Apocalypse as her authority, asserting that the heavenly city is to be distinguished from the earthly one: "Bot þe nwe, þat ly3t of Godez sonde, / Þe apostel in Apocalyppce in theme con take" (943–44).

[17]For a depiction of the New Jerusalem as a city, see for example, the Angers Tapestries in Planchenault (pl. 80); and for a representation as an abstract, map-like diagram see the Morgan Beatus (f. 222v), reproduced in Williams (pl. 20).

FIGURE 6. St. John Sees the New Jerusalem. N. Bataille, *Apocalypse of Angers*. Musée des Tapisseries, Angers, France. (Photo: Giraudon/Art Resource, New York.)

Later, when recounting his own vision of the New Jerusalem, the poet repeatedly tells us that he saw the city as John saw it and as John described it. At one point, the poet explains that he only knew the names of the jewels that he saw in the New Jerusalem because John had already named them: "As John þise stonez in write con nemme, / I knew þe name after his tale" (997–98). In all but one case (the *rybé*), the poet has not so much translated the names of the stones as transliterated them. For example, for *sapphyrus* he has *saffer*, and for *chrysoprassus*, *cryso-pase* (Apoc. 21.20 and *Pearl*, 1002, 1013).[18] The poet's detailed "pointing" of the New Jerusalem adds up to a dazzling vision, a shining bejewelled picture very like those found in illustrated Apocalypses,[19] especially the lavish Trinity Apocalypse, with its abundant use of gold leaf:

> As John þe apostel hit syȝ with syȝt,
> I syȝe þat cyty of gret renoun,
> Jerusalem so nwe and ryally dyȝt,
> As hit watz lyȝt fro þe heuen adoun.
> Þe borȝ watz al of brende golde bryȝt,
> As glemande glas burnist broun,
> With gentyl gemmez anvnder pyȝt. (985–91)[20]

[18]Andrew and Waldron have carefully glossed and footnoted many of the names of the gems, even providing a lengthy comment on what kind of stone a *calsydoyne* might be (101; note to 1003), but I believe the poet generally was little interested in what stone was meant—the only specific thing he had in mind was the word named in John's text, *carcidonius* or *calcidonius* (21.19). For a discussion of the one exception to this transliteration, the word *rybé* for *sardius*, see Gordon (79, note to 1007) and compare Gollancz, who emends to *sarde* (*Facsimile* 18), which seems to me correct since it would be in keeping with the poet's handling of the other terms.

[19]The term *"pointing"* is used by Burrow in describing the Pearl poet's craft (*Ricardian Poetry* 69–73; see my earlier reference in the Introduction, 13).

[20]It seems likely that the poet was visualizing the New Jerusalem as it was actually painted in illuminated manuscripts like the Trinity Apocalypse. See Nolan, who says that *glarye* (used later in the description, line 1027) refers to the egg white used in gold leaf, one of several pieces of evidence that the Pearl poet was drawing his terms from "the illuminators' craft" (200); in an earlier article Salter makes much the same point (149, note 24).

FIGURE 7. The New Jerusalem. The Trinity Apocalypse, Trinity College Library, R.16.2, fol. 25v (1230–1250). By permission of the Master and Fellows of Trinity College Cambridge. (Photo: Trinity College Library.)

The vision of the New Jerusalem is the most detailed and direct of the Pearl poet's borrowings from John's Apocalypse. Less visually realized and less dependent upon John's text, but equal in importance as a sign of God's kingdom in *Pearl*, is the Wedding of the Lamb, the focal figure for the love between the *Lombe* and *His meyny schene*. Here, in giving us more verbal references than visual description, the Pearl poet again reveals a faithfulness to John's text, and to the spirit of that text. For the visual and exegetical tradition of the Wedding of the Lamb comes from a complex iconographic and theological development, not from John's text. In fact, the Apocalypse provides no direct account of the Wedding, but only indirect references. In Chapter Nineteen, John says he heard a loud noise, like a great crowd saying:

> . . . . "Alleluia!
> Quoniam regnavit Dominus Deus noster omnipotens.
> Gaudeamus et exultemus et demus gloriam ei,
> quia venerunt nuptiae agni,
> et uxor eius praeparavit se."
> . . . .
> Et dicit mihi, "Scribe,
> Beati qui ad cenam nuptiarum agni vocati sunt."
> (19.6–7,9)

> [. . . . . "Alleluia!
> For the Lord our God reigns all-powerful!
> Let us rejoice and be glad and give Him glory!
> For the Wedding Day of the Lamb is come,
> And his bride has made herself ready."
> . . . .
> And he said to me, "Write:
> 'Blessed are those who are called to the Wedding Feast of the Lamb!' "]

The figure of the Wedding of the Lamb is carried over into the vision of the New Jerusalem, which immediately follows, when John writes that the heavenly city is "arrayed as a bride prepared to meet her husband" (21.2—"paratam sicut sponsam ornatam viro suo"). In addition, the tradition that developed around the Wedding of the Lamb drew upon the other visions of the Lamb in John's text, as well as upon scattered references in the gospels to wedding banquets or the coming of the bridegroom, and also upon elaborate allegorization of the Song of Songs as the heavenly marriage. In this case, we find John's visual descriptions combining with essentially verbal and nonvisualized signs to produce newly realized visual images in late medieval art.

Of John's visions of the Lamb, the ones that contributed most to the Wedding symbolism are those that describe his followers. The first of these is the opening of the fifth seal in chapters six and seven, which is a continuation of the first vision of the Lamb, and the opening of the sealed book (which in turn follows the first vision of the Throne and thereby connects the Lamb with the Enthroned One). When the Lamb breaks the fifth seal John sees the dead souls under the altar being given white robes (6.9–11). Later, after the opening of the sixth seal John sees 144,000 from the tribes of Israel and then a great throng from every nation, all robed in white and praising God and the Lamb. The angel tells John that these "veniunt de tribulatione magna / et laverunt stolas suas et dealbaverunt eas in sanguine agni" ("come from the great tribulation and have washed their robes and made them white in the blood of the Lamb"—7.14). These followers are linked to the 144,000 virgins of chapter fourteen, who are with the Lamb on Mount Sion and praising him with the *canticum novum* (14.1–5). The Lamb's followers, in one vision martyrs, in the other virgins, were thought of as his brides, especially in the later tradition of the virgin martyrs as brides of Christ. In John's text both references stand clearly in the apocalyptic tradition that insists upon purity and persecution as necessary to salvation.[21] This purity of the Lamb's followers is emphasized by the Pearl Maiden, with her repeated references to the *moteles meyny* (900;

[21]For an example of the emphasis on purity as necessary to salvation and to the separation of the saved from the wicked, compare the close of the Book of Daniel: "Go your way, Daniel, for the words are kept secret and sealed till the time of the end. Many shall purify themselves and be refined, making themselves shining white, but the wicked shall continue in wickedness and none of them shall understand; only the wise leaders shall understand" (12.9–10).

"withouten mote" then becomes the linking phrase of the following section, XVI).

Also important in developing the image of the Wedding of the Lamb, and especially significant for the Pearl poet, are the various references in the gospels to banquets and weddings. In particular, Matthew's parable of the Wedding Feast (22.1–14), in which Jesus tells the story of a king "qui fecit nuptias filio suo" ("who prepared a wedding feast for his son"—21.1), and Luke's version of this parable, which has only a banquet (*magna cena*, Lk. 14.16), sources for the parable in the prologue to *Cleanness*, were understood as references to the *aeterno convivo*, the eschatological banquet (*Glossa ordinaria*, *PL*, 114.155).[22] Through these connections, the Wedding of the Lamb is joined to all the iconography and symbolism of the eucharist. With the basic figure from the gospels—that the kingdom of God will be a joyous nuptial celebration, where the saved are united to God in an eternal feast—was added the passage in Paul's letter to Ephesians that compares the relationship of Christ and his Church to human marriage (Eph. 5.22–33). Finally, this figure was enriched by the allegorization of the Song of Songs, especially in Bernard of Clairvaux's sermons, the whole resulting in an extended metaphor of love, marriage, and feasting, which became available to artists and poets depicting the joy of the world beyond human time.[23]

[22]The *Glossa ordinaria* specifically identifies Matthew's *nuptiae* with Luke's *cena* and both with the *æternam convivium*. Modern biblical scholars point out that the celebration of the eucharist "anticipated the return of Jesus and the messianic feast with him in the immediate future" (Gager 153); there are numerous biblical texts that make this connection, including Mark 14.25 and 1 Cor. 11.26 (Gager 155, note 19). Furthermore, Matthew's version of the Parable of the Wedding Feast, by its use of the "tag line" (22.13) "introduces an eschatological note that changes the image of the wedding feast from the Church to the eschatological Messianic banquet" (McKenzie 100).

[23]I know of no one source that summarizes the complex traditions of exegesis and iconography that fed into the Wedding Feast. Bernard of Clairvaux's sermons contain the most extended allegorization of the Song of Songs and are considered a cornerstone of the late medieval figures of the mystical marriage and God as the Christian's bridegroom.

Several of the illustrated Apocalypses attest to the interest in the Wedding of the Lamb and include large illustrations of the Wedding Feast, even though as we have seen, John barely mentions the Wedding and says nothing whatsoever about a wedding feast. The Wedding Feast in the Morgan Apocalypse is a good example of the way this scene in the illustrated Apocalypses is created from all the interwoven traditions and symbols, especially the eucharist, the eschatological banquet, and the Wedding of the Lamb (MS.M524, fol. 17r). [Figure 8] The manuscript illustration combines divine power, eternal moment, and human tenderness: the bride enthroned on a high bench, her loving embrace of the Lamb, the sumptuous banquet laid out on the table, with one guest holding forth a chalice, and an angel emerging from the clouds above to blow a trumpet.

The Morgan's Wedding Feast appears on the same page with the better-known vision of Christ enthroned in glory, and together the two pictures provide a visual relationship between the sacrament of the eucharist and the transcendent reality of the Kingdom of God. The scene of Christ enthroned is the supreme image of the divine, beyond time and space, whereas the banquet depicted below includes the human and historical institution, Christ's church, along with the individual souls privileged to share in the beatific vision and the reign of God. The Wedding Feast is not only a vision of eternity, but a sacramental union, realizable on earth within time through the eucharist. The ritual offering of the chalice evokes the mass, at once both a symbolic act of the transcendent union of divine and human and also a commemoration of an historical event, an event which ultimately makes such a union possible.

As in John's text, in *Pearl* the Wedding of the Lamb is never actually pictured, but the joy of that union is referred to from the beginning of the dream. Like the visions of the adoration of the Lamb and the heavenly Jerusalem, and in fact closely bound to both of them, the Wedding of the Lamb is referred to twice in *Pearl*: once by the Pearl Maiden to the dreamer, and secondly by the poet himself. The context for the earlier refer-

FIGURE 8. Christ Enthroned; and the Wedding Feast of the Lamb. The Pierpont Morgan Library, New York, M.524, fol. 17v (mid-13th cen.). By permission of the Pierpont Morgan Library. (Photo: The Pierpont Morgan Library.)

ences, as well as the medium through which they are filtered, is the dreamer's obsessive and human love for his pearl, in answer to which the Pearl Maiden insistently refers to her love for the Lamb. By the end of the dream, following the vision of the New Jerusalem, the dreamer sees the Pearl's loving union with the Lamb in its heavenly context, visualized as a joyous celebration by the great crowd of the 144,000, all united to the Lamb. The pointed contrast between these two perspectives of love parallels the two contrasting Jerusalems: the historical Jerusalem, where the Lamb was slain, and the heavenly Jerusalem, where God's kingdom reigns and is celebrated with the "nwe songe" (881). Both the old Jerusalem and the mortal love that the dreamer has for his pearl are bound in human time and human space. However, the earthly Jerusalem has the validity of sacred history, a validity that the dreamer's obsessive, earthly love lacks.

Early in the dream the Pearl Maiden describes her marriage to the Lamb:

> Bot my Lorde þe Lombe þurȝ Hys godhede,
> He toke myself to Hys maryage,
> Corounde me quene in blysse to brede
> In lenghe of dayez þat euer schal wage;
> And sesed in alle Hys herytage
> Hys lef is. I am holy Hysse. (413–18)

In this passage the Pearl Maiden begins with the symbol of the mystical marriage and adds to it the image of a court of heaven and her election to that court. The image is further enriched by the evocation of the traditions of the heavenly wedding available through iconography and exegesis. Finally, in the last line the pun on "holy"—referring both to the sacredness and the unique exclusiveness of the Pearl Maiden's love for the Lamb—encapsulates the paradox implicit in the use of the metaphor: the love between the Lamb and the Pearl is both like and unlike human love. Like human love, the union with the Lamb insists that the lovers be all in all to each other; unlike human love, the Lamb's exclusivity is good and holy.

Towards the end of the Apocalypse, the Wedding of the Lamb is merged with the New Jerusalem. Here, in the passage in which John comes closest to actually envisioning a wedding, the New Jerusalem descends from heaven, "paratem sicut sponsam ornatam viro suo" [arrayed like a bride for her groom] (21.2). In *Pearl* the connection between the New Jerusalem and the Wedding of the Lamb is more logical and less figurative: the city is simply the place of the joyous union. As the Pearl Maiden tells the dreamer:

"Þe Lambes vyuez in blysse we bene,
A hondred and forty þowsande flot,
As in þe Apocalyppez hit is sene:
Sant John hem syȝ al in a knot.
On þe hyl of Syon, þat semly clot,
Þe apostel hem segh in gostly drem,
Arayed to þe weddyng in þat hyl-coppe,
Þe nwe cyté o Jerusalem." (785–92)

Later, when the dreamer is granted his vision of the New Jerusalem, it is in response to his specific request to go and see the place (*mote*) where the Pearl Maiden lives. This focus on the *mote* of eternal bliss serves to emphasize its otherness and to separate and celebrate the experience of union with God, rather than providing that experience itself. Likewise, much of the Pearl Maiden's earlier discourse with her *juelere* is about the Lamb's followers and their happiness, while the climax of the dreamer's own vision comes not with the appearance of the Lamb, but with the *nwe songe* sung by the Lamb's *meyny*. This emphasis is in keeping with the spirit both of John's text and of much of its artistic representations, the Moissac tympanum in particular.

The poem uses a number of different terms for the company of the blessed, some of them—the 144,000 or "maydenez" for example—taken directly from the Apocalypse, others more of the poet's own coining. The preeminent of these is "perlez," although it is indicative of the dreamer's situation in most of the poem that usually the term is in its singular form—"perle." Two of the narrator's own terms for the company of pearls are especially revealing: the first, used when he recounts the vision, is "his meyny schene" (1145); and the second, which comes in the final prayer, is "his homly hyne" (1211).[24] The term used in the poet's prayer is a humbler one, for although "homly" in Middle English is not as homely and inelegant as its modern equivalent, it does suggest a kind of ordinary domesticity, as does "hyne," a word used for common laborers and servants. "Meyny," on the other hand, is a little less lowly, for it is generally used for the followers or retinue of a lord, while "schene" elevates the company to the shining light of heaven. Characteristic of the Pearl poet (and indeed, as Burrow has shown, of much fourteenth-century poetry) is this combination of ordinariness and transcendence.[25] A pearl too, as the concrete, literal gem, combines these characteristics, for, while it lacks the dazzling light or colors of gems like rubies and emeralds, it is perfect in its roundness, a conventional figure for perfection and eternity, and in its spotlessness—a pearl is both *homly* and *schene*.

The Rivers in *Pearl* and the Apocalypse

In all the *fayre formez* of God and his kingdom that are quoted from John, described by the Pearl Maiden, and envisioned by the dreamer, there is an emphasis upon the dreamer's absence from the actual experience of theophany and from the company of blessed, of whom he is not yet a member. This separation and

[24]See Wood [Douglas] on the term "*hyne*" as it is used in the parable told by the Pearl Maiden.

[25]In the chapter on "Ricardian Style" in *Ricardian Poetry* (11–46), Burrow has a good discussion of this aspect of poetic style and discourse in late-fourteenth-century English literature. Burrow concludes: "Neither Chaucer nor his great contemporaries are often in [Arnold's] sense 'serious.' Their characteristic manner lies, to adopt a favourite phrase of the period, 'betwixt earnest and game.' This oblique and often humorous approach to great matters—God, sin, death—does impose undoubted limitations on the range of Ricardian poetry, however attractive it may be to post-Arnoldian taste" (45).

the dreamer's attempt to conquer it are very much a part of the story of *Pearl* and therefore belong to my later discussion of the *forme* as narrative pattern. However, there is also a *forme* as visual image that signifies the separation of the New Jerusalem from the dreamer's world and, as such, should be examined along with the other *formez* that refer to God's kingdom: that image is the river running through the dream landscape. Although it is usual to read this river as one and the same with the river that flows from the Throne envisioned at the end of the dream, such an identification is never made in the poem and is, I believe, totally wrong.[26]

The river that the dreamer sees flowing from the Throne is taken directly from John's Apocalypse, where it appears in the climactic vision: "Et ostendit mihi fluvium aquae vitae splendidum tamquam cristallum, / Procedentem de sede Dei et agni in medio plateae eius (22.1) [And he showed me the river of the waters of life, resplendent like crystal, / Proceeding from the Throne of God and of the Lamb into the middle of the city's street]. At virtually the same point in his own vision, the dreamer sees the same river: "A reuer of þe trone þer ran outryȝte / Watz bryȝter þen boþe þe sunne and mone" (1055–56). Traditionally, this river symbolizes the outpouring of God's gifts (Andrew and Waldron 104, note to 1055). It is a river that flows forth and that shines and was usually represented in art more as a living outgrowth than as a body of water to be crossed; the Morgan Apocalypse's river is especially remarkable in this respect. [Figure 9] In *Pearl* the river from the Throne is clearly part of the glorious splendor of the New Jerusalem, like the streets of gold and the jeweled walls.

The other river in *Pearl*—the one seen from the beginning of the dream, the one that separates the dreamer from his pearl,

[26]The identification of what I believe to be two different rivers is made in both Gordon's and Andrew and Waldron's editions. See also W. S. Johnson, who says that the river is both a boundary and a "means of passing" (41). This is the way the river Lethe works in Dante's *Purgatorio* (canto 33), but I do not think it is what we find in *Pearl*.

FIGURE 9. The River of Life. The Pierpont Morgan Library, New York, M.524, fol. 21r (mid-13th cen.). By permission of the Pierpont Morgan Library. (Photo: The Pierpont Morgan Library.)

and the one that he rashly tries to cross at the end—is not found in John's text and figures something very different from the river of the Throne. As the otherwise fairly inept artist who illustrated the Cotton Nero manuscript clearly saw and depicted in three of his four pictures accompanying *Pearl*, this first river is a line of demarcation, a visual sign symbolizing the separation of this world from the next. [Figure 10] This river is not sacramental, it is not the gifts of the Holy Spirit, it is not divine grace, and it is not the emanation of the divine into this world—it is the *separation* of the divine from the human and thus a symbol of the distance of God, not of His approach to humanity.[27] The river is the visual sign that corresponds to the insistence on the special experience of the visions that characterizes apocalyptic texts, with their sealed books and warnings of secrecy. The river in *Pearl* probably also reflects the iconographic tradition that showed John on Patmos, alone and set apart by the Bosphorus; the Morgan Apocalypse contains a particularly good example of this use of the sea as a separation between the ordinary world and the visionary one. [Figure 11] What we must remember, however, is that the dreamer is not in a position analogous to John's, for the dreamer in *Pearl* is on the wrong side of the river and therefore closer to the position of the boatman who is moving away from Patmos (and out of the picture) in the Morgan illustration.

In the last stanza, *Pearl* offers a resolution to the problem of the separatedness and distance of the otherworld and its joys:

> To pay þe Prince oþer sete saȝte,
> Hit is ful eþe to þe god Krystyin;
> For I haf founden hym, boþe day and naȝte,
> A God, a Lorde, a frende ful fyin.
> Ouer þis hyul þis lote I laȝte,
> For pyty of my perle enclyin,
> And syþen to God I hit bytaȝte,

[27]Hanning discusses the role of the river in *Pearl* as a separation marker and sees a connection between this and the river in *Navigatio sancti Brendani* ("Limit").

FIGURE 10. The River in *Pearl*. BL Cotton Nero A.x., fol. 42r. By permission of the British Library. (Photo: The British Library.)

FIGURE 11. John on Patmos. The Pierpont Morgan Library, New York, M.524, fol. 1r (mid-13th cen.). By permission of the Pierpont Morgan Library. (Photo: The Pierpont Morgan Library.)

In Krysteȝ dere blessyng and myn,
Þat in þe forme of bred and wyn
Þe preste vus scheweȝ vch a daye.
He gef vus to be His homly hyne
And precious perleȝ vnto His pay. Amen. Amen.
(1201–1212)

In this final stanza the poet, having left the visionary and apocalyptic mode altogether, turns to the sacramental, where he finds a *fayre forme* that is both visual—"þe forme of bred and wyn" that the priest "schewez" us—and verbal—the "lote" the dreamer "laȝte" on his hill. In the eucharist and the celebration of mass lies the dreamer's best hope for theophany and the joys of God's presence.

By concluding with the *fayre forme* of the eucharist, *Pearl* suggests that visions of future bliss are not available to most people, except secondhand. For all the beauty of John's visions of the *Lombe and his meyny* enjoying the bliss of the New Jerusalem, it is a beauty not immediately the dreamer's. He can see or hear or read secondhand representations of the New Jerusalem, but he cannot cross the river to join the *meyny schene* in singing the *nwe songe*. Furthermore, the dreamer's vision is definitely inferior to the certain truth of Scripture. John's vision is authoritative and reliable, but the narrator's own dream is subject to doubt. Unlike the *forme* of John's words, which are a true and accurate description, and unlike the visual *forme* of the bread and wine, which the priest shows him, the *forme* of the poet's dream is human and flawed. In *Pearl*, neither John's vision nor the eucharist deals with present reality—each works in a different mode, the modes of future time or sacrament, but their *fayre formez* are still more fully realized than those of the narrator's dream.

It remains to the other poems to introduce and develop other aspects of the *formez* made by God and those adapted or created by his creatures, in particular the *fayre formez* of biblical history and the Beatitudes, the *fayre formez* of sacrament and the promises of the beatific vision, and also the *contraré* of *fayre formez*, the signs of divine judgment and punishment.

TWO

Signs of the Divine in *Cleanness*, *Patience*, and *Sir Gawain and the Green Knight*

PEARL PROVIDES the most visual and the most apocalyptic images of the divine found in the Pearl poet's works. The other three poems are less explicitly and less exclusively concerned with the *formez* of God and his kingdom. Indeed, when taken in their respective order in the manuscript, the latter three poems move progressively further and further away from visualized and apocalyptic images of the divine. *Cleanness* is in many ways the most apocalyptic of the poems after *Pearl.* While picking up on the figures of the Wedding Feast, with references to the "frelych feste" (162) to which many are called, *Cleanness* mostly emphasizes what *Pearl* neglects: images of the crises of the Last Days before the establishment of God's kingdom and the importance of God's action in past history, not just in the future. *Patience*, on the other hand, moves away from a concern with either future or past and toward a more present and more internalized representation of the divine, a representation that is markedly less visual than that found in *Pearl* or *Cleanness*, and that is based not on apocalyptic visions of the world to come, but rather on the "heuen-ryche" (14 and *passim*) spoken of by Jesus in the gospels. Finally, *Sir Gawain and the Green Knight* leaves behind explicitly biblical and Christian signs for the supposedly otherworldly, but finally human and fallen, wonders of romance and fairytale, the "ferlyes on þis folde" (23) so beloved of medieval courtly audiences. The authority of scripture and the fairness of divine signs that are established by the first three poems in the manuscript provide a context for reading *Sir Gawain and the Green Knight*, a poem which lacks any authoritative *formez* whatsoever. When approached through his other poems, the Pearl poet's best loved and most read work stands not as a denial but rather as an affirmation that the fairest *formez* are God's—those in his sacred text, those in the sacraments, and those in his kingdom.

Cleanness and the "Frelych Feste"

Like *Pearl*, *Cleanness* grants authority and primacy to the sacred word, and, like *Pearl*, *Cleanness* looks to the eucharist as the fairest *forme* immediately available to God's creatures in this world, the closest humans can get now to the beatific vision. But the context and content of *Cleanness* are otherwise quite different. *Pearl* focuses on the *fayre formez* of God's kingdom, *Cleanness* on the *contraré* (paradoxically enough since this is the poem that speaks explicitly about *fayre formez*). Whereas *Pearl* omits all of the Apocalypse's signs of the catastrophes, wars, judgment, and punishment that are to precede the establishment of God's kingdom, in *Cleanness* the visual signs of divine judgment, especially punishment, predominate. In *Pearl* references to judgment are few and to punishment even fewer, and when the question of judgment does occur, the biblical source is the Parable of the Vineyard from Matthew's gospel, and the medium verbal discourse and debate, not visual symbol, much less apocalyptic vision. *Cleanness* too avoids using the signs of divine judgment provided in the Apocalypse; otherwise it does convey an apocalyptic sense of cataclysmic loss and terror, using *formez* of punishment found in the Old Testament. Even the *fayre formez* in *Cleanness*, which are few, have very little connection to John's Apocalypse, but rather are drawn primarily from the recorded words and deeds of Jesus in the gospels. In other words, while *Pearl*, at least until the last stanza, looks to the future and to visions and dreams, *Cleanness* turns to biblical history for its *fayre formez* and their *contraré*.

The images of divine judgment in *Cleanness*, particularly the flood and the fire, are supremely biblical, for they were favorites not only of post-biblical exegetes and preachers, but of the prophets, Jesus, and the apostles, as well.[1] The visualization of these signs in *Cleanness* comes directly from their Old Testament accounts, the original historical contexts of these popular types of the End. *Cleanness* is thus the poet's most typological and also his most historical poem.

While the poet uses his remarkable craft of *pointing* to expand the visualization of each sign, his additions to the biblical accounts are not extensive, and are primarily a kind of highlighting of some aspect of the apocalyptic moment of crisis and judgment. In the retelling of the Flood story, for example, the coming of the flood itself is expanded from a few verses in Genesis to over sixty lines in *Cleanness* (361–424; cf. Gen. 8.11–12, 17–21). However, it is not the actual process of flooding that the poem elaborates upon—that is taken care of, with brilliantly effective alliteration, in eight lines:

> Þen bolned þe abyme, and bonkez con ryse,
> Waltes out vch walle-heued in ful wode stremez;
> Watz no brymme þat abod vnbrosten bylyue;
> Þe mukel lauande loghe to þe lyfte rered.
> Mony clustered clowde clef alle in clowtez;
> Torent vch a rayn-ryfte and rusched to þe vrþe,
> Fon neuer in forty dayez. And þen þe flod ryses,
> Ouerwaltez vche a wod and þe wyde feldez. (363–70)

Except for this passage, it is the description of the experience of the victims that occupies the bulk of the flood passage in *Clean-*

[1]See, for example, Wisdom 10.4–6; Luke 17.26–29; 2 Pet. 2.4–9. In the Lucan passage, Jesus compares the events of the Last Days to Noah's Flood and Sodom and Gomorrah, saying that "sicut factum est in diebus Noe" (17.26) [as it was in the days of Noah] and "sicut factum est in diebus Loth" (17.28) [as it was in the days of Lot], so it will be "in diebus Filii hominis" [in the days of the Son of Man]. The Petrine epistle, which is strongly eschatological and apocalyptic, also refers to the fall of the angels, and has been seen by Cuffe (115) as important for understanding *Cleanness*, since it draws together three of the poem's narratives.

ness. In a sense, this is a matter of narration, not of visual description, but it is precisely upon the visualization of the doomed creatures that the poet focuses our attention, in order to illustrate the wrath of God and the form of divine punishment. The description begins with the flight of the victims, particularized as a mother with her children:

> Fyrst feng to þe flyȝt alle þat fle myȝt;
> Vuche burde with her barne þe byggyng þay leuez
> And bowed to þe hyȝ bonk þer brentest hit wern,
> And heterly to þe hyȝe hyllez þay haled on faste.
> (377–80)

The flight of the wild creatures follows, the passage climaxes in the last desperate pleas for mercy from the Creator, and the poet sweeps away the scene, as ruthlessly as God's flood obliterates his creation:

> Luf lokez to luf and his leue takez,
> For to ende alle at onez and for euer twynne.
> By forty dayez wern faren, on folde no flesch styryed
> Þat þe flod nade al freten wyth feȝtande waȝez. (401–404)

In the second major narrative, Sodom and Gomorrah, the apocalyptic catastrophe is handled somewhat differently. The poet pays less attention to the victims of the catastrophe, and instead uses his craft to recapture the fire itself:

> . . . . þe wyndez He [God] callez,
> And þay wroþely vpwafte and wrastled togeder,
> Fro fawre half of þe folde flytande loude.
> Clowdez clustered bytwene kesten vp torres,
> Þat þe þik þunder-þrast þirled hem ofte.
> Þe rayn rueled adoun, ridlande þikke
> Of felle flaunkes of fyr and flakes of soufre,
> Al in smolderande smoke smachande ful ille,
> Swe aboute Sodamas and hit sydez alle,

Gorde to Gomorra, þat þe grounde laused,
Abdama and Syboym, þise ceteis alle faure
Al birolled wyth þe rayn, rostted and brenned,
And ferly flayed þat folk þat in þose fees lenged. (948–60)

Giving more detail than that found in Genesis, the poet also connects the fire directly to the flames of hell:

For when þat þe Helle herde þe houndez of heuen,
He watȝ ferlyly fayn, vnfolded bylyue;
Þe grete barreȝ of þe abyme he barst vp at onez,
Þat alle þe regioun torof in riftes ful grete,
And clouen alle in lyttel cloutes, þe clyffez aywhere,
As lauce leuez of þe boke bat lepes in twynne.
Þe brethe of þe brynston bi þat hit blende were,
Al þo citees and her sydes sunkken to helle. (961–68)

The visualization in *Cleanness* of hell opening up and the cities sinking into it comes not from Genesis, but reflects rather the images of Babylon's fall in the illustrated Apocalypses, as well as the ubiquitous depictions, in every medium from stone to stained glass, of hellmouth swallowing the evil and the damned. [Figure 5]

In the third major narrative in *Cleanness*, Belshazzar's Feast, the poet concentrates his visual descriptions upon the sinful acts and upon the message of judgment, rather than upon the punishing catastrophe or the suffering of the victims. The two chief visual images of the divine in this section of the poem are the holy vessels and the writing on the wall. In both cases the poet is providing us with descriptions of the symbols of the divine, instead of giving us the direct account of a divine action, as he does for the Flood and for Sodom and Gomorrah.

The lavish description of the vessels is a poetic tour-de-force, comparable to the craft and the richness that Solomon used, "with alle þe syence þat hym sende þe souerayn Lorde" (1454), when the vessels were first created. The poet's description involves an intricate layering of symbol and mimetic image: vessels of holiness, as signs of God's presence, are crafted by humans in gems and precious metals, in the likeness both of God's creation, and of humanity's as well:

> Couered cowpes foul clene, as casteles arayed,
> Enbaned vnder batelment with bantelles quoynt,
> And fyled out of fygures of ferlylé schappes.
> . . . .
> Pinacles py3t þer apert þat profert bitwene,
> And al bolled abof wyth braunches and leues,
> Pyes and papejayes purtrayed withinne,
> As þay prudly hade piked of pomgarnades;
> For alle þe blomes of þe bo3es wer blyknande perles,
> And alle þe fruyt in þo formes of flaumbeande gemmes.
> (1458–60, 1463–68)

Though a human creation, the vessels have "ben blessed bifore wyth bischopes hondes" (1445) and therefore are sacred signs. Furthermore, the landscape that the vessels mimic in turn invokes God's kingdom, since, like John's New Jerusalem and other traditional paradises, it is made with jewels.[2] There is a complex, and potentially confusing, distancing in all this: signs that recreate signs; verbal descriptions of physical signs that point to other physical signs; and finally God's own symbols from nature, mimicked visually by Solomon's craftsmen, and then verbally by the Pearl poet's craft.

The writing on the wall is an image that works in reverse of that of the vessels. Writing is very much a human enterprise, and this is emphasized by the poet. The hand looks like a human hand, it writes with a stylus, and it writes upon a wall made by humans. Yet all is transformed into an otherworldly image of horror:

[2]See Patch (190) and W. S. Johnson (35); jewels, of course, characterize the heavenly paradise as well as the earthly.

Forþy a ferly bifel þat fele folk seȝen;
Fyrst knew hit þe kyng and alle þe cort after:
In þe palays pryncipale, vpon þe playn wowe,
In contrary of þe candelstik, þer clerest hit schyned,
Þer apered a paume, wyth poyntel in fyngres,
Þat watz grysly and gret, and grymly he wrytes;
Non oþer forme bot a fust faylande þe wryste,
Pared on þe parget, purtrayed lettres. (1529–36)

A vision of a human part, "non oþer forme bot a fust," using a man-made tool, nonetheless turns out to be a divinely created sign, a message straight from God.

Although, as we are warned in the Prologue, signs of uncleanness and more exactly of its punishment are dominant in *Cleanness*, the poem does contain some *fayre formez* as well. These include: the Wedding Feast, God enthroned in his *cort*, the Nativity, and the beatific vision. Interconnected in various ways, all of these are signs of the joy of God's Kingdom.

The vision of God enthroned is evoked explicitly several times in the poem, the first of these in the opening lines:

He is so clene in His courte, þe Kyng þat al weldez,
And honeste in His housholde, and hagherlych serued
With angelez enourled in alle þat is clene,
Boþe wythinne and wythouten in wedez ful bryȝt.
(17–20)

The visual basis of this image of God and his court is the *Maiestas Domini*, the enthroned deity, "þat Syre vpon throne" (1112), but the verbal focus is generally upon God's court and household, not upon the divine sovereign himself. In this, *Cleanness* is like *Pearl*, which focuses on the Lamb's *meyny* and their pure heavenliness, on those celebrating the theophany of the world beyond, rather than on theophany itself.

In the Prologue to *Cleanness*, this emphasis upon the court of the reigning God is primarily achieved through the retelling of the Parable of the Wedding Feast (51–160) and the poet's own "mini-parable," the latter given in the form of a question about the appropriate attire for approaching a ruler in his court (33–48).[3] Since both the parable and the mini-parable develop the imagery of a court gathered for a feast,[4] their visual emphasis in *Cleanness* is upon the gathering and the celebration, not upon the "vrþly haþel þat hyȝ honour haldez" (35) and who "sette[z] solempnely in a sete ryche" (37). The emphasis upon the court and the guests, not upon God, is made clear in *Cleanness* at the conclusion of the parable, when the narrator tells us:

> Thus comparisunez Kryst þe kyndom of heuen
> To þis frelych feste þat fele arn to called. (161–62)

By beginning with a reference to the Matthean *nuptiae* and then ending with the Lucan motif of a *cena*, the poet underscores the connection between God's court and the eschatological banquet or wedding banquet. Through its immediate context in the Prologue, the *frelych feste* as a sign also refers both to the eucharist and to the beatific vision. The eucharist is invoked in the extended analogy between priests and poets (7–10), while the sixth beatitude, which promises the beatific vision to whoever is "*mundo corde*" (Matt. 5.8) or "clene of his hert" (27), is explicitly recalled in commmenting on the "*clannesse*" (26) of "þe Kyng þat al weldez" (17).

Later in the poem, in the Incarnation passage, the *fayre formez* of God's kingdom are developed further and related to the historical events of the Incarnation and Christ's ministry and also

[3]I have coined the term "mini-parable" to stress that the poet has provided a very brief *exemplum* that is much like the parables told by Jesus, especially in its use of its audience's own cultural references in order to illustrate its message. Matthew's Parable of the Wedding Feast and Luke's Parable of the Great Banquet are both eschatological, or as modern scholars term them "parables of the kingdom" (Dodd; Kelly and Irwin 255).

[4]As several readers have noted, in retelling Matthew's parable the poet creates the setting of a late medieval feast, very like the one at the Arthurian court that opens *Gawain*, and also like the similar and parallel feasts at Hautdesert. See, for example, Spearing (*The Gawain Poet* 45) and Edward Wilson (85).

to the sacramental signs of eucharist, baptism, and penance. This passage, which stands out as intrusive and digressive (deliberately so, I believe), comes between the story of Sodom and Gommorah and the story of Belshazzar's Feast (1069–1132). Here, by elaborating the paradoxes of God's *clanness* and *cortaysye*, the poem underscores the divine ineffability of the *fayre formez* of past history, future joy, and present life.

The passage opens with the startling metaphor of sexual romance for humanity's relationship to God—startling because it comes in a poem that stresses sexual purity. The poet does not merely speak of humanity's love for God as romantic (an analogy so commonplace as to carry little force); he even uses overtly sexual words:

> If þou wyl dele *drwrye* with Dryȝtyn þenne,
> And lelly louy þy Lorde and His leef worþe,
> Þenne confourme þe to Kryst, and þe clene make.
> (1065–67; emphasis mine)[5]

The paradox of chastely loving God like a sexual lover is followed by the paradox of the Incarnation, which is pictured as a pure taking-on of flesh, a clean enclosing within a corrupt world—"For non so clene of such a clos com neuer er þenne" (1088)—and a clean breaking into an unviolated enclosure:

[5]*Drwrye* is a term used primarily for sexual love (often unlicensed sexual love); it is used as an epithet for the *luflace* the lady gives Gawain in *Gawain* (1805, 2033). Cf. *MED*, which lists "love between God and man" as a figurative meaning for the word (the third meaning after romantic or sexual love and flirtatious behavior). However, the *MED*'s instances of this figurative use are few indeed; in fact there are only two citations given, one the line in question from *Cleanness*, and one from *Ancrene Wisse*: "þe deore druerie þet he haueȝ to his deore spuse" (89b). But this really begs the issue, since it's obvious that in each of these cases the author has deliberately chosen a word with very strongly sexual and passionate nuances in order to give force and life to the metaphor. Furthermore, many of the citations for *druerie* used in a romantic or sexual sense are from the Pearl poet's works, primarily *Gawain*.

For, loke, fro fyrst þat He lyȝt withinne þe lel mayden,
By how comly a kest He watz clos þere,
When venkkyst watz no vergynyté, ne vyolence maked,
Bot much clener watz hir corse, God kynned þerinne.
(1069–72)

The climactic paradox of this passage, which keeps stressing both the untouched purity and the passionate closeness of divine love, finally contradicts the poem's thesis that the unclean cannot enter the divine presence:

And ȝif clanly He þenne com, ful cortays þerafter,
Þat alle þat longed to luþer ful lodly He hated,
By nobleye of His norture He nolde neuer towche
Oȝt þat watz vngoderly oþer ordure watz inne.
Ȝet, comen lodly to þat Lede, as lazares monye,
Summe lepre, summe lome, and lomerande blynde,
Poysened and parlatyk, and pyned in fyres,
Drye folk and ydropike, and dede at at þe laste,
Alle called on þat Cortayse and claymed His grace.
(1089–97)

The force of the "ȝet" is very strong in this passage and calls attention to its apparent contradiction. The clue to that paradox is *cortayse*, which mediates between *clanness* and *grace*, between the preservation of pure holiness and the welcoming of all would-be followers, between final irrevocable judgment and merciful forgiveness. In the midst of this poem about *clanness*, with its narratives of sexual, religious, and moral filth, narratives that place great stress upon the preservation of the pure and holy and the guarding against violation, we get an extended lyric meditation on Christ's *cortayse*, which apparently contradicts his *clanness*. Christ, who arrives "clanly" is "ful cortays þerafter"; his pure divinity becomes open, and "cortayse" is the word used by the poet to describe that openness.

The "cortayse" that comes "þerafter" is exemplified in Christ's ministry, in his healing, in his institution of the eucharist, and finally in his passion and resurrection. These last two, the central historical events in Christ's life and in all history, are not recounted or even mentioned explicitly in *Cleanness*, but are only evoked implicitly through the reference to the eucharist. As the description of Christ's breaking of the bread shows, although the crucifixion seems the ultimate violence, it, like the incarnation, is a pure, non-violating act. Since the eucharist is a reenactment of Christ's sacrifice, and the priest's act of breaking the bread in the mass is a dramatic, visual symbol of the breaking of Christ's body, the poem's reference to Christ's breaking the bread refers simultaneously to: the crucifixion, the Last Supper, the resurrection (the Supper at Emmaus, when the disciples recognized Christ "at the breaking of the bread," is one of the resurrection appearances, recorded in Luke 24.13–35), and the Christian community's celebration of the eucharist. The passage referring to the breaking of the bread emphasizes the "cleanness" of Christ's handling, so clean that he needs no knife or blade:

> So hende watz His hondelying vche ordure hit schonied,
> And þe gropyng so goud of God and Man boþe,
> Þat for fetys of His fyngeres fonded he neuer
> Nauþer to cout ne to kerue with knyf ne wyth egge;
> Forþy brek He þe bred blades wythouten,
> For hit ferde freloker in fete in His fayre honde,
> Displayed more pryuyly when He hit part schulde,
> Þenne alle þe toles of Tolowse moȝt tyȝt hit to kerue.
> (1101–1108)

This breaking is a pure act; the divine is not corrupted by violation, but rather purifies the corrupt that it encounters, and it does so without intermediary or human assistance (without the use of knives).[6]

Implicit in the *fayre formez* of the Prologue and the Incarnation

[6]Christ's unique way of breaking the bread, barely implied in the gospel account, eventually developed into the idea that he did it better and more

passage is the fairest *forme*, the beatific vision. The King in his court and the *frelych feste*—as historical Last Supper, present sacrament, and eschatological banquet—are figures of the beatific vision, particularly of the experience of the beatific vision by those enjoying it. This experience is grounded in the historical act of Christ's birth, which is celebrated with music:

> And þer watz solace and songe wher sorȝ hatz ay cryed;
> For aungelles with instrumentes of organes and pypes,
> And rial ryngande rotes and þe reken fyþel,
> And alle hende þat honestly moȝt an hert glade,
> Aboutte my lady watz lent quen ho delyuer were.
> (1080–84)

This angelic adoration of Christ at the moment of his birth is a *canticum novum* and represents a theophanic moment within time. Its role in *Cleanness* as the historical realization of God's presence is consistent with its representation in art. From earliest times, the depiction of the Virgin and Child, in stone, wood, stained glass, and painting, has been used as a focal point of adoration; it can be found on and above altars and on tympana. Even when part of a narrative cycle on the life of Christ, the Nativity often has a transcendent iconic quality. In the passage in *Cleanness* however, the Pearl poet has again avoided theophany by focusing our attention on those witnessing and celebrating the nativity.

In *Cleanness* the nativity is thus presented as an angelic celebration, not as a visualized scene. The closest to an actual description of the beatific vision in the poem is a typological one: the appearance of the Three Visitors to Abraham. Traditionally, this episode has been seen by Christian exegetes as both a sign of the Trinity and also a prefiguration of the sacra-

cleanly than a sharp knife could—a typical medieval literalization and rationalization. See, for example, references to Christ's "clean," knifeless cutting in the N-Town play of "Christ's Appearances to the Disciples" (Happé, 592–606, esp. 602, stanza 36).

ment of the eucharist. A fifth-century mosaic at Santa Maria Maggiore, for example, provides a striking visualization of the event and of its typological significance.[7] [Figure 12] The Pearl poet presents the scene in a way that manages to introduce a certain subtle vagueness, so that a visual "appearance" rather than actual theophany is suggested:

> Þenne watz he [Abraham] war on þe waye of wlonk
> Wyȝez þrynne;
> If Þay were farande and fre and fayre to beholde
> Hit is eþe to leue by þe last ende. (606–608)

Unlike the statement in Genesis that announces the historical fact of God's appearance to Abraham—"Apparuit autem ei Dominus in convalle Mambre" [Then the Lord appeared to him in the valley of Mambre] (18:1)—the poet has given us only a statement of Abraham's consciousness of God's appearance. Furthermore, there is no direct description of the Visitors, only a secondhand comment that they must have been "fayre to behold." The fullness of that *fayre forme* can only be judged at "þe last ende." The signs of God's kingdom in *Cleanness*, the *fayre formez* that the poet implicitly warns us in the Prologue will not be his task, are few enough, and none of them, not even the fairest of *formez*, the beatific vision, receives the kind of full visual description accorded to the *contraré* signs like the Flood. The *pointing* the Pearl poet is so justly famous for is certainly found in *Cleanness*, but it is lavished on the signs of horror and catastrophe, not on those of joy.

[7]Abraham's Visitors "regularly served to represent the Trinity, evidently because the text of Genesis affirms the theophanic character of Abraham's vision, and the presence of three figures in this theophany led to its acceptance by Christian theologians as a manifestation of the Trinity" (Grabar 114). See also *Glossa ordinaria* on this passage (*PL* 113.126), which connects the event to the eucharist, as well as interpreting the three men as the Trinity; and see the comments in Morey (277; cf. pl. 178).

FIGURE 12. The Hospitality of Abraham (mosaic). S. Maria Maggiore, Rome (5th cen.). (Photo: Scala/Art Resource, New York.)

Patience and the "Heuen-ryche"

Although using different forms, and different biblical texts as sources for those forms, *Pearl* and *Cleanness* are alike in two important ways: in the strongly visual quality of their particular *formez* of God and his kingdom, and in the essentially apocalyptic quality of those forms. *Patience* is markedly different in both respects. The dominant *fayre forme* in *Patience* is the *heuen-ryche*, and it is most deliberately nonvisual and nonapocalyptic, unlike the vision of the New Jerusalem in *Pearl*, and unlike the description of the courts and feasts that represent the kingdom of God in *Cleanness*. This lack of visualization of God's kingdom in *Patience* derives in large part from the Beatitudes, the biblical source used for the *heuen-ryche*. The Beatitudes, though somewhat eschatological, are not at all apocalyptic or visual. Matthew (like Luke in a shorter version) deemphasizes the visual image of heavenly joy, by focusing on the abstract, internal quality of blessedness that characterizes the *regnum caelorum*. In addition, the Beatitudes are placed in a frame of present time, thereby undercutting some of the suggestions of a distant visionary future. Whereas all the other Beatitudes look to the reward of future joys, the first and last Beatitudes, which specifically promise the Kingdom of God, assert the present reality of the Kingdom for those who are *pauperes spiritu* and who *persecutionem patiuntur*:

> Beati pauperes spiritu quoniam ipsorum *est* regnum caelorum. . . .
> Beati qui persecutionem patiuntur propter iustitiam quoniam ipsorum *est* regnum caelorum.
> (Mt. 5:3, 10; emphasis mine)

> [Blessed are the poor in spirit for theirs *is* the Kingdom of Heaven. . . .
> Blessed are those who endure persecution for justice's sake for theirs *is* the Kingdom of Heaven.]

Thay are happen þat han in hert pouerté,
For hores *is* þe heuen-ryche to holde for euer;
. . . .
Þay ar happen also þat con her hert stere,
For hores *is* þe heuen-ryche, as I er sayde.
(*Patience*, 13–14, 27–28; emphasis mine)

The use of the present tense, by both Matthew and the Pearl poet, makes it clear that this is no mythic kingdom, no conventional paradise or New Jerusalem, but an internal state, one that is not visualized, but is fully realized. The *pauperes spiritu* do not gain the Kingdom of God—they have it already within them, as a non-visual condition.[8] The subsequent exegesis offered in the Prologue to *Patience* continues in this non-visual mode and resorts to personifying the virtues in order to emphasize the internalization of the Kingdom. *Pouert* and *Pacyence*, two of the "ladyes" of the Beatitudes (30–33) are seen as the narrator's "playferes" (45), and his reluctant submission to their presence is an allegory of the proper conditioning of his heart. The mode of personification allegory is rare for this poet and is used here, I believe, in order to emphasize the internalization and non-visual quality of the Beatitudes.

The Prologue of *Patience* is unique in the Pearl poet's works—over fifty lines without a single visual detail, much less any well-pointed description. The rest of *Patience* is not without visualization, however, not even without visual signs of the divine, but they are primarily images of divine action, and more particularly of divine judgment. Like *Cleanness*, *Patience* has a strongly visualized description of apocalyptic disaster by water, although in *Patience* the disaster is the threat of shipwreck, not the actuality of flood. The storm that God raises when Jonah is running away to Joppa is typical of apocalyptic warning, and it so functions in the Book of Jonah. The Pearl poet, drawing on his superb craft of alliterative description, expands on the passage

[8]For an earlier and fuller discussion of this feature of *Patience*, see Prior, "*Patience*—Beyond Apocalypse."

in his biblical source in order to create a climactic moment of terror and cosmic disaster:

> Anon out of þe norþ-est þe noys bigynes,
> When boþe breþes con blowe vpon blo watteres.
> Roȝ rakkes þer ros with rudnyng anvnder;
> Þe see souȝed ful sore, gret selly to here;
> Þe wyndes on þe wonne water so wrastel togeder
> Þat þe wawes ful wode waltered so hiȝe
> And efte busched to þe abyme, þat breed fysches
> Durst nowhere for roȝ arest at þe bothem. (137–45)

After this vivid description of the storm, which is a paraphrase and an expansion of a single verse in the Bible (Jon. 1.3), the poet has added seventeen lines detailing the damage to the ship, before picking up with the next verse in the Bible, the one narrating the terror of the sailors and their prayers for help. The heightened drama created by the Pearl poet's expansion is obvious, but the increased visualization is not always noted. The effect of such visualization is similar to that of the illustrated Apocalypses: the meaning of the symbols is not elaborated nor extended, but the impact is. Whether it is through the vivid colors of the Trinity Apocalypse artist, or the life-like grimaces sculpted on the damned in the Conques Last Judgment, or the power of the Pearl poet's alliterative descriptions—the horror of divine punishment comes home to the viewer/reader.

While thus employing at least one traditional, iconographic sign of divine punishment and judgment, and focusing on a nonvisual image of God's kingdom, *Patience* avoids, for the most part, the popular images of the divine, that is, of God himself. There are some references to iconographic images of God, notably the apocalyptic image of God enthroned and the image of Christ crucified, but these are encouched in irony. When Jonah first receives the call to preach to Nineveh, he grumbles:

> "Oure Syre syttes," he says, "on sege so hyȝe
> In His glowande glorye, and gloumbes ful lyttel
> Þaȝ I be nummen in Nunniue and naked dispoyled,
> On rode rwly torent with rybaudes mony." (93–96)

The first of these two sacred images is the apocalyptic one of the eternal God enthroned, the latter of the historical Christ crucified. The clear visualization in which these two images are combined and presented in *Patience* owes much to the many late medieval representations of Christ on the cross, with God the Father above and behind him, as well as to the vision of Christ enthroned with the angels bearing a cross behind the Throne. The representation of the Trinity in this way—God the Father behind Christ enthroned, with the Holy Spirit as a dove hovering somewhere in the middle—is especially common in the small English alabasters from the fourteenth and fifteenth centuries and no doubt would have been quite familiar to the Pearl poet and his audience. [Figure 13] But Jonah's way of combining the images and applying one to himself is not only wrong—it is blasphemous. As the audience of *Patience* knew very well, the one seated on the throne in "glowande glorye" is the same as the one suffering on the cross, although they are in different times, one in history and one in eternity. Jonah's willful and selfish confusion here, by the way, effectively distances him from the crucified Jesus and works against seeing Jonah as a Christ figure—Jonah may make the identification, but attentive readers should not.[9] To underscore the irony of Jonah's foolishness, the narrator later tells us, when Jonah is floundering in the whale:

> Bot he watz sokored by þat Syre þat syttes so hiȝe,
> Þaȝ were wanlez of wele in wombe of þat fissche,
> And also dryuen þurȝ þe depe and in derk walterez.
> (261–63)

[9]See Andrew, "Jonah and Christ," for an argument for the importance of the Christ figure; compare Schleusner, who says that the poet "does not make a great deal of Jonah's figural status" (961).

There is one other visualized sign in *Patience* that points both to God (or rather to his Son) and also to divine judgment and divine action—Jonah in the whale's belly. This is actually a group of signs, some made highly visual by the poet, some drawing on a long tradition of interpretation and allegorization. They all merit close examination, since they serve as an interesting and unusual example of how the poet handles a "loaded" sign, one with both a strongly visual image, or series of images, and also with a complex iconographic and exegetical meaning, or series of meanings.

As the commentators are well aware, Jonah in the whale's belly is exegetically distinctive, since it is one of the few Old Testament signs singled out by Jesus for typological and allegorical import. Jesus's famous reference is in Matthew's gospel:

> "Generatio mala et adultera signum quaerit.
> Et signum non dabitur ei nisi signum Ionae prophetae.
> Sicut enim fuit Ionas in ventre ceti tribus diebus et tribus noctibus,
> Sic erit Filius hominis in corde terrae tribus diebus et tribus noctibus." (Mt. 12:39–40)

> [An evil and false generation seeks a sign. No sign will be given to them, except for the sign of the prophet Jonah. For just as Jonah was in the belly of the whale for three days and three nights, so the Son of Man will be in the depths of the earth for three days and three nights.]

The implicit, and explicit, exegesis given by Jesus himself is thus to his own suffering, death, burial, and resurrection. The three days' sojourn in the whale is an unmistakable reference to Christ's death and descent into hell, and, by extension, Jonah's release from the whale has always been read as a reference to the resurrection. The *Glossa ordinaria*, for example, tells us simply: "Sicut ejectus est in aridam, sic Christus surrexit in gloriam" (*PL* 114.128). [Just as he (Jonah) was thrown out onto

FIGURE 15 (ABOVE). Initial "S" from "Salvum me" (Psalm 68/69). BL MS. Egerton 2908, fol. 176v (14th cen.?). By permission of the British Library. (Photo: The British Library.)

FIGURE 13. The Trinity, with Crucifixion (English alabaster, ca. 1400). Victoria and Albert Museum, London. (Photo: Victoria and Albert Museum.)

FIGURE 14 (BELOW). Jonah and the Whale (relief from the catacomb of Priscilla) Louvre, Paris. (Photo: Giraudon/Art Resource, New York.)

dry land, so Christ rose to glory.] Iconography used this event as a sign of the resurrection—it was especially popular in early Christian art, either as a single episode or often as a sequence that combined Jonah's emergence from the whale with his sleep under the woodbine, as in a relief from the catacomb of Priscilla. [Figure 14]

The *signum Ionae* can also be read as a story of individual suffering and salvation, since, according to the earliest theological discussions, everyone has the opportunity to participate in Christ's death and resurrection. Paul writes in Romans:

> Have you forgotten that when we were baptized into union with Christ Jesus we were baptized into his death? By baptism we were buried with him, and lay dead, in order that, as Christ was raised from the dead in the splendour of the Father, so also we might set our feet upon the new path of life. (Romans 6.3–4)

Both a prefiguration of the crucifixion, and also a type of the universal human experiences of pain, grief, loneliness, and death, the *signum Ionae* has been associated with the suffering servant passage in Isaiah and Psalms 21/22 and 68/69.[10] Psalm 68/69 is particularly important for the *signum Ionae*, since its opening verses contain verbal parallels to the "Jonah-Psalm" of the Book of Jonah:[11]

> Salvum me fac Deus quoniam intraverunt aquae usque
> ad animam meam.
> Infixus sum in limum profundi et non est substantia.
> Veni in altitudines maris et tempestas demersit me.
> Laboravi clamans raucae factae sunt fauces meae.

[10]The Passion, in both the liturgy and the gospels, incorporates passages from the Old Testament, especially the Suffering Servant passages in Isaiah (42.1–4, 49.1–7, 50.4–11, and 52.13–53.12) and Psalms 21/22 and 68/69.

[11]For a modern discussion of the "Jonah Psalm" and its relationship to the ones that are of the same genre in the Book of Psalms, see Landes.

Defecerunt oculi mei dum spero in Deum meum.
(Ps. 68:2–3)

[Save me, O God, for waters surround me even to my life's breath. I am sunk into the mud of the deep, and there is no firm ground. I have come into the depths of the sea, and the waves sink me down. I have struggled, calling out, my voice made hoarse. My eyes turn away (or close?), while I hope in my God.]

Clamavi de tribulatione mea ad Dominum et exaudivit
me.
De ventre inferni clamavi et exaudisti vocem meam.
Et proiecisti me in profundum in corde maris et flumen
circumdedit me.
. . . .
Circumdederunt me aquae usque ad animam abyssus
vallavit me.
Pelagus operuit caput meum.
Ad extrema montium descendi,
Terrae vectes concluserunt me in aeternum.
(Jon. 2:3–4, 6–7)

[I called out in my tribulation to God and he heard me. Out of the belly of the deep I called out, and thou heardest my voice. Thou hast cast me into the depths, in the midst of the sea, and the flood closed around me.. . . The waters closed around me; the ocean swallowed me even to my life's breath. The sea covered over my head; I sank to the uttermost depths, and the bars of (that) land enclosed me in eternity (or forever).]

The above passages have traditionally been understood to represent the agony and suffering of Jesus on the cross, Psalm 68/69, as well as the passage from Jonah. Jerome, in his commentary on the Psalms, points out both the Christological significance of Psalm 68/69, and also its implication for all of

Christ's followers: "Iste psalmus de passione Christe sonat, et ex persona memborum suorum" [This psalm sings about the passion of Christ and of his role in behalf of his people (lit. members, i.e. of his body)] (*PL* 25.1189; trans. mine). The illuminations in late medieval psalters, however, usually point to the general human, rather than to the specifically Christological, reading of Psalm 68/69, for they often depict a man in the curve of the "S" (the initial letter of "Salve"), literally drowning in the depths, with his hands raised in prayer—he is clearly not Christ, for there is no nimbus, and Christ usually looks down on him from the upper curve of the "S." [Figure 15] The Christological reading does occasionally appear in some of the illuminations of this psalm. Most interesting in this regard is the illuminated "S" of the York Psalter. [Figure 16] Here both curves of the "S" are used: in the lower one is Jonah/everyman emerging from the whale, while in the upper is Christ emerging from the tomb (using the most common iconography, angels and Christ with banner, although the sleeping soldiers so often found in the empty tomb scene are not depicted).

These illustrations of Ps. 68/69 indicate that the typology and symbolic references for *signum Ionae* are not simply to Christ, but to all Christians suffering death, and not only literal death, but also the metaphorical death of loneliness and grief, and the spiritual death of sin. The highly personal, first-person voices in Ps. 68/69 and in the Jonah psalm convey primarily a human, not a Christological, experience. Of course, in one sense, Christ's suffering is a type of human experience; for the theologians, this is central to the fact of Christ's humanity. Furthermore, in the schematic system of allegorization exegetes would see the tropological reference to everyman as well as the allegorical prefiguring of Christ. However, for the Pearl poet, and anyone else concentrating on the figure of Jonah, there are important differences between Jonah as everyman, and Jonah as Christ, the most essential being that Christ's sojourn in hell was not a suffering experience (although his ordeal in Gethsemane and on the cross was). Christ's descent into hell is a victorious event, the moment of deliverance for the just souls in hell.

FIGURE 16. Initial "S" from "Salvum me" (Psalm 68/69), York Psalter. BL MS. Additional 54179 (ca. 1260). By permission of the British Library. (Photo: The British Library.)

In liturgy, in the Gospel of Nicodemus, and in art, Christ enters hell with triumphant banner in hand, to the confident strains of "Adtollite portas, principes, vestras" [Lift up your gates, princes] (Ps. 23/24; and the Gospel of Nicodemus, 473). Jonah, on the other hand, is everyman; he is Adam, Isaiah, and all those waiting to be released—he is not releasing anyone else.

The Pearl poet has taken this rich and complex sign of the *signum Ionae* and adapted it for his own purposes. By focusing on the actual, individual experience of Jonah in the whale, the poet shifts the references away from Christ as savior, and toward Jonah as representative of fallen humanity. In *Patience*, the poet expands Jonah's sojourn in the whale from the biblical source, so that one chapter of eleven verses becomes almost a hundred lines in *Patience* (249–342).[12] This expansion, proportionate to that in the rest of the poet's retelling, includes an important addition: a prayer for help inserted before the Jonah psalm. As Davenport has effectively shown (119–30), the poet's addition of the first prayer helps detail and make more consistent Jonah's gradual conversion to God's will. Although the implications of these additions for the narrative do not concern me in this chapter, I do want to point out that anything that emphasizes Jonah's conversion process can scarcely refer to Jonah as a Christ figure. Underscoring Jonah's humanity, the poet in *Patience* portrays Jonah whimpering in desperation to his God:

> 'Now, Prynce, of þy prophete pité þou haue.
> Þaȝ I be fol and fykel and falce of my hert,
> Dewoyde now þy vengaunce, þurȝ vertu of rauthe;
> Thaȝ I be gulty of gyle, as gaule of prophetes,
> Þou art God, and alle gowdez ar grayþely þyn owen.
> (282–86)

[12]In *Patience* somewhat less than one-fourth of the 460/62 lines given to the story of Jonah describe the experience in the whale. Cf. the Book of Jonah: 4 chapters of 10 or 11 verses each, except for ch. 1, which has 16 vss—the sojourn in the whale occupies all of ch. 2. For full analyses of the sojourn in the whale, see Davenport (119–30) and Spearing (*Gawain Poet* 83–88).

A man, even a prophet, so conscious of his own sinfulness and utter unworthiness to be saved, can in no way resemble, let alone prefigure, the saving, crucified Christ.

In addition to these all-too human reactions, in *Patience* the actual scene of Jonah in the whale is more earthly and more fleshly than spiritual. The physical interior of the whale dominates the description of Jonah's suffering there:

> He glydes in by þe giles þurȝ glaym ande glette,
> Relande in by a rop, a rode þat hym þoȝt,
> Ay hele ouer hed hourlande about,
> Til he blunt in a blok as brod as a halle;
> And þer he festnes þe fete and fathmez aboute,
> And stod vp in his stomak þat stank as þe deuel.
> (269–74)

The poet does, in this passage and in the line immediately following, liken the whale's interior to hell; indeed the gross details of foul smells, slimy surfaces, and darkness everywhere, are typical of late medieval depictions of hell, which often are vivid representations of hell's horrors.[13] However, such is not the way Christ experienced hell, but the way sinners have and will. Furthermore, with his usual gifts for mimetically creating individual perceptions and points of view, the Pearl poet has brought out Jonah's very human succession of impressions: his sliding down the guts, which seem like a road to him, and his tumbling head-over-heels until he is able to get his feet fastened underneath him and stand up.[14] It is difficult, if not impossible, to see Jonah as Christ at this point—for all their free-wheeling ability to mix the blasphemous and the sacred, medieval Chris-

[13]See, for example, the detailed description of hell in the thirteenth-century, Middle English *Sawles Warde* (250–52), itself a paraphrase of Hugh of St. Victor's *De Anima*.

[14]For a more detailed and, in some respects, slightly different reading of this scene, see Stanbury, esp. 80–82. Stanbury examines the way the poet denotes "each stage of Jonah's journey into the whale through references to perception, either tactile or imaginary" (81).

tians would probably not place Jesus in a vaudeville routine of pratfalls.

The *signum Ionae* has an authority and a weight that cannot be ignored, even by the Pearl poet, but even so the poet manages to deflect most of the specifically Christological symbolism of *signum Ionae*, partly through his use of other traditions associated with the sign, and partly through his attention to the mimetic, visual detail of the whale's interior. The Pearl poet's adaptation goes even further, for in the same episode, Jonah's sojourn in the whale, the poet includes another sign, the *hyrne* within the whale, which is the principal visual sign of God's kingdom in *Patience*, complementing the verbal sign of the *heuen-ryche*. The poet has done something quite remarkable here. First he has taken the visual aspects of the *signum Ionae*, but adjusted their meaning from Christ in hell to everyman in hell, and then he has placed within the visually mimetic everyman's hell a sign of God and his presence and continuing care, a paradise, in other words, that has all the meanings and import of heavenly paradise and virtually none of its visual characteristics. This lack of visualization is in keeping with the Prologue, in which, as we have seen, the central image of God's kingdom is in a mode that is pointedly non-visual.

There is a difference, however, between the non-visualization of God's kingdom in the Prologue and the non-visualization of the *hyrne* in the middle of the poem. The entire Prologue is abstract, generalized (except for the narrator's few personal references), and non-visual, whereas the later passage is replete with the graphic and sensory details of the whale's stomach and Jonah's personal experience there. Unlike the *heuen-ryche* of the Prologue then, the *hyrne* Jonah finds in the whale stands in sharp contrast to everything that surrounds it. The narrator stresses that the *hyrne* is free of the disgusting characteristics of the rest of the whale's stomach:

> With þat he hitte to a hyrne and helde hym þerinne,
> Þer no defoule of no fylþe watz fest hym abute;
> Þer he sete also sounde, saf for merk one,

As in þe bulk of þe bote þer he byfore sleped.
So in a bouel of þat best he bidez on lyue,
Þre dayes and þre nyȝt, ay þenkande on Dryȝten,
His myȝt and His merci, His mesure þenne. (289–95)

As the above passage makes clear, we are to note several things about Jonah's *hyrne* in the whale: its safety and comfort; its darkness; its similarity to Jonah's hiding place in the boat; and its emotional and spiritual closeness to God. Two of these, the safety and the closeness to God, are qualities associated with the *regnum caelorum*, captured visually, for example, in the iconography of the Apocalypse illustrations of the childlike souls carried tenderly to heaven.[15] In the passage in *Patience*, the loving security of the *hyrne*, emphasized in the first and last characteristics, frames the second and third characteristics, the darkness and sleep. Both the "merk one," which usually characterizes the absence of God, and the willful, escapist sleep of sinners, are qualities normally associated with hell, whether the mythic realm or the self-imposed spiritual alienation of sin.

In *Patience* then we have been given an image of the kingdom of God that is, in part, a negative paradise. Furthermore, the poet connects this negative paradise to two other refuges of Jonah's: his *hyrne* in the bottom of the boat and his bower under the woodbine, refuges in which Jonah escapes into sleep. Most readers have noticed the parallel situations of Jonah's two *hyrnes* and their similarity to his behavior under the woodbine;[16] indeed, the poet makes sure we do not miss the connection, at least between the first two, since he calls them both "hyrnes"

[15]The charming childlikeness of this scene, especially notable because it is so unlike the grander visions of heavenly bliss, is clearly connected to the iconography of Lazarus in the bosom of Abraham (the Parable of the Rich Man and Lazarus, Lk. 16. 19–31).

[16]Such uses of parallels and contrasts are, after all, generally seen as very characteristic of the poet's craft. See especially Howard on *Gawain* ("Structure and Symmetry"). I know of no one, however, who has pointed to the irony of placing a divinely granted refuge within a figural "hell."

(178, 289).[17] I think, however, we need to ask ourselves what are the implications of comparing escapes and separations from God to union with God in his kingdom. In effect, it is heaven and hell that have been made analogous.

Jonah's first sleep, the one in the bottom of the boat, is the nadir of his disobedient and foolish attempt to escape from God and his will, an escape that draws forth from the narrator twelve lines of angry, sarcastic comment (113–24). This literal running away from God, which culminates in Jonah's sleep, is considered by the exegetes to be a type of spiritual sloth. Jerome, for example, likens Jonah's sleep in the boat to that of the apostles in the Garden of Gethsemane, both of which typify "hominem torpentem . . . erroris sopore" [torpid man in the deep sleep of sin] (*PL* 25.1179). Similarly, in the Woodbine episode, when Jonah "slydez on a sloumbe-slep sloghe vnder leues" (466), sleep comes as the final act in a series of Jonah's movements away from God: verbally grumbling and threatening suicide (413–28); physically withdrawing from Nineveh "on est half of þe hyȝe place" (434); and literally building his own world, a bour, completely enclosed, with only a "nos on þe norþ syde" (451), where Jonah can once again hide from God, this time from God's loving mercy towards Nineveh, as earlier he hid from God's command to preach to Nineveh.

It is to these two sleeps of escape and disobedience, explicitly to the first, and implicitly to the latter, that the poet compares Jonah's refuge in the whale. A *hyrne* in God's protection is likened to the ungodly actions of deliberate disobedience and willful removal from God's kingdom, both of which are enclosed in darkness, universally a sign of God's absence. By so drawing attention to the paradoxically hellish and sinful qualities of a time and place of union with God, the poet thereby undercuts the reliability of visual and sensory signs. He thus directs our attention, as he does in the Prologue, to the inner quality of

[17]Actually, the hiding place in the bottom of the boat is only indirectly called a "hyrne," since the discovery of Jonah comes during the general hunt for all passengers who are "herȝed out of vche hyrne" (178).

God's kingdom. In *Patience* holiness, union with God, safety, comfort, and joy are abstract, inner qualities, not visually perceived paradises or mythic realms of jewel-bedecked cities.

Sir Gawain and the Green Knight and the "Ferlyes in þis Folde"

The signs of God and his kingdom are often paradoxical and generally non-visual in *Patience*, but they are not ambivalent or innately contradictory. In *Patience*, we are shown that God and the *heuen-ryche* can be found in visually and symbolically unlikely places. In *Sir Gawain and the Green Knight*, however, we are left with no sense of where God and those called to his kingdom can be found. Although many critics, especially those who subscribe to the allegorizing principle in interpreting medieval literature, read *Gawain* as a Christian moral poem, it is first and foremost secular—secular in its setting and sources (the medieval court and Arthurian literature principally) and secular in its genre as romance. The basic *formez* of *Gawain* are obviously and strikingly different from those of *Pearl*, *Patience*, and *Cleanness*, so that analyzing it in terms of its signs, especially signs of God and his kingdom, is a very different enterprise. Nonetheless, *Gawain* is a poem with a number of strongly visual images, sometimes bearing a long tradition in iconography and exegesis, but almost invariably undercut with irony or ambivalence. There are so many of these unreliable signs, and the poem has been so widely and deeply analyzed that I will select only a few of the most obvious, focusing first upon the the ambivalent signs that have some connection to the Bible and the Apocalypse, since those are the *formez* that dominate the other poems, and then moving to a consideration of the poem's two most important signs: the pentangle and the *luflace*.

Sir Gawain and the Green Knight is a poem filled with *ferlyes in þis folde*, wonders but earthly ones, for the poem contains practically no authentic explicitly biblical signs. The few that one can discern are either buried in oblique and complex allusions or are so overladen with their post-biblical iconographic traditions that they are hard to recognize. (The one sign, the pentangle, that the narrator seems to set up as biblical is no such thing.) While there are no straightforward biblical *formez* in *Gawain*, there are a number of apocalyptic images that have some connection to apocalyptic passages in the Bible, although they owe more to subsequent exegesis and iconography than to the Bible, and they are treated with ambivalence in the poem. Precisely because of this ambivalent treatment, these images reveal much about the poet's attitude toward such *formez* and therefore are worth examining in light of the *fayre formez* of the three other poems.

The dominant apocalyptic images in *Gawain* are those of judgment. The motif of judgment is introduced by the Green Knight, who sets himself up as the judge of Arthur's court and of Gawain, and, by extension, of chivalric, courtly culture and the individual, Christian knight. Judgment is an important feature of apocalyptic texts and traditions, especially John's Apocalypse, although, as we have seen and as the Pearl poet implicitly acknowledges with his narrative choices in *Cleanness*, the actual Last Judgment is a small episode in the Bible (and, of course, is not a recorded event, but a visionary scene). On the other hand, judgment in general and its corollary, the punishment of evil, are dominant themes in many Old Testament narratives, especially in the readings given those stories by the Pearl poet and by other medieval writers and exegetes. Judgment reveals God's plan, shows his power, and renews creation by cleansing it of its evil. While the Green Knight's authority is in doubt, his would-be role as a judge is fairly clear, although it takes the Arthurian court and the narrator quite a while to figure out this role, and they never really get it straight (nor do we).

The Green Knight's appearance in King Arthur's court is beset with contradictory and ambivalent images and responses, which have been analyzed by a number of critics, preeminently Burrow (*Gawain* 12–23) and Borroff (*Study* 104–16). The narrator's description mingles physical details of the Green Knight—his size, color, and his dress—with frequent references to the court's (and the narrator's) responses to this outlandish creature (136–202). In particular, the holly bob and the axe, the Green Knight's "attributes"—that is, his iconographic signs—are used by the narrator, and King Arthur, and us, to read the Green Knight's purpose and meaning (203–32). King Arthur eventually concludes that the axe means battle, particularly since the Green Knight has declared that he will not join the feast, because "to won any quyle in þis won hit watz not myn ernde" (257). However, the Green Knight corrects Arthur's misreading by pointing to his lack of suitable armor (a lack already noted for us by the narrator [202–05]), as proof that battle with the "berdlez chylder" is not what the Green Knight seeks. The axe rather is a sign of judgment, and as such is the closest thing to an authoritative biblical sign that the poem contains.

The axe's iconographic associations are part of a larger cluster, a cluster that includes swords and that serves as biblical signs of judgment. The sword's most explicit connection to the Last Judgment occurs in the vision of the coming of *Fidelis et Verax* ("Faithful and True") in John's Apocalypse:

> Et vidi caelum apertum,
> et ecce equus albus
> et qui sedebat super eum vocabatur Fidelis et Verax vocatur.
> Et iustitia iudicat et pugnat.
> Oculi autem eius sicut flamma ignis,
> et in capite eius diademata multa,
> Habens nomen scriptum quod nemo novit nisi ipse.
> Et vestitus erat vestem aspersam sanguine,
> et vocatur nomen eius Verbum Dei.
> Et exercitus qui sunt in caelo sequebantur eum in equis albis,
> vestiti byssinum album mundum.
> Et de ore ipsius procedit gladius acutus ut in ipso percutiat gentes. (19:11–15)

[And I saw heaven open.
And behold there was a white horse,
And the One who sat upon it was called Faithful and is called True.
And he judged and waged war with justice.
His eyes were as the flames of fire,
And on his head were many diadems.
He had a name written (upon him) which no one could know except himself.
And he was clothed in a cloak sprinkled in blood,
And his name is called the Word of God.
And his armies which were in heaven followed him on white horses,
(And they were) clothed in pure white linen.
And from his mouth came a sharp sword for smiting the nations.]

The axe itself has an even more direct association with the Last Judgment, since it was depicted as the instrument used for cutting down the bad fruit tree. In a heavily apocalyptic passage at the conclusion of the Sermon on the Mount, Jesus speaks of the fate of the tree that has borne bad fruit:

Non potest arbor bona fructus malos facere
Neque arbor mala fructus bonos facere.
Omnis arbor quae non facit fructum bonum exciditur et in ignem mittitur. (Matt. 7:18–19)

[A good tree cannot bear bad fruit,
nor can a bad tree bear good fruit.
Every tree that does not bear good fruit shall be cut down and thrown into the fire.]

Vincent of Beauvais gives a clear explication of the traditional understanding of this passage and its allusion to the fire and the sword, the two principal symbols of the Last Judgment:

> Ecce duplex paena reprobis praeparata, scilicet excisio, vel separatio a regno, et cruciatus in inferno. Hae sunt securis et ignis de quibus dicitur in evangelio, omnis arbor, quae non facit fructum bonum excidetur, et in ignem mittetur. Quarum, scilicet paenarum priorem afferit ibi Chrysostomus omnibus tormentis esse graviorem.
>
> [Behold there are two punishments prepared for the damned, namely the cutting down, or separation from the kingdom, and torment in fire. These are the axe and the fire of which it is spoken in the gospel, for every tree that does not bear good fruit will be cut down and thrown into the fire. Of these, Chrysostomus asserts that the first punishment will be the worst of all torments.]
>
> (epilog., cxviii, f. 1328; trans. mine)[18]

In addition, it is possible that the poet and his audience thought of another apocalyptic association for the beheading axe, namely the execution of Elias as it is depicted in the Morgan-Bodleian Apocalypse. [Figure 17] This latter use of the axe is closer to the *ferlyes* often found in chivalric romances, where uncouth giants and other such barbaric and fairytale creatures wield axes instead of the more courtly, more civilized sword.

The axe borne by the Green Knight in the first fitt of *Gawain* is thus unequivocally associated with judgment and justice, but whether it is the divine justice of *Fidelis et Verax* that removes only bad fig trees, or the parodic and demonic justice enacted when Antichrist has the two witnesses executed in John's Apocalypse, or the earthly and arbitrary acts of fairytale monsters assuming pseudo-divine powers—that is not clear. The ambivalence surrounding the axe of the first fitt lies not only in its iconographic associations, but also in the contradictory com-

[18]Mâle, in a discussion of the Last Judgment symbols, cites the same passage from Vincent of Beauvais and points out that the sculpture on the archivolts of Amiens depicts the fruit-bearing and still flourishing tree, with the barren, felled tree lying next to the axe (*Gothic Image* 388–89).

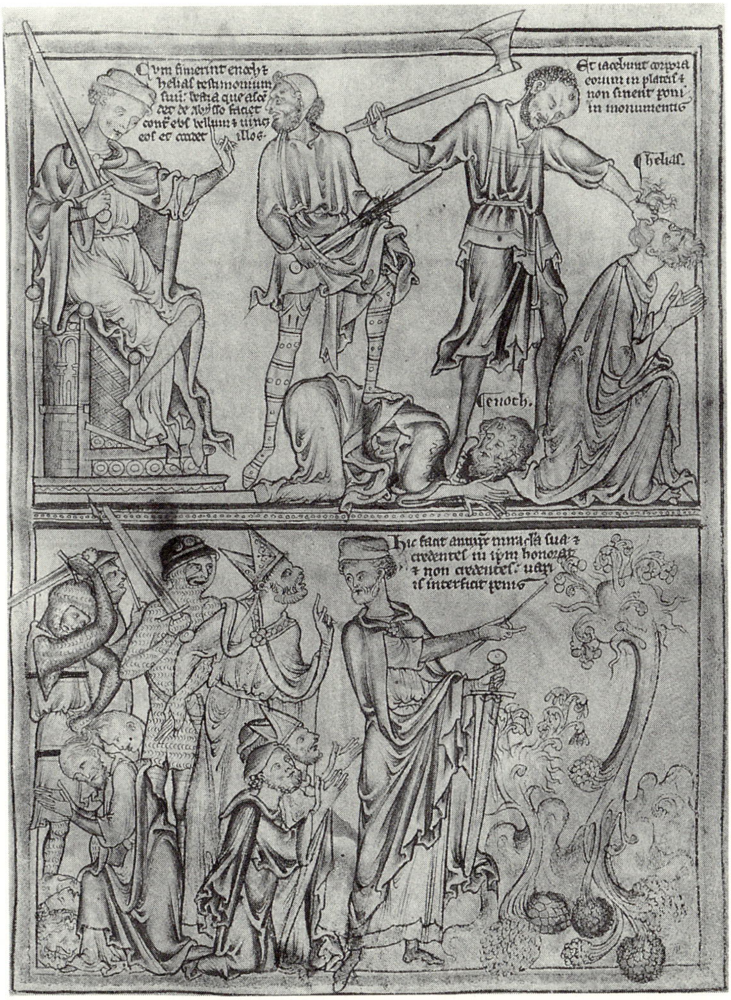

FIGURE 17. The Slaying of Enoch and Elias. The Pierpont Morgan Library, New York, M.524, fol. 7r (mid-13th cen.). By permission of the Pierpont Morgan Library. (Photo: The Pierpont Morgan Library.)

ments made about it by the narrator. On the one hand, it is a huge and terrible weapon, almost four feet long with a grim and fearfully sharp blade of a half-moon shape, and with a spike sticking up from the blade (208–13); on the other hand, it is an elegant artifact, made of green steel and bright gold, and "al begrauen with grene in gracios werkes" (216). In this latter respect, the axe corresponds to the courtly aspects of the Green Knight's own appearance and attire and is appropriate to the mood of game and Christmas interlude insisted upon by the Green Knight:

> Forþy I craue in þis court a Crystemas gomen,
> For hit is Ȝol and Nwe Ȝer, and here ar ȝep mony.
> (283–84)

Both the color and this festive association for the axe and the Green Knight's game are closely linked to his other attribute, the holly bob, "þat is grattest in grene when greuez ar bare" (207). Though dropped after this brief mention, the holly bob is implicitly a sign of the season and presumably also of peace, comparable to the dove's olive branch at the end of Noah's flood.[19]

At the end of the first fitt, Arthur too speaks of the axe and the gruesome beheading scene as parts of a courtly game, "such craft vpon Cristmasse" (471), like "laykyng of enterludez, to laȝe and to syng" (472). This kind of game seems to be one of the *ferlyes in þis folde*—scary in a playful, horror-movie way, the stuff of holidays and good stories. Such a mixture, according to Jonassen, is quite characteristic of the seasonal games of Mummers. Jonassen points out that in *Gawain* the poet creates "a tension beween frivolous game and life-and-death seriousness" and that the Green Knight "is both a playful organizer of games

[19]See Andrew and Waldron (215, note to lines 206–7), who point out that the holly is in keeping with the Christmas season and that it is carried as a sign of peace, just as an olive branch often was by messengers in the Middle Ages.

and a purveyor of death."[20] In this same spirit, of celebration and playful horror, the axe is hung above the court at Arthur's orders:

> And hit watz don abof þe dece on doser to henge,
> Þer alle men for meruayl myȝt on hit loke
> And bi trwe tytel þerof to telle þe wonder. (478–80)

Although the narrator typically omits telling us what the wonder is that is told, we can assume it is the aura of *ferlyes*, the fairy magic surrounding the Green Knight, but it may also be the wonder of the Green Knight's challenge and his threat of judgment.

The hint of doom in the Green Knight's axe becomes stronger in later images of axes. The next image of an axe occurs in the second fitt, when Gawain is pictured asleep under overhanging icicles:

> Ner slayn wyth þe slete he sleped in his yrnes
> Mo nyȝtez þen innoghe, in naked rokkez
> Þeras claterande fro þe crest þe colde borne rennez
> And henged heȝe ouer his hede in hard iisseikkles.
> (729–32)

This clearly visualized, physical threat points immediately to the cold hostility of the wilderness and implicitly to the beheading by axe that hangs over Gawain's story. It is noteworthy that here the poet has used the icicles as a stand-in for the actual image of an axe, which in turn is the vehicle that conveys the meaning of doom.

The third and final axe image is, like the first, not an image but the thing itself, but in this last the literal axe is closer to the metaphorical meanings created by the axe-like icicles. By this

[20]In an informative and interesting article, Jonassen argues that the drama (both the Mummers' Play and certain cycle plays) provided an important influence and source for the holiday mixture of gaiety and seriousness in *Gawain*.

last fitt, the Green Knight and his emblemmatic axe have each gathered together meanings and simultaneously been separated from some. Now the axe and its wielder betoken death and judgment, supernatural (or at least magical) powers, and green and primitive wilderness. The *ferlye* quality has taken over, at least for the first part of this scene, while the courtly aspects of the Green Knight, symbolized by the elegant engravings on the axe and prominent in his interest in Christmas games, have since been split from him and co-opted by his other persona, Bertilak, the genial, game-loving host of Hautdesert.[21] The Green Knight that we and Gawain meet in Fitt IV is, until the very end of the scene, hardly a player of games, nor is there anything courtly about him.

As an attribute of the Green Knight, the axe provides a putative sign for reading him, although it is as complex and ambivalent as the Green Knight himself. Not only is there a question of what as a sign the axe signifies, but the axe shifts from signifier to signified. This slipperiness of the signs belonging to the Green Knight is exemplified in his physical setting in Fitt IV, which is otherworldly but in a fairytale way, not a biblical one. In particular, the Green Chapel and the river, the two most important signs in the scene, carry biblical or Christian associations that are either undercut or conflated with a pagan context, making this highly visual, iconographic scene especially difficult to read.

The river functions as a separation, like the river in *Pearl* and thereby creates a strong sense of otherworldliness. On one side of the river is Gawain and the Green Chapel, while on the other side is the Green Knight, heard, but not seen, sharpening his axe in a climax of suspense and terror. Though the river functions as a boundary, it is a boundary soon crossed by the Green Knight:

[21]As Laura Hibbard Loomis has pointed out, after testing (I would say judging) Gawain, the Green Knight "drops on the instant his role of magic horror and becomes again the gallant, benevolent Bercilak, full of warm good-will" (20).

And þe gome in þe grene gered as fyrst,
Boþe þe lyre and þe leggez, lokkez and berde,
Saue þat fayre on his fote he foundez on þe erþe,
Sette þe stele to þe stone and stalked bysyde.
When he wan to þe watter, þer he wade nolde,
He hypped ouer on hys ax and orpedly strydez,
Bremly broþe on a bent þat brode watz aboute,
    On snawe. (2227–34)

The Green Knight's crossing of the river in an almost playful way, a kind of giants' leapfrog, is a significant action and moment. As both defining limit and sign of the otherworld, the river, like all the defining boundaries and signs in the story, is easily crossed and it, like its meaning, virtually effaced. This is in sharp contrast to the river in *Pearl*, which cannot be transgressed as a boundary; boundaries in secular romances are apparently as slippery as their other limits, unlike the divinely sanctioned boundaries between the eternal kingdom and our human existence. Earthly *ferlyes* are both otherworldly and of this world, as the vagueness of the boundaries in Celtic tales and Breton lais attest. Hills, oceans, and woods usually separate the everyday world from the fairy, but they are not impassable nor do they stay fixed. In Marie de France's *Yonec*, for example, the separate fairy realm of the Hawk-knight is entered by the Lady only after an arduous quest, following her lover's blood along a road, into a dark cave and through a hill; yet later in the tale the Lady, with her husband, son, and a guide, comes upon the fairy castle while travelling to a festival.

Similarly, the Green Chapel (which is, by the way, on the wrong side of the river, since it presumably belongs to the Green Knight's world, not Gawain's) is a strange conflation of visual and verbal images with conflicting interpretations.[22] The

[22]Vantuono gives a concise summary of the many scholars who have tried to identify the Green Chapel with specific places, either saints' shrines or pagan Celtic sites (342–43, note to lines 2171–84). Some of this research is interesting, but its usefulness is limited, since what's most important about the Green

Green Chapel is both a *ferlye* and of this world. Expecting, like Gawain, a literal chapel (that is, some kind of man-made building for Christian worship) we then, with Gawain, find "non suche in no syde . . . / Saue, a lyttel on a launde, a lawe as hit were, / A balȝberȝ" (2170–72).

The first words actually describing and identifying the Green Chapel in the last fitt thus place it in nature, a green and natural part of a green and natural scene. While Gawain's initial inspection reveals the chapel to be "nobot an olde caue" (2182), his first spoken observation, given in the wheel of the stanza, pushes the chapel into a less neutral, more sinister context:

> "We! Lorde," quoþ þe gentyle knyȝt,
> "Wheþer þis be þe Grene Chapelle?
> Here myȝt aboute mydnyȝt
> Þe Dele his matynnes telle!" (2185–88)

Gawain's response here might seem to be an overreading, but it is reasonable enough, since both the story and the Green Knight have led us to expect a "chapel"—and if it is not a Christian chapel, then it must be a demonic one.[23] By now, the meaning of the "Green Chapel" in this poem has moved from the holy, Christian place of worship the name alone implies, to the natural thing it appears to the eyes, to the unholy and evil place interpretation makes it—a series of changes that correspond to the unfixed boundaries represented by the river.

Chapel is that we do not know where it is (or *what* it is, or even *if* it is). Of course, if the Green Chapel were an obvious reference for the poet and his original audience, perhaps the effect would be different, but, given the enormous number and kinds of places proposed by scholars as the "real" Green Chapel, it seems unlikely that the poet expected his audience to make a connection to a specific place.

[23]Furthermore, folklore in western Europe and England traditionally associated the devil with caves, barrows, and wastelands (Silverstein, *Gawain* 162, note to lines 2163–84).

Like the axe, like the river, like the Green Chapel, but even more so because he subsumes them all, the Green Knight is a mixture of shifting and often contradictory visual and verbal signs. By the last fitt, as Borroff has explained in "Judgment," he is somewhat shrunken and domesticated, having been laundered, as it were, through his alter-ego Bertilak.[24] But, if finally less of an otherworldly giant, the Green Knight is yet older, wiser, and more experienced than either Gawain or his king. Attaching to the Green Knight have been a few biblical and Christian overtones—judgment suggested by the axe, prayer and worship by the chapel, and otherworldly by the river. By Fitt IV, all these have been undercut or contradicted. Yet the Green Knight remains, at the end, a *ferlye* figure, of wonder and authority, and the roles he undertakes—teacher and mentor (to say nothing of confessor)—suggest verbally what the visual images do not: that the Green Knight is judging, with informed and rational and Christian opinions, both Gawain as a human individual and the Arthurian court as a human institution. As Borroff argues, the judgments the Green Knight makes "are, indeed, the *only* considered judgments the poem provides" ("Judgment" 106; emphasis hers).

Just as we and the narrator and Gawain have trouble reading the Green Knight and his signs, so do we and the narrator stumble over Gawain as a figure and his story as an exemplum, both of which are simultaneously treated as frivolous hero and courtly game and also invested with implications of Christian holiness. Like the Green Knight with his axe and chapel and holly bob, Gawain has iconographic attributes that embody and exemplify the contradictions in him and in his story—his shield with the picture of the Virgin Mary on one side and the pentangle on the other side, later to be replaced by the girdle given to him by the Lady. The pentangle and the luflace in particular have been extensively and exhaustively examined ever since we first recovered the poem in the nineteenth century, most re-

[24]The point is Borroff's ("Judgment" 113), although the term "laundered" is mine.

cently by Shoaf, who sees them as "the two most portentous signs in the poem, at least after the Green Knight himself" (" 'Syngne of Surfet' " 154).[25] It is worth taking one more look at these two formez in order to see just how central to the poem the process of interpreting them is.

What is seldom acknowledged is that the complexity and ambiguity of these *formez* as visual signs is much more the point of the poem than their fixed meanings (which, in any event, do not exist).[26] Even more than the Green Knight's axe, Gawain's attributes change and develop with the process of the story and with the point of view of those involved with them. Indeed the biggest change is that, as so many readers have noticed, the girdle replaces the pentangle—the Green Knight at least sticks to axes, although, as some readers fail to note, not the same axe.[27] The narrator's (perhaps it is better to think of it as the poet's) role in the handling of the pentangle and the *luflace* is curious, for he sometimes misleads us and generally seems to know more than we as readers do. In contrast, with the Green Knight and his attributes, readers usually share the narrator's point of view, often the same as Gawain's—assuming what they assumed when they assumed it (for example, that the Green Chapel is a Christian place of worship, or that the axe perhaps betokens battle with an Arthurian knight) and having those assumptions contradicted or modified when they are for Ga-

[25]Shoaf's article, "The 'Syngne of Surfet' and the Surfeit of Signs in *Sir Gawain and the Green Knight*" (which I read after completing this part of my discussion), examines most of the same passages that I cover, but many of our conclusions differ. Shoaf ends with an intriguing study of the poem's signs as *knots* (160–67), which strikes me as a useful way to see these signs, especially since it works with the poet's own figures, as I have tried to do in other cases.

[26]Shoaf's " 'Syngne of Surfet' " is one notable exception. See also Hanning's article, "Red Herring." While Hanning is not discussing the poem's signs, but rather certain specific scenes, his point—that "our frustration as would-be exegetes of *Sir Gawain*'s highly decorated images epitomizes our difficulties with the poem as a whole" (6)—is close to the one I make, and indeed inspired mine in part.

[27]The first axe is presumably still hanging above Arthur's court, when in Fitt IV, the Green Knight hops across the stream, with his freshly sharpened axe.

wain or the court or the narrator. The pentangle and *luflace* are a different story altogether, since from the first, they are surrounded by misleading or false information, information which is supplied by the characters within the story and even by the narrator. In fact, the introductions of the respective attributes for Gawain are given by the narrator (for the pentangle) and the Lady (for the girdle), which makes for the curious and unsettling situation that the narrator and the Lady are partners in providing us (and Gawain) with untrustworthy exegesis.

The pentangle, for example, is, the narrator claims, an authoritative biblical sign:

> And quy þe pentangel apendez to þat prynce noble
> I am in tent yow to tell, þof tary hyt me schulde.
> Hit is a syngne þat Salamon set sumquyle
> In bytoknyng of trawþe, bi tytle þat hit habbez. (623–36)

It is nothing of the sort, of course, since any development of the pentangle as a symbol is post-biblical and largely the creation of the poet.[28] In the context of the Pearl poet's works, poems that so frequently reproduce and evoke biblical iconography, it is particularly striking that so much importance and attention should be paid to a minor and nonbiblical Christian symbol. The pentangle, painted on the front of Gawain's shield, is described and analyzed at length, but the much more established iconographic image, that of the Virgin Mary on the reverse of the shield, is mentioned quickly and never described visually. The Virgin Mary, like the judgment and authority of the Green Knight, is more of a verbal than a visual reality in the poem.

Though the pentangle lacks the biblical ancestry claimed for it by the narrator, it does bear Christian associations and mean-

[28]Several scholars provide extensive information on the background of the pentangle, which had a full history in the Middle Ages, although as the "Seal of Solomon," not "pentangle." See, for example: Silverstein (*Gawain* 129–31, note to lines 619ff); and Tolkien-Gordon (92–93, note to line 620). No one, however, notes the irony involved in this most biblical of poets citing a biblical authority (Solomon) for a symbol that is nowhere in the Bible.

ings. In contrast, the *luflace*, which by the end of the poem has replaced the pentangle as Gawain's emblem, comes from a completely nonchristian and nonbiblical world. The *luflace* is not a divine *forme*, but a human creation of gems and cloth; female and fleshly, it is supposedly endowed with magical properties. In reality, it embodies deceit and is not life-preserving, but life-threatening. By the last lines of the poem, this nonchristian and nonchivalric artifact has come to symbolize, for Gawain, Christian penance and holy protection, and, for the Arthurian court, chivalric honor and knightly fellowship:

> "Bot your gordel," quoþ Gawayn, "—God yow forȝelde!—
> Þat wyl I welde wyth guod wylle, not for þe wynne
> golde,
> Ne þe saynt, ne þe sylk, ne þe syde pendaundes,
> For wele ne for worchyp, ne for þe wlonk werkkez;
> Bot in syngne of my surfet I schal se hit ofte,
> When I ride in renoun remorde to myseluen
> Þe faut and þe fayntyse of þe flesche crabbed,
> How tender hit is to entyse teches of fylþe.
> And þus, quen pryde schal me pryk for prowes of armes,
> Þe loke to þis luf-lace schal leþe my hert. (2429–38)

> Þe kyng comfortez þe knyȝt, and alle þe court als
> Laȝen loude þerat and luflyly acorden
> Þat lordes and ledes þat longed to þe Table,
> Vche burne of þe broþerhede, a bauderyk schulde haue,
> A bende abelef hym aboute, of a bryȝt grene,
> And þat, for sake of þat segge, in swete to were.
> For þat watz acorded þe renoun of þe Rounde Table
> And he honoured þat hit hade, euermore after. (2513–20)

The *luflace* gains its two meanings (apparently, but not completely, contradictory) from the poem, more particularly from the role played by the girdle in the story, and also from the meaning the poem's characters choose to give it. In this way, the *luflace* is, I believe, the preeminent image of *Gawain*, the archetypal *ferlye forme*,[29] and typifies an important aspect of the poem: namely, that the poem creates, or recreates its own signs and images, and endows them with its own meaning (or meanings, actually). The *luflace* is a *forme* "of þis folde," made by human tradition and poetic craft (and female ingenuity). The way the *luflace* works as a sign, though but a stronger version of the way other signs and images work in this poem, is very different from the way the New Jerusalem, or even the river, works in *Pearl*; it is different too from the Flood or the feast in *Cleanness*; it is even different from the *hyrne* or the *signum Ionae* in *Patience*, although *Patience* comes closest to *Gawain*, in its readjustment, recreation, and reinterpretation of visual signs.

In *Gawain*, the poem's creation and recreation of its own visual and verbal signs, along with the conflicting interpretations it provides for them, are explicitly a matter of great interest to the narrator. Reading signs and tokens is often a matter of knowing the story, as is the case of the pentangle, and even more with the girdle. However, the story can be read in various ways, and so can the signs. Several times during the story, the narrator pauses to point to a symbolic sign and to discuss its meaning, or to offer the interpretations given by different characters within the poem; on most of these occasions, the narrator uses terminology appropriate to theoretical discussions of signs and symbols.

Syngne is a word the poet uses primarily for a particular visual symbol, which betokens a specific meaning or series of meanings. A *syngne* can be an iconographic image, like the pentangle that "is a syngne þat Salamon set sumquyle / In bytoknyng of trawþe" (625–26), or simple visual evidence, like the kind Gawain is searching for at the Green Chapel, when he sees "no syngne of resette bisydez nowhere" (2164). When Gawain and his story have endowed the *luflace* with meaning, then that becomes, in Gawain's words, "a syngne of my surfet" (2433) and a "token of vntrawþe" (2509). In the latter statement, Gawain

[29]Shoaf calls the *luflace* "the most *critical* sign in the poem" (" 'Syngne of Surfet' " 156; emphasis his).

uses the word "token" as a virtual synonym for *syngne*; elsewhere *token* tends to point to meaning and significance, at least as much as to the image of the thing itself (a conflation of signifier and signified).[30]

Another word frequently appearing in the poet's explicit discussions of signs is *tytel*. After Arthur has instructed that the axe be hung above the dais, he says: "þer alle men for meruayl myȝt on hit loke / And bi trwe tytel þerof to telle þe wonder" (479–80). The word "tytel" here conveys not the sense of "name" or "label," but rather "evidence" or "right" (corresponding to our verb "entitle"), with some suggestion of "symbol."[31] Enshrined in its Arthurian setting as an emblemmatic artifact that inspires storytelling, the axe is now even more associated with courtly games, but not with the games of warriors and knights, rather with the games of poets, ministrels, and artists. "Tytel" (like the related word "tytelet") is used in the context of story and fiction. Signs, like the axe, are images of meaning, but they are also proof of meaning.

The past participle "tytelet"—"entitled" or "giving evidence"—is used by the Lady in one of the passages in which she evokes Gawain's literary ancestry:

> And of alle cheualry to chose, þe chef þyng alosed
> Is þe lel layk of luf, þe lettrure of armes;
> For to telle of þis teuelyng of þis trwe knyȝtez,
> Hit is þe tytelet token and tyxt of her werkkez

[30]Compare Shoaf's claim that "the green girdle is often mentioned in the same breath with words for *sign* and *signifying*" (" 'Syngne of Surfet' " 155).

[31]Silverstein translates *bi trwe tytel* as "by the authority of its visible presence" and calls it "a kind of legal phrase" (*Gawain* 125, note to line 480); Andrew and Waldron render the two lines: "where everyone could look at it in amazement and relate the wonder of it by true right." Andrew and Waldron also note the syntactical ambiguity: "Possibly, however, *to telle* is grammatically parallel to *to henge* [in the preceding line]: the axe would tell its own wonderful story (cf. 626); in this case we should read *þerof* with *tytel* rather than with *wonder*" (225, note to 479f.)

How ledez for her lele luf hor lyuez han auntered,
Endured for her drury dulful stoundez,
And after wenged with her walour and voyded her care
And broȝt blysse into boure with bountées hor awen.
(1512–19)

These lines and the Lady's entire speech are rich in ambiguity and self-consciousness about literature and texts—a veritable goldmine for modern critics. The Lady has placed Gawain in a literary tradition, in which he has a long-standing reputation, despite his being "so ȝong and so ȝepe . . . at þis tyme," and she, based on her own, presumably authoritative, knowledge of the literature, attributes to him an authority on chivalric literature and customs. In this case, it is not Gawain as the protagonist of his own story, or the narrator, or Arthur's court, but the reader—the Lady—who decides what deeds Arthurian narratives should recount and what is the most praiseworthy thing in the chivalric world: "þe lel layk of luf, þe lettrure of armes." In making this evaluation of the literature and its meanings and its values, the Lady simultaneously passes back to Gawain the ultimate authority and knowledge, along with the power to instruct others:

"And ȝe, þat ar so cortays and coynt of your hetes,
Oghe to a ȝonke þynk ȝern to schewe
And teche sum tokenez of trweluf craftes." (1525–27)

The process of asserting the authority to read and to interpret and to judge, while looking elsewhere for that authority—for something other, something outside—characterizes the way Gawain's story is read by all the inscribed audiences, except the Green Knight. The Green Knight thus becomes the closest to a substitute for God in the poem, not only because he at times seems to be supernatural, but also because he never questions his own right to assert the literary fame of the court, and his even greater right to challenge that fame, to test it, and finally to pass judgment upon it. However, if the Green Knight does not question his authority, we do, because implicitly the narrator does, both by the ambiguity created in the figure of the Green Knight and also by the structure of the narrative, which does not allow the Green Knight the last word.

The almost obsessive concern with signs and their meanings, and with visual perception and verbal interpretation, is part of the poem's larger context, the post-biblical world of British history and secular romance. *Sir Gawain and the Green Knight* is the only one of the Pearl poet's works that does not have strong roots in biblical texts; without that authoritative text and provider of verbal signs and iconographic images, *Gawain* is left afloat in a secular world, of courts and wilderness, of human *ferlyes* instead of divine *formez*. The lack of biblical authority is partly reponsible for the poem's search for something equivalent to sacred canonicity and certainty and for its effort to establish a secular canon of history, events, and figures. This search is reflected in the poem's famous use of parallels and contrasts: King Arthur and the Green Knight, King Arthur and Bertilak, Hautdesert and Camelot, the *luflace* and the pentangle, the foxskin and the *luflace*, and more—all noted and analyzed by many of the poem's best critics.[32]

Some of the parallels are parallels in episodes and scenes and more properly belong to my discussion of narrative patterns. For now, we can note the way so many of these paired motifs, figures, and images are contrasted in terms of their legitimacy and canonicity. King Arthur is an actual historical figure (or so the poem's audience believed) and a Christian, civilized king, while Bertilak is a lord belonging to no land and no time, and his other persona, the Green Knight, is half-giant/fairy and half-man. The pentangle is a sacred symbol, attested to in some texts, if not in ancient ones, while the foxskin is animal and consigned to the devil, and the girdle is female and fleshly and bears suggestions of deceit, cowardice, and lust. The women in the story offer a similar interesting series of parallels and con-

[32]See, for example, Donald Howard, "Structure and Symmetry" and Benson, *Art and Tradition* (160–65).

trasts, less often seen in critical readings.[33] Guinevere is young, beautiful, and good (at least here, though not in all Arthurian literature, of course);[34] the Virgin Mary is young, beautiful, and a saint; Morgan, old, ugly, and a witch; Bertilak's lady young, beautiful, and bad.

It is important in understanding the poet's use of images of God and his kingdom to see how often, in these myriad juxtapositions, the offically Christian is contrasted with the ostensibly pagan or *ferlye*. Furthermore, the officially Christian also tends to be civilized and literary and partriarchal, like the pentangle, or even the axes (at least the first one), and like, of course, King Arthur's court; whereas the *ferlye* is presumably pagan, usually primitive or wild, folkloric or oral, and frequently female, like the Green Knight, the Green Chapel, and the *luflace*, all of which ultimately belong to a magical world ruled by a woman. Bertilak, though he is such a masculine figure and has more maturity and more power than is ever demonstrated by King Arthur, is, he finally tells Gawain, the pawn of the all-powerful Morgan.

In this alignment—of the literate, historical, and patriarchal versus the oral, romantic, and matriarchal—we find the former officially triumphant and privileged, and the latter implicitly present and still undermining the victory of the patriarchal.

[33]But see the provocative, feminist analysis of the poem by Fisher, and also Heng.

[34]The character of Guinevere suffered through the centuries. In Chrétien's *Erec and Enide*, Guinevere is a gracious and powerful (but good) queen; admittedly, she is a more problematic figure in Chrétien's *Le Chevalier de la Charette* (though not, I believe, as negative as some read her). However, as the Queen's love affair with Lancelot began to dominate so much Arthurian literature and increasingly was read as the cause of Arthur's fall, Guinevere became more and more the type of woman cited in all the misogynist texts, the ones that list Eve, Delilah, and others as examples of women who have been the ruin of men and civilization. It is thus remarkable that in *Gawain*, alone among surviving fourteenth- and fifteenth-century English literature, we are given such a positive view of Guinevere, and that moreover, in the poem's own misogynist passage, the one spoken by Gawain (2414–28), Guinevere is not only not mentioned, but seems implicitly to be an exception to the rule.

Gawain returns to King Arthur's court, the women disappear (partly because Gawain refuses to go back and spend more time with them), and the masculine warrior culture welcomes its hero and listens to his tale of heroic, though faulty, deeds. At the same time, the signs and symbols of the *ferlye*, particularly the *luflace*—the pagan, the oral, the folkloric, and the female—assert their importance and survive in the official, supposedly historical world, to which "þe Brutus bokez . . . beres wyttenesse" (2523).

Two women rule this poem: Gawain is Mary's knight, while King Arthur and Gawain and Bertilak are all Morgan's relatives and her dupes. The chivalric *bauderyk* worn in honor and fellowship is a lady's very personal article of clothing and, to some, betokens moral failure. In the last lines of the poem, there is no more resolution to this set of dichotomies than to any of the other important ones throughout the poem. The tension and ambiguity are maintained until the end. And that, as Hanning has argued ("Red Herring"), is what the poem is about. More particularly, I would claim, *Sir Gawain and the Green Knight* is concerned with human, as opposed to divine, *formez*—with images and patterns, with verbal signs and visual signs—and with the attractions and the problems, both of making them, as well as of reading them and of relying on them as signifiers of truth.

The explicit concern with interpretation, reflected in the detailed descriptions of visual images (the poet's renowned *pointing*) and the quest for verbal *syngnes*, constitutes the poem's response to the Arthurian world's signs and visions and therefore corresponds to the *luflongyng* experienced by the Dreamer in *Pearl*; both are mortal responses to manifestations of the divine and hence radically different from the immortal response, the *nwe songe* sung by the 144,000. The questioning nature of the response in *Gawain* sets it apart from the biblical world of certainty and authoritativeness, which is embodied in the Pearl Maiden, enacted in *Cleanness*, and evoked in the final speech of God in *Patience*. For all its Christian, chivalric, and courtly trappings, *Sir Gawain and the Green Knight* is more romance than history, more magical than "real," more pagan than Christian, more feminine than masculine, more human and fallen than divine and immortal. *Gawain* is a human story, a *ferlye in þis folde*, and in it there are no clear signs of God or his kingdom, except the sign of the crown of thorns in the second-to-last line and the sign of the cross made by Gawain several times in the poem. Otherwise God is absent, and so are his *formez*.

The confusion and loss caused by this absence are greater than the discontent of Jonah in *Patience*, greater than the grief of the Dreamer in *Pearl*, greater even than the plight of the flood victims in *Cleanness*, who at least know who is who and what is what. The beauty of the *fayre formez* evoked in the opening lines of *Cleanness* is not just the fairness of God's kingdom and its signs, but the clarity and serenity of authority. This kind of *fayre form* is missing from *Gawain*, but in its place is another kind of artistic beauty, a less authoritative, less solid, but nonetheless beguiling fairness, the kind found in fairytales and the kind found in Chrétien and Chaucer—wondrous, exciting, merry tales told with the elegant, witty, ingenious artistry of courtly poetry.

THREE

Formez of Sacred History in *Cleanness* and *Patience*

IN THE previous chapters I have been concentrating on the poet's use of *formez* as visual and verbal signs. In addition to these meanings in the context of semiotics, the term *fayre formez* must refer as well to the outlines and rhetorical structures of discourse—such is the more obvious use of the term in the context of rhetoric, and such is the primary meaning of *fayre formez* in the opening lines of *Cleanness*.[1] Although *fayre formez* should not be translated simply as *exempla*, *exempla* does constitute one aspect of the rhetoricians' broader meaning for *formez*, a meaning which includes the more general sense of narrative and structural patterns. *Formez* can thus refer to larger narrative frames, as well as to smaller units like *exempla*, and even to versification and other patterns in poetry. We can be fairly sure that the Pearl poet had in mind this rhetorical usage of *fayre formez*, since formal aspects of literary composition were apparently of great concern to poets in late medieval England. According to Burrow, Ricardian poetry is characterized by "well-marked formal structure" (*Ricardian Poetry* 61), "numerical composition" (61), and a "strict formal enclosing of narrative material" (68). With these rhetorical senses of *formez* then, I would like to examine the structures and narrative development of the four poems. Since I feel the poet's art is grounded in the Bible, I will look first at the two biblical poems, *Cleanness* and

[1]The rhetorical applications of the term probably related to the use of "*forma/forme*" in philosophical discourse, in which, however, "idea," became the preferred term in English. See Tayler, *Donne's Idea of A Woman* (23–28).

Patience, for they rely on the Bible not only for their stories, but for their formal patterns as well.

Just as the fairest images and signs are those made by God and provided in the Bible and in the sacraments, so too are the fairest narrative patterns those of the Bible and of sacred history. It has often been said that the Judeo-Christian pattern of history is linear and progressive, that salvation history starts with creation and the beginning of time and moves forward to an end in time when God's Kingdom will be restored. While, in the largest sense, Providence, God's planned form for history, is progressive, it is not, as Tayler has shown in his work on Milton, unequivocally linear.[2] It is more precisely circular, since the end is described as a return of God's Kingdom.[3] Prophets (especially those following the diaspora), apostles, Jesus, and John in his Apocalypse—all emphasize this circularity, this idea of return. For example, in Isaiah, the Lord says:

> I say to Jerusalem: Be inhabited;
> to the cities of Judah: Be rebuilt;
> I will raise up their ruins. (44.26)

John in the Apocalypse echoes the idea of restoration, adding, as we have seen, that the promised land will be new:

> Then I saw a new heaven and a new earth, for the first heaven and the first earth had vanished, and there was no longer any sea. I saw the holy city, new Jerusalem, coming down out of heaven from God, made ready like a bride adorned for her husband. I heard a loud voice proclaiming from the throne: "Now at last God has his dwelling among men! He will dwell among them and they shall be his people, and God himself will be with them. He will

[2]See particularly the Introduction to *Milton's Poetry: Its Development in Time* (1-17).

[3]See Lynn Staley Johnson, who says that "the men of the Middle Ages . . . saw time as a diminishing spiral" (46); but in the end, when the restoration is complete, the pattern has to be seen as progressive.

wipe every tear from their eyes; there shall be an end to death, and to mourning and crying and pain; for the old order is passed away!" (21.1–4)

The loss suffered by Adam and Eve when they were driven from paradise, and subsequently by Israel when she was conquered by neighboring nations, will be restored when God renews Jerusalem, his people are his once again, and he is their God. In the Apocalypse, this return is a return to Christ, who is the beginning and the end, Alpha and Omega. Tertullian comments on the pattern and movement implied in this; he says:

> [T]he two letters of Greece, the first and the last, the Lord assumes to himself as, figures of the beginning and end which concur in Himself: so that, just as Alpha rolls on till it reaches Omega, and again Omega rolls back till it reaches Alpha, in the same way He might show that in Himself is both the downward course of the beginning on to the end, and the backward course of the end up to the beginning; so that every economy, ending in Him through whom it began—through the Word of God, that is, who was made flesh,—may have an end correspondent to the beginning. (*On Monogamy* V; p. 29)[4]

The linear, progressive *forme* of salvation history is modified not just by this circular sense of return, but also by the smaller *formez* within the larger framework, *formez* that also begin at a beginning and move forward to an end, but which, because they are repeated, begin to look more cyclical than linear. Augustine, for example, writes of the little judgments that precede and prefigure the Last Judgment:

> And when we speak of the day of God's judgment, we add the word last or final for this reason, because even now God judges, and has judged from the beginning of human

[4]See Tayler, who quotes this passage (*Milton's Poetry* 219, note 12).

> history, banishing from paradise, and excluding from the tree of life, those first men who perpetrated so great a sin. Yea, He was certainly exercising judgment also when He did not spare the angels who sinned, whose prince, overcome by envy, seduced men after being himself seduced.
> (*The City of God*, xx.1; Dods 710)

The practice of typology reflects a mindset that sees repetitions and a cyclical pattern, although the concepts of foreshadowing and fulfillment acknowledge progression in addition to repetition. This is why the spiral is a better spatial analogue for Christian time and Christian history.

The smaller *formez* within the full framework of salvation history are patterns of judgment, narratives of loss that are seemingly contradictory to Providence's ultimate pattern of restoration. The pattern of judgment is the structure followed in many prophetic writings: creation and blessing (Israel's gifts from God), then sin (Israel's breaking of the covenant), and finally punishment (Israel's loss of peace, power, prosperity, and homeland). Jeremiah, for example, proclaims, in God's name, that all of Israel's troubles and losses are punishments for faithlessness:

> Is Israel a slave? Was he born in slavery?
> If not, why has he been despoiled?
> Why do lions roar and growl at him?
> Why has his land been laid waste,
> why are his cities razed to the ground and abandoned?
> . . . .
> Is it not your desertion of the Lord your God that brings all this upon you?
> . . . .
> It is your own wickedness that will punish you, your own apostasy that will condemn you. (Jeremiah 2.14–15, 17, 19)

Just as the joyous and triumphal *forme* of any particular blessing follows the same pattern as the cosmic, comedic one of Providence, so the grievous pattern of loss or separation from God provides the paradigm of judgment and punishment at the End.

This latter pattern, what Morse calls the "pattern of judgment," is the *contraré forme* referred to in the Prologue of *Cleanness*.[5] The *contraré forme*, as is obvious from the stories the poet has chosen to recount in *Cleanness*, is characteristic of apocalyptic texts. Just as the signs of flood and fire are apocalyptic *formez*, so also the pattern of judgment is an apocalyptic *forme*. Apocalyptic signs and stories are part of the fairest *forme* of sacred history, the conversion *forme* that ends in restoration. Moreover, *contraré formez* that are judgment patterns are meant to function in a conversion context; that is, the horror of the threatened punishment is meant to cleanse the evil (including the evil beings if they cannot be converted) from God's creation, so it can be restored to his kingdom.

In *Cleanness* the focus is, with a few notable exceptions, wholly on the judgment and the punishment, and the cleansing involves eradicating sinners, rather than converting them. In *Patience*, on the other hand, the poet has shifted the focus to the larger conversion *forme* of salvation history, and he thereby makes plain to us the way apocalyptic threats fit into the fairest *forme* of conversion. Significantly, *Patience* ends by moving into the present, post-Incarnation, time, whereas *Cleanness* ends firmly in the as-yet-unredeemed world of the pre-Incarnation past. To the Christian exegetes, even the earliest ones included in the New Testament, that pre-Incarnation time was a time of rebellion, the "*diem temptationis in deserto*" [the day(s) of testing in the desert], when the Israelites provoked God's anger. For example, the Holy Spirit (in a variation on the prophets' formula of "thus said the Lord") says, in the Epistle to the Hebrews:

[5]Morse is explicit about the pattern of judgment, since it is the thesis and title of her book, and yet oddly she never connects the term *formez* in the opening lines of *Cleanness* to "pattern" as Morse uses it. See also Kittendorf, who, while she claims that "structural unity" in *Cleanness* "is completely absent" (319), does see in both the Flood and the Sodom and Gomorrah stories "destruction symbolic of the apocalyptic end of things" (325).

Today if you should hear his voice,
harden not your hearts as at the revolt
in the day of testing in the desert,
When your fathers tested and tried me
and saw my works for forty years.
Because of this I was angered with that generation
and I said, "They have always been of erring heart,
and have never known my ways."
Thus I swore in my anger,
"They shall never enter into my rest." (Heb. 3.7–10)

Cleanness

Because the manuscript (and, I believe, the poet) would have us read *Cleanness* before *Patience*, I want to examine the *contraré formez* in *Cleanness* first and then move to a study of the way *Patience* fits the apocalyptic narrative patterns of judgment into the larger conversion *forme* of salvation history. *Cleanness* begins with Lucifer in heaven and Adam in paradise and ends with Belshazzar dead, Darius the new ruler, and Israel scattered—God's earthly kingdom is no more. Significantly, in the last narrative, Belshazzar's Feast, Daniel and the Jews are not mentioned after Belshazzar is killed and Babylon conquered. *Cleanness*'s major narratives thus recount the Christian view of the Old Testament relationship of God with his people Israel. God is the God who intervenes in history with direct action, who is often angry and vengeful, and who sometimes speaks directly to his people and other times sends them signs that apocalyptically reveal his judgment and his plan. Like much of the Old Testament—especially Genesis, from which come all but one of the stories—the narratives in *Cleanness* are public and historical accounts of actual events. These events are directly recounted; there is almost no intrusion of a narrative voice, no suggestion, except in Belshazzar's Feast, that this story is a contingent one that varies with its telling or that requires interpretation.[6] The events in *Cleanness* are the literally true events of history, its characters actual, historical personages, and its divine messages sent from God.

The Old Testament stories of *Cleanness*, while alike, are not identical; for in each story there is some variation in how God acts and speaks, how present he actually is, and how straightforward and direct the plot and the action are. There is a progress, or more precisely a regress, in God's presence, from simple and direct action without speech, to direct speech between God and his people, and eventually to the increasingly indirect means God uses to interact with his creatures. As God's actions become less decisive and his message less direct, so also the progress of the narrative becomes more limited and indirect, until we end with the most apocalyptic section, in which God resorts to arcane written messages, and the story is told with discontinuous and imbedded narratives.

The two Fall narratives that begin the narrative section of *Cleanness* are short and simple paradigms of divine judgment, involving no speech by God, only his judgment swift and sure. In fact, the only spoken words in either story are Lucifer's:

> Bot his Souerayn he forsoke and sade þyse wordez:
> "I schal telde vp my trone in þe tramountayne,
> And by lyke to þat Lorde þat þe lyft made."
> With þis worde þat he warp, þe wrake on hym ly3t.
> (210–13)

The paradigmatic narrative begins, as history begins, with the wrong action of a created being, and is followed, as all human history will be, by the punishing and correcting action of the Creator. There is no discussion of emotions, no dialogue, no

[6]Cf. for example, the intruding narrators in other medieval texts, including *Sir Gawain and the Green Knight* and *Patience*, as well as much of Chaucer's poetry. For a discussion of the aspect of narrative that focuses on the *process* of the narration, as distinguished from the *récit* of the events themselves, see Jordan (15–16) and Genette (140–43), the latter used extensively by Jordan.

argument, noticeably no anthropomorphic regrets attributed to God. The damnation of Lucifer is not only swift and complete; it is eternal, though as much through Lucifer's inability to get a second chance, and consequently extend the story, as because God has closed off the narrative.

Even more than the Fall of the Angels (which at least contains a vivid description of the actual fall through the cosmos), Adam's fall and the consequent sentence of mortality are reduced to the briefest and most matter-of-fact treatment:

> Þe defence watz þe fryt þat þe freke towched,
> And þe dom is þe deþe þat drepez vus alle;
> Al in mesure and meþe watz mad þe vengiaunce,
> And efte amended with a mayden þat make had neuer.
> (245–48)

Adam's fall is further distinguished from Lucifer's by its single-line glimpse into the distant future, when the story of the *culpa* will be reversed and become the story of the *felix culpa*. This important suggestion indicates that the *contraré* pattern dominating the stories of *Cleanness* is part of a larger *forme* and that the story of the Fall is but part of an open narrative that ends in restoration, a restoration that will be accomplished through the Incarnation, the subject of the lyric meditation that precedes the last Old Testament narrative in *Cleanness*. In the meantime, the focus remains on the closed, conclusive narrative of sin and punishment.

Following the brief accounts of the two Falls come the poem's three major narratives: Noah's Flood, Sodom and Gomorrah, and Belshazzar's Feast. Of these, the first, the Flood, is the simplest—the one with no plot variations, no imbedded smaller narratives, no introductory portions. The Flood is also the story that describes the most straightforward relationship between God and humanity, so that the passage has a quality of directness and simplicity that, in its lack of doubt or confusion, creates a mood of reassurance. In retelling the story of the Flood, the poet has stayed remarkably close to the Vulgate text, making only occasional changes, most of which have improved the narrative structure.[7] In contrast, for example, to the Noah mystery plays, which gain dramatic tension through the addition of apocryphal material, the Flood story in *Cleanness* has been pruned of the repetitions and inconsistencies present in the biblical account.[8]

One example of the way the poet simplifies the narrative is the change he makes in the episode in which Noah releases the raven and the dove. According to Genesis, in order to learn if the waters have receded, Noah first sends out a raven that never returns, next a dove that comes back without any evidence of dry land, then seven days later a dove that returns with an olive branch, and finally, after another seven days, the same dove that this time does not return at all. In *Cleanness* the poet omits the last occasion, so that the account is briefer and the narrative less delayed and more climactic. The focus of this episode in *Cleanness* is on the joy and awe-filled moment of the dove's return:

> What! ho broȝt in hir beke a bronch of olyue,
> Gracyously vmbegrouen al with grene leuez;
> Þat watz þe syngne of sauyté þat sende hem oure Lorde,
> And þe saȝtlyng of Hymself with þo sely bestez.
> Þen watz þer joy in þat gyn where jumpred er dryȝed.
> (487–91)

[7]A strict adherence to the biblical text is all the more remarkable since there was so much rich apocryphal material on the Flood, material that appears in the cycle drama, in some of the art, and even in secondhand references, like the ones in Chaucer's Miller's Tale. (See Prior, "Miller's Tale," for a summary of this Flood apocrypha.)

[8]The repetitions and contradictions in Genesis that are attributed by modern scholars to an imperfect conflation of the original sources (imperfect by modern standards for a coherent narrative, that is) have concerned exegetes from the beginning. See, for example, Augustine's attempt to resolve the inconsistencies in *Quaestionum in Heptateuchum* (3–5, esp. questions viii and xiv).

The moment is so important that the narrator's voice breaks in with an exclamatory "What!" and, lest we miss the import of the scene, he goes on to explain its significance before describing the joyful response of the ark's passengers. After this it would be anticlimactic to have Noah double-check the state of things by sending the dove off again, and it would also lessen the force of the dove's faithfulness.

Instead of gaining final proof through the dove's disappearance as in Genesis, in *Cleanness* Noah and his family wait in the ark for word directly from God that it is time to disembark:

> Vchon loued oure Lorde, bot lenged ay stylle
> Tyl þay had tyþyng fro þe Tolke þat tyned hem þerinne.
> Þen Godez glam to hem glod þat gladed hem alle,
> Bede hem drawe to þe dor: delyuer hem He wolde.
> (497–500)

The omission here of part of the Genesis account and the resulting simplification of the plot also strengthen the role and presence of God, who in *Cleanness* communicates even more directly with Noah than he does in the Bible and does so almost exculsively with words, and only one visual sign—the olive branch. The poet has made other changes, both additions and omissions, that make God's active role clearer. For example, an important addition to the biblical account is the narrator's insistence that the ark had no human means of steering or of power—nothing but the loving care of God and the force of the wind and waves (417–24). Of the various deletions of biblical material, probably the most striking omission is the rainbow, a favorite symbol of God's covenant in Genesis. In *Cleanness* there is no mention of a rainbow or any other reminder of God's covenant; God simply gives the words of his promise, in an emphatic triple negative: "Now, Noe no more nel I neuer wary / Alle þe mukel mayny on molde for no mannez synnez" (513–14).

In the *Cleanness* version of the Flood almost nothing stands between God and his creatures. With the single exception of the dove with the olive branch (and that is soon followed and confirmed by the divine words themselves—"Godez glam"), the story has no signs, no symbols, no messengers. God speaks, and his righteous followers hear and obey. He judges and rewards, and the just are saved; he judges and damns, and the wicked are lost. Although the divine actions in this story are terrifying, God's words can be tender, comforting, and secure, as in the promise made to Noah, or simple and direct as in the original, unquestioned commands to build an ark. As God's role has increased, so humanity's role has diminished. Noah has less to do in this version than in most medieval depictions of the Flood, or even than in the original version in Genesis. Relieved of almost all responsibility, humanity in the Flood story in *Cleanness* is also relieved of hope for change. There is no suggestion in this story that God's creatures could avert the apocalyptic doom through penance and conversion.

The remaining stories in *Cleanness* are more complicated than those of the two Falls and the Flood. Their plots move forward less directly and sometimes contain subplots and even imbedded stories, some of which do hint at an alternative to apocalyptic disaster. In these last two of the *þrynne wysses*, just as God's judgment is not so swiftly decisive, so too his Word is not so simple and unequivocal. Furthermore the Word does not come as the pure voice of God speaking to man, but rather as a message delivered by prophet, angel, or other intermediary. Altogether in these later narratives the Word is less direct and the divine presence less felt. In both the Sodom and Gomorrah story and its sub-narrative of Abraham's Visitors, there is nothing quite so reassuring as the loving God who speaks to Noah in "comly comfort"; neither is there anything so horrifying as the wrath of the Creator who regrets his own creation. In the Sodom and Gomorrah section there is also more possibility for equivocation, for arguing with God's Words, or for disobeying. Humanity and their words take on greater force and become increasingly important, attaining in Sodom and Gomorrah a certain real power in salvation history, albeit as often for evil as for good. God is further away, and his role is less active. Once humanity has an opportunity to speak to God with more than Noah's simple answers of assent, the question of delaying or mitigating God's judgment arises. This more complex relationship of God with his people leads to a more complicated narrative. In the story of Abraham's Visitors, which serves as a kind of prologue to the Destruction of Sodom and Gomorrah, the announcement to Abraham of the fate of the two cities has not the finality of God's first speech to Noah, and the Word of God quickly turns into a debate in which Abraham has an essential part to play.

Furthermore, unlike the pure voice in the Flood story, which is simply identified as God, the Visitors who appear to Abraham are not God, but an appearance of him. Although visualized, Abraham's Visitors are paradoxically less present and less real than the unseen voice of the Lord in the Flood story. In this respect they are more messengers from God than God himself.[9] In *Cleanness* the Visitors evoke God, but they behave like any honored guests, talking to Abraham, sharing a meal with him and explaining God's plan. The Pearl poet casts the episode in a well-realized scene, with the trappings of human civilization; to what already exists in Genesis are added more details to give us a pleasant picture of a medieval picnic. All of this is markedly different from the conversations between God and Noah, which seem to exist in no earthly space. It is as though God's Word has been domesticated in the scene with Abraham. The effect is much the same as the change from the otherworldly, awe-inspiring, early apocalyptic manuscripts to the homier, more humanized ones of the thirteenth and fourteenth centuries.

Both the more human guise of Abraham's Visitors and the narrator's reluctance to provide a direct description of them are in keeping with the Pearl poet's (and the Bible's) avoidance of visual theophany. Full theophany is reserved for the end of time, "þe last ende" (608), when we will know the beauty of

[9]This is one of the ways of interpreting the Visitors, along with the more common reading of them as a representation of the Trinity (cf. Chapter Two, 73, note 7).

Abraham's guests in their full being as the Trinity. I have already argued in Chapter Two that the story of Abraham's Visitors evokes two *fayre* signs, the eucharist and the beatific vision, but what we need to see in addition is the importance of the phrase "þe laste ende." This single phrase obliquely reveals the connection between *fayre formez* as signs and *fayre formez* as patterns, or between *fayre formez* as images and pictures and *fayre formez* as narrative structures. The complete *forme* as pattern, when God closes history and restores his creation, is, as apocalyptic writing assumes, the ultimate revelation, the moment when we will see all clearly, whereas, as Paul says, "videmus nunc per speculum in enigmate" [now we see through a mirror in puzzling shadows] (1 Cor. 13.12). The *fayre formez* we have now, whether sacramental signs like the eucharist, or verbal and visual symbols of the New Jerusalem or of the beatific vision, will at "þe last ende" become real and present in all their fullness. They will no longer be signs pointing to the fulfillment but fulfillment itself.[10] *Þe laste ende* is not only a time when the *fayre formez* sent from God will be fulfilled; it is in itself a *fayre forme* since it completes the pattern of sacred history. But for now, humanity has only the promise of the beatific vision and lacks even the reality of God speaking directly as he does with Noah.

The main narrative in the Sodom and Gomorrah story, the actual condemning of the cities and the saving of Lot, further develops the possibilities for modifying God's Word that are found in Abraham's bargaining session. Lot is allowed to converse freely with the bearers of God's Word. When he does not understand how he will escape God's wrath, he questions the angels in anguish:

[10]See Augustine, who explains that "when this life has passed, we will no longer seek that bread which the hungry man seeks, nor will we receive the sacrament at the altar, because there we will be with Christ, whose body we now receive" (Sermo 59, p. 7; trans. mine).

Þen laled Loth: "Lorde, what is best?
If I me fele vpon fote þat I fle moȝt,
Hov schulde I huyde me fro Hym þat hatz His hate
kynned
In þe brath of His breth þat brennez all þinkez?"
(913–16)

Lot is all too aware of the power of God's wrath, but he is assured that he will be allowed to flee, and he is given the right to name his own place of refuge. Lot's speech is freer than Abraham's—less formal, less couched in humble, apologetic civilities. Furthermore, Lot's role in saving his family is greater than Abraham's or Noah's. Lot is left to rouse his family, to choose his destination, and even to defend, or attempt to defend, his sacred visitors when they fall under the threat of the Sodomites' sexual desires. However, as the human role in the divine plan increases, the plan seems less conclusive, and God's *forme* loses some of its awesome power. Similarly, in their conversations with God, in this story God's people do not merely say "yes" with ready obedience as Noah does; instead they discuss the details of the providential plan, a plan that begins to be contingent, not final.

Some of God's creatures do more than argue politely like Abraham and Lot. Sarah, Lot's wife, and the Sodomites at Lot's door—all challenge and even scorn God's judgment. Sarah laughs at the promise of a son (655–56); Lot's wife not only scoffs at the command to use no salt in the cakes (822–24) but flatly disobeys the prohibition, resulting in defilement of the holy angels. The ultimate scorn of God and the most obscene defilement of his *forme* come with the "harlotez speche" (874) of the Sodomites at Lot's door, whose filthy sin they would even extend to God's representatives.

The pattern of judgment in the Sodom and Gomorrah story becomes, even more than in the Flood, not just a punishment of the disobedient, but a cleansing, and a cleansing of an evil that threatens God's fairest *formez*. The sins against *clanness* call forth the wrath of God in a way that mere disobedience does not. At the same time, in Sodom and Gomorrah God's anger is less starkly revealed and more subject to mitigation, while God himself and his protective love are also less evident. It is as though the increasing ugliness and perversion of the world have driven him away, for, as the poet explains, "He is so skoymos of þat skaþe" (598). And the further away God is, the less direct and straightforward his actions and his words, the more complicated and contingent his judgment, and the less conclusive the narrative.

The last of the *þrynne wyses* (1805), Belshazzar's Feast, shows God even more distant and his Word even more indirect. In this narrative God does not appear, nor does he speak directly to Belshazzar, nor does he even send his messengers, as he does to Abraham and Lot. Although reminders of God are present at Belshazzar's celebration, in the *formez* of the sacred vessels and in the Writing on the Wall, God himself is far removed from the blasphemous and idolatrous scene, which is the *contraré* of his fairness. From the paradigmatic Word of God speaking to Noah, through the modifications of this pattern in the second major narrative, the poem comes to a time when the Word is not spoken, but written, necessitating that people be able to read and interpret. God's punishments are likewise less direct; no longer "acts of God," they now require human agents, the scourges of God.

The result is in many respects a typically apocalyptic text, in which tyrannical rulers practice all sorts of abominations and desecrations, and armies war against armies in gruesome, bloody battles. Blood is spilled, women are raped, innocent children slain, holy places and people are desecrated; and behind it all the absent God allows, indeed he ordains, these horrible ends of human civilization. Yet, unlike John's Apocalypse or medieval commentaries on John's text, the apocalyptic battles in *Cleanness* are not conducted by mythic and allegorical creatures, nor do they refer directly or indirectly to contemporaneous figures; instead, they are actual events peopled by historical personages.[11] However, the scope of the punishment is limited in this last story in *Cleanness*, for the punishment affects only Belshazzar and his court (or in the earlier account of the fall of Jerusalem, only one city), unlike the Flood, which wipes out all of the created world that is not on board the ark, and unlike the fire that destroys all four cities and their inhabitants except for Lot and his family. This geographical limitation tends to render the story of Belshazzar's Feast less cosmic and less mythic and makes it harder for the narrative to function as a type of the End. At the same time, the story contains features like the arcane message of the Writing on the Wall that are characteristic of apocalypses.

Significantly, Belshazzar's Feast is a complicated narrative. Its plot is less spare and less focused than the earlier stories, making its *forme*, like the relationship between God and his people, less clear. Belshazzar's Feast includes not one apocalyptic battle, but two, one at the beginning and one at the end, thereby emphasizing the repetitive form of the narrative pattern; and it contains an interpolated flashback—Daniel's recounting of Nebuchadnezzar's conversion (1641–1708)—which suggests that there is an alternative *forme* for divine action, namely a pattern of conversion instead of a pattern of judgment. Although literally true, the stories of Belshazzar's Feast and the Babylonian captivity are so complex and varying in their several Old Testament sources and have been so often used in apocalyptic texts and traditions (from the prophets, through John's Apocalypse, to medieval iconography and exegesis) that in *Cleanness* the symbolic and iconographic nature of

[11]The fall of Jerusalem to the Babylonians is an historical event recounted in 2 Chronicles (36.11–21) and often referred to in the Old Testament, including the Book of Daniel, the primary source for this section of *Cleanness* (1.1–2). Similarly, the subsequent conquering of Babylon by Darius the Mede, which is briefly recounted at the end of *Cleanness*, is an historical event (or more precisely the conflations of several events) mentioned in Daniel 5.30–31. Cf. other accounts, in 2 Chronicles (36.17, 22–23) and the Book of Ezra (1.1–4 and 4.3–5), which make it clear that Babylon's kingdom passed into the kingdom of the Persians, led by Cyrus, and later by Darius, a Mede by birth.

the events almost takes over their historicity. With symbolism and complexity of narrative come the need for interpretation, for Daniel to read and interpret the writing on the wall and for the narrator to describe and explicate the sacred vessels.[12]

In every respect, including its narrative patterns, Belshazzar's Feast is the most thoroughly apocalyptic story in *Cleanness*. Whereas the poem's earlier narratives are apocalyptic in the sense that they are types of the End, they lack some distinctive features we associate with apocalyptic texts: the emphasis upon written and secret messages and the resultant need for a seer to interpret—notable features of the last narrative. On the other hand, these same characteristics that make the story of Belshazzar's Feast more apocalyptic also render it a more humanized *forme*. At every stage, human action, human speech, human art, and human interpretation figure in ways they do not in the earlier stories. God's action is narrowed in scope, and this part of sacred history does not feature patriarchs engaged in major events, but instead a seer/interpreter, who reads instead of acting. The divine *forme* has lost its purity and clarity and become less *fayre*. The emphasis here is on the hiddenness of apocalypse and the implied distance of God.

Belshazzar's Feast exemplifies the paradoxes and contradictions inherent in the apocalyptic mode. For, while an apocalypse is by definition a "revelation," apocalyptic texts unfold their mysteries only through complex interpretation, and they frequently are at pains to disguise these revelations in arcane symbolism. Whereas the revelation of divine purpose and of God himself is presumably the goal of apocalyptic vision, theophany is rare in most apocalypses and the words of God less present and less real than they are in either the Pentateuch or the prophets. Finally, although almost always eschatological, apocalyptic texts generally lack conclusiveness and closure, in part because, like John's Apocalypse, their narrative line is

[12]The vessels, as we have seen in the previous chapter, are not just themselves but suggest other things that they are not: "as casteles arayed" (1458) or like birds "as þay prudly hade piked of pomgarnades" (1466).

weak, and they repeat catastrophic ends so often that the catastrophes become cycles and not ends, and in part because the catastrophes are not meant to be the final end but the "last things"—the cleansing that comes before the final end, which is the restoration of God's kingdom.

Furthermore, apocalyptic preaching and writing function in a conversion context: if the apocalyptic warning is sent and received, it is meant to force people to repent and change their ways, so that the promised disaster can be averted. In *Cleanness*, the first four narratives give little hint that the catastrophic end serves as a warning. There is no forecast of Adam's and Lucifer's falls, although the account of Adam's fall hints of the restoration to come through the Incarnation. Noah's foreknowledge of the Flood serves only as a warning to save the righteous (Noah and his family), not as a threat that will induce the conversion of the wicked. Similarly, the Visitors' prophecy of the destruction of Sodom and Gomorrah is meant only to give Abraham a chance to save the guiltless, not to allow the guilty to repent. In none of these cases is there a suggestion that the wicked could avert the promised end through penance.

If *Cleanness* is meant to be a kind of apocalyptic warning, to offer a *forme* of loss and punishment as an inducement to conversion, it only gives hints of this. The *formez* that structure the poem's larger framework and the major narratives within that framework are all in the *contraré forme* of punishment and disaster. While *Cleanness* does, as we have seen, contain in the Prologue *fayre formez* that are visual images of the joys of God's kingdom, these are only signs, not formal patterns that show how conversion and salvation might follow disaster (or the warning of disaster). With the story of Nebuchadnezzar, however, the poem at least alludes to a *fayre forme* as a pattern of restoration; and, in addition, *Cleanness* contains an extended passage on the Incarnation, the divine intervention that reversed the *contraré* pattern of Israel's history forever.

Even Nebuchadnezzar's Fall works against a narrative sequence, since, although itself a straightforward story, it has been imbedded within the narrative of Belshazzar's Feast. Instead of placing Nebuchadnezzar's story first, where chronologically it should be, the poet makes it a tale within a tale by having Daniel recount it at the feast.[13] Daniel's story of Nebuchadnezzar's fall takes this particular narrative out of chronological history and holds it forth as an *exemplum*, much in the same way that the Christian exegetes use the Incarnation as a breaking into human time—both provide an alternative to the seemingly inexorable pattern of history as a cycle of sin followed by punishment and loss.

Nebuchadnezzar's Fall has been analyzed as an *exemplum* of penance by several critics,[14] but while the story follows a conversion pattern, it does not relate a tale of penance. Nebuchadnezzar, portrayed by the Pearl poet at the beginning of the story of Belshazzar's Feast in a remarkably favorable light, turns out, according to Daniel, to have at one time fallen into the sin of pride, setting himself up as a rival to God. (In this respect Nebuchadnezzar's guilt is closer to that of Adam and Lucifer than to either the Sodomites' or the flood victims' sexual sins.) Like Lucifer, no sooner does Nebuchadnezzar challenge God than he is brought down, although not spatially down to hell but rather metaphorically down the chain of being. For seven years Nebuchadnezzar suffers the privations and indignities and even the ontological confusion of an irrational beast:

> His hert heldet vnhole; he hoped non oþer
> Bot a best þat he be, a bol oþer an oxe.
> . . . .

[13]It should be noted, however, that to some extent the Book of Daniel itself takes the tale out of chronology. There Daniel also tells the story at Belshazzar's Feast (5.18–21). However, this is a recapitulation; the first account of Nebuchadnezzar's Fall is given earlier (4.26–33), in proper chronological sequence, that is, during the reign of Nebuchadnezzar and before Belshazzar. In *Cleanness*, on the other hand, we hear of the Fall only when Daniel tells the story; the earlier account of Nebuchadnezzar is quite laudatory and includes only a brief mention of his pride (1327–28).

[14]Compare Doob (65–75) and L. S. Johnson (135). See Doob also for a thorough treatment of the traditions surrounding Nebuchadnezzar's madness, in literature and iconography.

Þus he countes hym a kow þat watz a kyng ryche.
(1681–82; 1685)

Having lost his reason, which, of course, is what distinguishes human beings from animals, and having therefore lost his sense of who and what he is, the Nebuchadnezzar in *Cleanness* is, if not strictly animal, surely not too human. He is not a rational creature.[15] Nebuchadnezzar is therefore not strictly speaking a penitent, for he makes no conscious act, and speaks no word on his own that would show him entering his mad state out of a distraught consciousness of his sin, much less from a need to practice extreme penance. His suffering begins when he "*is outkast* to contré vnknawen" (1679; emphasis mine—note the passive). Once Nebuchadnezzar regains self-knowledge, he is returned to his throne, a return that follows upon and externalizes the return to his senses. The narrator describes this process as an action by God, who restores Nebuchadnezzar's reason:

Þenne he wayned hym his wyt, þat hade his wo soffered,
Þat he com to knawlach and kenned hymseluen;
Þenne he loued þat Lorde and leued in trawþe
Hit watz non oþer þen He þat hade al in honde.
(1701–04)

The restoration of Nebuchadnezzar makes his story clearly different from the narrative pattern of Belshazzar's Feast, but although Nebuchadnezzar's madness is suggestive of a conversion pattern, in its context it actually functions as a minor variation or exception to the judgment pattern. In this respect, it is like the story of Noah and his family, or of Lot and his family, and represents the saved remnant that is otherwise miss-

[15]Furthermore, there is no mention of a crown, a critical detail in art, which keeps Nebuchadnezzar looking human. In this emphasis upon the bestiality of Nebuchadnezzar, the Pearl poet seems to be going further than the traditional understanding, which was that Nebuchadnezzar remained a human being throughout his madness. See Doob (79), although Doob later points out that in Gower's version the king is really transformed into an animal (87).

ing from the account of Belshazzar and the fall of Babylon. In fact, Daniel's hint of a conversion ending as an alternative to the doom prophesied by the Writing on the Wall is not realized. The story of Belshazzar's Feast ends abruptly and finally with catastrophe:

> And þus watz þat londe lost for þe lordes synne,
> And þe fylþe of þe freke þat defowled hade
> Þe ornementes of Goddez hous þat holy were maked.
> He watz corsed for his vnclannes, and cached þerinne,
> Done doun of his dyngneté for dedez vnfayre.
> (1797–1801)

Only a dozen lines follow, most of them in the conditional mode of prayer and sacrament and wholly removed from the historical past, and thus the poem ends.

The real exception to the *contraré forme* of punishment in *Cleanness* is not an alternative narrative *forme*, but an alternative genre and mode—the lyric meditation on the Incarnation that is inserted between the stories of Sodom and Gommorah and Belshazzar's Feast. Because it is essentially lyric the Incarnation passage lacks the sequentiality of narrative, the historicity of past event, or the linear process of cause-and-effect.[16] The only historical event included in the Incarnation passage is the nativity itself, and this, as we have seen in the previous chapter, is not the Lucan narrative of birth in Bethlehem, but the iconographic scene of the Virgin and Christ Child adored. The poet presents the scene as a theophanic moment, prefiguring the eschatological *nwe songe* raised in praise of God. However, rather than *pointing* the picture, the Pearl poet meditates on it, resorting to puns, paradoxes, and oxymorons, the usual ways

[16]Compare Morse, who believes that the story of Belshazzar's Feast is meant to be analogous to the contemporary Christian period, since, for one, it follows the Incarnation passage (134); but, as I have stressed, it is clear that the Incarnation passage is intrusive and digressive and stands outside chronology and time (and in fact is not a narrative).

for stretching human language to make it more appropriate as a vehicle for the divine.

Moreover, in the Incarnation passage the narrator does not proceed sequentially; he follows neither the chronology of history nor the progression of logic, but rather leaps from one image to another, impelled by the suggestiveness of the words. Whereas the rest of the poem is a series of narratives arranged in linear and chronological sequentiality (except for the tale within a tale of Nebuchadnezzar's fall), the Incarnation passage is a lyric meditation, floating free of human time. This atemporality and the lack of logical progression are characteristic not just of lyric poetry, but of the sacramental mode. In fact, in this passage the poet is using words, the poet's *formez*, in much the same way the Church uses sacraments—both poetic language and the sacraments can transcend the earthboundness of human experience and mediate between Creator and creation.[17]

The similarity between sacraments and language in the Incarnation passage is significant, since it is in this part of the poem that the poet makes clear the role of the sacraments, as the means by which God allows humans to change their narrative from one of judgment to one of conversion. Whereas throughout *Cleanness* the explicit message is that humanity's filth will condemn them to God's wrath, at the end of the Incarnation section we are told that penance can purify the unclean for the beatific vision. Employing the image of the pearl, the narrator concludes the passage by describing the role of the sacraments in making us worthy to approach the Kingdom of God:

> . . . þaȝ þou be man fenny,
> And al tomarred in myre whyl þou on molde lyuyes;

[17]This use of verbal wit as a way of dealing with the problem of ineffability is a common device among mystics and certain Christian exegetes (Paul relies upon it heavily, especially in Romans), but it is not much used in Middle English literature, except in *Ancrene Wisse*, certain late lyrics, and *Piers Plowman*, the last notably in a passage on the Incarnation (Skeat ed., B 1.146–56, C 2.147–55).

Þou may schyne þurȝ schryfte, þaȝ þou haf schome
serued,
And pure þe with penaunce tyl þou a perle worþe.
(1113–16)

Later, using an extended metaphor of the pearl, the narrator asserts that a dirty pearl can be cleansed with wine: "Nobot wasch hit wyth wourchyp, in wyn, as ho askes" (1125). These allusions to the sacraments of penance and the eucharist follow an earlier one to baptism:

For alle arn laþed luflyly, þe luþer and þe better,
Þat euer wern fulȝed in font, þat fest to haue. (163–64)

Together these three passages on the sacraments make explicit the role of the eucharist, baptism, and penance as the divinely given means of our salvation and welcome into God's kingdom.

The poet has accomplished a tour de force with the Incarnation passage, for, while explicitly recommending the sacraments to his audience, he also imitates in his verse the extratemporal and transcendent qualities proper to sacrament. Furthermore, not only does the Incarnation passage transcend historical event and more particularly historical past, it also transcends the explicit messages given in the rest of the poem. This passage ignores and even contradicts *Cleanness*'s emphasis upon religious, dietary, sexual, and moral purity. The Incarnation passage specifically denies the *contraré* insistence that the unclean can never approach God (since the filthy and grotesque quite explicitly limp right into the divine banquet—1093–96), and finally, it does not focus solely upon God's intervention in human history or upon his unilateral, unequivocal, and direct acts of judgment and purification. Furthermore, here the poem provides a demonstration of the connection between poetry and sacrament that is implied in the Prologue, in the lines that set up an analogy between the *fayre formez* of priests and the *fayre formez* of preachers, rhetoricians, and poets, for in the Incarnation passage the Pearl poet uses his craft to transform his *contraré forme* into a *fayre* one.

Nonetheless, rather than using the restoration pattern as a narrative framework, the poet has enclosed these *fayre formez* within the stories of loss and punishment, thus leaving *Cleanness* still effectively a *contraré forme* in its largest outline. With the exception of the Incarnation section and the various allusions to the sacraments, *Cleanness* is a poem bound to human time and anchored in human history. In *Cleanness* God's actions are historical and chronological and therefore follow in succession, one after the other. He can judge, and he can speak, but were he to speak one judgment and then follow it with a different one, his actions would seem contradictory and unreasonable. If he is angry at corruption, impurity, and violation, then he must follow that anger with pure vengeance. Although the later narratives in *Cleanness* show God's Word seemingly less conclusive, in this case it is not the pure Word itself but rather its various representations and interpretations that equivocate. The frustration of history and time is that one act of purification does not purify forever, but is followed by another lapse into corruption, for only outside history are purity and holiness eternally pure and holy. *Cleanness* further demonstrates that, before the eschaton, the sacramental mode is the closest humanity can come to that pure holiness. Christ's ability to be freed from the necessity of final action and his paradoxical purity and openness, which are described in the Incarnation section, are shown by the poet to be available through the eucharist and the other sacraments to those who are, to use Kermode's words, in "the middest."[18] But the beauty of that *fayre forme*, like the eschatological bliss in God's Kingdom, can only be seen in the light of

[18]On the term and concept of "the middest" and also on the role of the eschaton in structuring narrative fiction, see Kermode, esp. p. 8, and my earlier note in the Introduction (note 20). (However, Kermode has not, as far as I know, discussed time or the End in terms of the sacramental mode.) For the importance of providential history, see Schleusner.

history and of that "kark and combraunce huge" (4): God's absolute hatred of corruption, filth, ugliness, and sin.

The "kark and combraunce huge" of writing about uncleanness and recounting God's historical actions of judgment also apply to the ostensible finality and linearity of the human story. Christian history is not in fact linear and sequential, but rather cyclical and spiral, discontinuous and continuing. The human story is openended and—as Jesus keeps telling his followers—near and yet unpredictable.[19] It is the present moment that counts, for while, as Augustine explains, a real present belongs only to eternity and God (*Confessions* 11.11; pp. 230–33), there is a sense in which "now" is all that matters for humanity—the past exists only as our present memory of it, and we cannot know the future (*Confessions* 11.18; pp. 247–51). All of this is only paradoxically implied in *Cleanness*, although the interpolation of the Incarnation passage makes the point somewhat more forcefully. It remains to the next poem in the manuscript, *Patience*, to make explicit the presentness of sacred history.

Patience

Set in the pre-Incarnation past and based very closely upon an Old Testament text, *Patience* reveals the fairest *forme* of history: a narrative pattern of conversion that tells a human story that is present and continuing. The suggestions scattered through *Cleanness*—that God is not solely responsible for humanity's return to him and his kingdom, that his creatures have a role in history, and that their story may not end apocalyptically—these suggestions are all made explicit in *Patience*. *Patience* goes further and demonstrates the contingency of

[19]Many of Jesus's teaching and parables, especially in the synoptic gospels, stress the nearness of the end, as well as its unpredictability. Toward the end of Matthew's gospel, for example, Jesus speaks much of the End and its calamaties, but adds: "As for the exact day or hour, no one knows it, neither the angels in heaven nor the Son, but the Father only" (24.36).

history, the possibility of postponing the promised end, even of changing it.

The problem of determining the pattern and especially the end of history is an important issue in the New Testament, reflecting the early church's concern with the timing of God's final acts of judgment, particularly the apparent delay of the imminent eschaton so often mentioned by Jesus. The longer the day of the Lord was delayed, the more awkward the church's position became. It is this problem which is addressed in the Second Epistle of Peter, in a passage that is explicitly relevant to *Patience*:[20]

> Caeli autem qui nunc sunt et terra eodem verbo repositi sunt,
> igni servati in diem iudicii et perditionis impiorum hominum.
> Unum vero hoc non lateat vos carissimi,
> quia unus dies apud Dominum sicut mille anni
> et mille anni sicut dies unus.
> Non tardat Dominus promissi,
> sed patienter agit propter vos
> nolens aliquos perire,
> sed omnes ad paenitentiam reverti.
> Adveniet autem dies Domini ut fur
> in qua caeli magno impetu transient
> elementa vero calore solventur.
> . . . .
> Novos vero caelos et novam terram
> et promissa ipsius expectamus in quibus iustitia habitat.
> (2 Pet. 3.7–10, 13)

> [The heavens and earth which are now have been set aside by that same Word,

[20]In addition to serving as an important general source for apocalyptic views, 2 Peter, as Cuffe has noted, contains a passage that has specific relevance for the poem *Cleanness*—see 2 Pet. 2.4 and Cuffe, in a 1951 dissertation cited by Kelly and Irwin (244).

Preserved for the fire in the day of judgment and of the ruin of impious men.
Let not this one thing be hidden from you, beloved friends,
For one day in the Lord is like 1,000 years and 1,000 years like one day.
The Lord does not delay with his promises, but rather he acts patiently, since he does not wish you others to perish, but all to return to repentance.
Even so, the day of the Lord will come like a thief,
On which day the heavens will disappear with a great force and the elements will dissolve in a fierce heat.

. . . .

Truly we await new heavens and a new earth, where, in accord with his promises, justice will reside.]

In this passage the apparent conflict between God's desire for our return to him and his inevitable judgment and punishment of evil is resolved by his patience. The end will eventually come, the judgment will then be final, and the evil cast out forever, but in the meantime God awaits patiently. He endures the history of humanity's repeated failures, and his endurance is paradoxically an *act of patience* (*Dominus . . . patienter agit*), not passive inaction or failure to intervene.

The problem raised in the passage from the Petrine epistle is crucial to the understanding of *Patience* and indeed has bearing upon the Book of Jonah as well. *Patience*, in recounting the story of Jonah, presents us with a very fallible prophet—wrong thinking as well as wrong acting. What Jonah needs to be taught is that God is not just the Lord above history, but also the loving Yahweh within history, who holds each individual and every society in his continuing care. Jonah has a tendency to focus on the end of history and to take divine signs for human signs that are susceptible to his own manipulation and misinterpretation; he uses God's *formez*, whether pattern or visual symbol or verbal image, as finite human ones. For example, Jonah acknowledges God as Creator of the earth, but then expects that Creator to be confined to one locale. Furthermore, while Jonah looks ahead to cleansing acts of divine judgment, he seems unwilling to acknowledge humanity's own responsibility for reform and repentance.

The lesson for Jonah, and for the poem's audience, is to stop concentrating on the distant apocalypse and instead to bring God's Kingdom into the present—and thus paradoxically to go one step beyond apocalypse. Going beyond apocalypse involves moving away from the linearity of an eschatological perspective and replacing the linear *forme* of judgment with the circular and openended *forme* of conversion. The paradox of going beyond the eschaton, which is to redefine it, is closely connected to the paradox embodied in *pacience* and to the poem's "narrative redefinition of patience" (Kirk). The poet's use and definition of *pacience* make it an active virtue, a divine quality that characterizes not just God's long sufferance but also his involvement in human history. By extension, patience becomes the virtue best suited to God's servants and prophets in "the middest," those who must work within history, who must cease looking to a distant, timeless future and become instead responsive to the present reality of God and his will.[21] For Jonah, having finally delivered God's warning, responds with anger when Nineveh is spared the threatened destruction. In the Bible the prophet regrets God's well-known patience and mercy (Jon. 4.2); in *Patience* the poet has added to Jonah's complaint words that strikingly echo those used in the argument of the Petrine epistle:

> Wel knew I þi cortaysye, þy quoynt soffraunce,
> þy bounté of debonerté and þy bene grace,
> þy *longe abydyng* wyth lur þy *late* vengaunce.
> (417–19; emphasis mine)

[21]According to Tayler, this is Milton's position, made clearest in *Paradise Regained*. Tayler argues that the church could never successfully rationalize away the prolonged wait for the supposedly imminent Second Coming, and so "[h]ere lies the fundamental reason for the preeminence of patience as a Christian virtue, the fundamental necessity for enduring the 'tempestivity of time.' The greater hero knows how to play the waiting game" (152).

The last line of this passage specifically accuses God of delay. Jonah's error here should be obvious, for, as 2 Peter tells us, *Dominus non tardat.*

In *Patience* the movement beyond the apocalypse, from future to present, which is more explicit than in the Petrine epistle, is accomplished in several ways, most of them owing to the poem's two biblical sources: the Book of Jonah and Matthew's Beatitudes. First, in *Patience* the Word of God is not the Johannine Logos nor the apocalyptic Judge, but the Old Testament Word, namely God's spoken words, heard first by his prophet and then delivered to his people.[22] Second, the bearer of the spoken Word is not a visionary seer and scribe but a prophet—prophets work primarily in the present, and they hear and then speak, whereas apocalyptic visionaries see into the future and write for the future.[23] Third, God's justice in *Patience* is characterized by mercy, not vengeance, and the corresponding virtue for humanity is *patience*, not *clanness* (purity, righteousness, or godliness—the distinguishing characteristics, according to *Cleanness* and its sources, of the elect beyond history). Finally, *Patience* and the Beatitudes do not look to the new heavens and new earth of the future, but to the Kingdom of God which is realizable now within each of God's creatures.

We have already seen in Chapter Two how the Prologue of *Patience* uses the Beatitudes to represent the Kingdom of God as a present and internalized reality instead of a mythic future world. Following the Prologue, *Patience* demonstrates in its narratives that the opportunity to enjoy the Kingdom of God now is inseparable from humanity's responsibility in salvation history. Unlike the apocalyptic focus on God's final and future acts of judgment, purification, and redemption, Jonah's mission to

[22]For the Logos, see John 1.1–14; for the apocalyptic Judge, see Apoc. 19.11–16. Compare the opening of the Book of Jonah. "Et factum est verbum Domini ad Ionam" [And the Word of the Lord was given to Jonah], a formula found in other books of the prophets; see, for example, Joel 1.1, Jer. 1.2.

[23]On the importance of the written text and the role of the apocalyptic seer as scribe, see McGinn (5), Russell (118–22), and my discussion in Chapter One (24–25, and note 1).

Nineveh exemplifies what humanity can do by undertaking its own conversion rather than awaiting God's judgmental action. This moral and doctrinal revision parallels the poem's revision in narrative structure, from the linear and closed to the circular and open. As God adjusts Jonah's thinking about judgment and action, mercy and patience, so also he adjusts Jonah's and the reader's views of history. A providential plan does not mean a simple straight line, which is the limited narrative structure of the stories within *Cleanness*, and a promised end does not mean a foregone conclusion.

The story of Jonah, both in the Bible and in *Patience*, comprises three linked narratives of conversion: the major one is the story of Jonah himself; the other two are the story of Nineveh and the story of the sailors. Jonah's story contains some of the most unusual features of a conversion narrative and is the most complex and most significant plot in *Patience*. However, before turning to Jonah himself, we should look first at the Ninevites' and the sailors' stories, in order to distinguish the basic pattern of a conversion narrative in its simpler forms.

In *Patience* we learn that the people of Nineveh have fallen into wicked ways; they are full of "vilanye and venym" (71) and are not behaving in accord with God's plan. God then takes the first action and sends his prophet to warn Nineveh of divine vengeance. Nineveh responds by embarking on a full-scale program of repentance. Led by their king, all the Ninevites, including the animals, do penance. God then, "þaȝ He oþer bihyȝt" (408), withholds his vengeance.

The story of the Ninevites illustrates that the purpose of God's Word is to save and restore his creatures, not to destroy them; the other two narratives make even clearer how much this act of restoration involves God's patience and how it apparently delays the promised end. The story of the sailors' conversion is less impressive than the complete turning to God by the Ninevites. To begin with, the sailors are not introduced to us as a wicked people, and, in their lack of knowledge regarding God's plan, they seem more neutral and less guilty than the Ninevites. On the other hand, unlike the Ninevites, the sailors do not respond immediately when Jonah tells them about the true God. They ignore the Word of God spoken by his prophet and bend even more energetically to their rowing. When they do finally respond to the message with a patient acceptance, then their story has a happy ending—there is "louyng on lofte" as they reach land (237).

In the story of Jonah himself, we find two special features not found in the Ninevites' or in the sailors' narratives: Jonah's story is individualized and internalized, and it is openended. Although Jonah's narrative has what could be a happy ending, it does not end there, but goes on to a conclusion that for many (including Jonah himself) lacks finality and is anticlimactic. Both the internalization and the openendedness of Jonah's conversion allow us to witness the continuing progress of salvation history and the corresponding divine patience required in such a pattern. Jonah's conversion is a gradual change of heart, one that has psychological plausibility as well as dramatic suspense, both of which have been traced in detail by various critics (for example, Spearing, *Gawain-Poet* [83–88] and Davenport [119–30]).[24] One way of viewing Jonah's development is as a re-education in salvation history, "*re*-education" because all along Jonah betrays a knowledge of God and his purposes without, however, accepting the full implications of such knowledge. Jonah first recalls God's roles as sovereign and creator; later he learns the full extent, through time and space, of the Creator's power and loving concern; finally, Jonah is taught the lesson, stressed in the Petrine epistle, that the Lord does not want his creatures to perish, but to be restored to him (2 Pet. 3.9). As readers we learn with Jonah that the neat and tidy conclusiveness of a closed narrative is not the *fayre forme* of salvation history.

The revision to Jonah's understanding of history and of God's action within history corresponds to a revision in Jonah's reading of the divine signs, which tends to be overly apocalyptic. We

[24]For other analyses, which differ in several respects, see Diekstra and L. S. Johnson (6–22).

have already seen in the previous chapter how the poet handles ironically Jonah's understanding of the reigning Lord, who Jonah claims "syttes . . . on sege so hyȝe / In His glowande glorye" (93–94), not caring about the suffering of his poor creatures and his beleaguered prophets. Equally narrow in its application, if less immediately ironical, is Jonah's recognition of God as the Creator. Early in the poem, while on shipboard, Jonah explains to the sailors:

> Þat Wyȝe I worchyp, iwysse, þat wroȝt alle þynges,
> Alle þe worlde with þe welkyn, þe wynde and þe sternes,
> Alle þat wonez þer withinne, at a worde one. (206–08)

But this same prophet, who speaks so eloquently of the all-powerful Creator and Ruler, assumes that he can run away from God, that there can be some place beyond his power. This assumption calls forth great scorn from the narrator, who interrupts the narrative to expend thirteen lines attacking the "wytles wrechche" (113).

Jonah needs first a few basic lessons about divine power, the kind of lesson apocalypses teach by stressing cosmic judgment: that the Lord's power is limited neither by time nor space and, furthermore, that he can and will do anything to bring about his will. And so Jonah is exposed to a whole range of apocalyptic horrors: a divinely sent, cosmic storm, imminent shipwreck and destruction, and a deathlike sojourn in the hellish belly of the whale. The prophet's first turning away from rebellion and toward God is a direct response to these threats and perils. So far Jonah is behaving as do the Ninevites and the sailors, who heed the apocalyptic threat and do God's will because of God's power to destroy, although Jonah's response is even more delayed than the sailors' is.

The second lesson Jonah needs to learn is that these apocalyptic disasters are not the end, but promises of the end. The ship does not sink, the storm does not destroy the sailors, let alone all the created world (nor, as far as we know, does it hurt anyone or anything), Jonah does not die in the whale, and

Nineveh is not destroyed. Some of these changes are simply adjustments in plot direction, as with Nineveh and the ship, so that the sub-plot ends happily. Somewhat different is the sojourn in the whale, which represents not only a change in promised outcome (Jonah lives instead of dies), but, as we have seen, involves a radical adjustment of the sensible *forme*, so that signs of death and separation become signs of life and God's loving care. Furthermore, Jonah's three days in the whale also shift the poem's setting, from public to private, and from external and cosmic to internal and individual. Coming at the exact center of the poem, this episode is critical in the poem's revisions and conversions; it is meant to change Jonah's (and the reader's) views—of history, of the prophet's role, and of the meaning of divine signs. It is in the whale that readers are taught to go beyond apocalypse, for it is in the whale that readers first learn with Jonah to read differently and to see the openendedness of history and the ambiguity, or at least the paradoxical richness, of visual signs.

I have detailed in Chapter Two how the poet has played with traditional images and signs within the whale, so that a place that mimetically and typologically evokes hell comes to be a temporary Kingdom of God for Jonah. At the same time that the poet inverts the divine signs for Jonah, he also provides a narrative account of the corresponding inversion, which is a conversion, within Jonah's heart. This conversion, as the Pearl poet recounts it, includes a prayer not found in the Bible, in which Jonah acknowledges his sinfulness and seeks God's protection:

> "Now, Prynce, of Þy prophete pité Þou haue.
> Þaȝ I be fol and fykel and falce of my hert,
> Dewoyde now Þy vengaunce, þurȝ vertu of rauthe;
> Thaȝ I be gulty of gyle, as gaule of prophetes,
> Þou art God, and alle gowdez are grayþely þyn owen."
> (282–86)

The addition of this prayer, along with other changes from the biblical text, serves to rationalize Jonah's conversion.[25] While challenging Jonah and the reader with paradoxical reversals of our expectations about signs, the poem also explains the process of change within Jonah. Because the narrative account makes sense, we can accept the seeming contradiction that Jonah is close to God when he is in hell or a hellish world.

We are thus ready for the paradoxes of Jonah's deliverance from the whale, which concludes Jonah's deathlike journey. Traditionally seen as a figure for resurrection, Jonah's release from the whale is explicitly presented in *Patience* as an emergence from sin into new life:

> Þenne he swepe to þe sonde in sluchched cloþes:
> Hit may wel be þat mester were his mantyle to wasche.
> (341–42)

There is a potential allusion to John's Apocalypse here, to the often-used image of the elect whose white robes have been washed and "made white in the blood of the Lamb" (Apoc. 7.14)[26] But, as with the whale as a figure for hell and death, these typological suggestions of resurrection and the Last Judgment are undercut. Jonah's mantle is not new or white—the poet only says it "may wel be," if the clothes were washed. ("May wel be" could be translated either as "might well be" in the sense of "could have been," or else as "would be well" in the sense of "would be a good idea.") Moreover, Jonah's story does not conclude with this deliverance, since he has been delivered not into

[25]See Davenport (106–09) for a fine analysis of the poet's adaptation of the Jonah psalm, as well as of other changes. For a modern discussion of the problems and inconsistencies arising from the Jonah psalm, see George Landes. See also Jerome's commentary on this passage (*PL*, 25.1189). Jerome is explicit about the problem in the narrative, a problem that the Pearl poet is obviously solving through his changes and additions.

[26]See also Andrew and Waldron (199–200, note to line 342). Note especially their citation of the passage in *Piers Plowman* (B 13.272ff), when the sinful Haukyn is told to wash his dirty cloak.

the otherworld, but back to the created world, from which he tried to escape and in which he has a mission to perform.

This lack of a final "happy ending" that really ends, this openendedness, not only distinguishes Jonah's conversion from the Ninevites' or the sailors' stories, it also marks the "presentness" of providential history and the continuing need for the prophet's role. It remains to the Woodbine episode to make explicit both the openendedness of the narrative and the divine patience required by that openendedness. Not only does God mercifully forgive Nineveh, but his patience endures (*Dominus . . . agit patienter*) through Jonah's very gradual conversion in the whale and even through the prophet's new foolishness and escape under the woodbine.

In the Woodbine episode Jonah, angry because Nineveh is spared, runs away and builds a *bour* for himself. God first causes a woodbine to grow and give shade and beauty to Jonah's *bour*, and then, on the very next night, has the woodbine destroyed in order to teach Jonah another lesson in divine patience and mercy. For, having learned that the Lord, who sits "on sege so hyȝe" (93), does care about him and having personally experienced God's mercy, Jonah now needs to be reminded that this mercy and love extend to all creatures and to all creation. The Woodbine episode thus completes the second lesson that Jonah learns, the lesson that humanity must move beyond apocalypse and must learn not just that "*non tardat Dominus*" (2 Pet. 9), but also that both the whole creation and each individual creature within it are important to the reigning Lord.

One way of seeing this development is as a resolution of the dichotomy between the cosmic scale of an apocalyptic view of God and his creation and a personal focus upon the individual and his change of heart. As *Patience* finally makes clear, personal eschaton and individual conversion do not replace universal salvation; rather, they help accomplish the progress of history toward the realization of God's Kingdom. Jonah's conversion therefore has been not for his sake alone, but for Nineveh's, even though Jonah is slow to acknowledge this. Jonah's failure to comprehend fully God's purposes, even after his experience in the whale, is proof that the self-awareness gained in the whale has become self-concern, self-consciousness, and self-aggrandizement.

While Jonah's foolish preoccupation with his own status can hardly be missed, many readers have not noticed that the poet has extended Jonah's selfishness to include a kind of self-joy, as well as self-pity. This self-joy characterizes Jonah's behavior under the woodbine; for even though the prophet's retreat begins in anger and sulky sleep, it eventually takes on a mood of great delight. The poet describes Jonah's gaiety under the woodbine vividly and makes its excessiveness unmistakable:

> Þenne watz þe gome so glad of his gay logge,
> Lys loltrande þerinne lokande to toune;
> So blyþe of his wodbynde he balteres þervnder,
> Þat of no diete þat day þe deuel haf he roȝt.
> And euer he laȝed as he loked þe loge alle aboute,
> And wysched hit were in his kyth þer he wony schulde,
> On heȝe vpon Effraym oþer Ermonnes hillez. (457–63)[27]

Several details point to the disproportion of Jonah's delight in this bower. Most striking is his forgetting the human need for food;[28] and, even worse, he ignores the rightful place of things in the world. Jonah appears to have lost all sense of God's order

[27]There is some stress placed on Jonah's happiness even in the Vulgate, which repeats the root *laet*: "Et laetatus est Iona super hedera laetitia magna" [And Jonah was joyful, with a great joy, over the gourd plant] (Jon. 4.6).

[28]Vantuono glosses *diete* as "day's journey," admittedly another meaning of this word in Middle English, but the hyperbole does not really work with this meaning. Vantuono says "the prophet is too comfortable now to think of such a task" (that is, another day's journey to preach, as he made to Nineveh in line 355), but there is nothing remarkable in this, since Jonah never wanted to preach to Nineveh in the first place. What is remarkable is that under the woodbine Jonah is so comfortable that he does not care for something normally needful and good. In other words, consigning a trip to Nineveh to the devil is what Jonah in fact tried to do earlier; consigning food to the devil is something else again (and note that, unlike an ascetic, Jonah offers his fasting not to God but to the devil).

in space and time, and he stays in the dark away from the sun without even a "mountraunce of a lyttle mote" shining upon him (456). Also excessive is Jonah's childish way of enjoying his bour; it is hardly with the dignity of a prophet that he "balteres þervnder" (459), *balteres* suggesting a kind of faltering dance with a bounce, a graceless joy.[29] Jonah's retreat under the woodbine reaches its culmination when he "slydez on a sloumbe-slep sloghe vnder leues" (466), where he enjoys "wyl dremes" (473), not the first time that Jonah uses sleep to escape from God's plan and God's will, although this time the sleep is part, not of a lazy avoidance of responsibility, but of a subtler though more general retreat from the world.

By destroying the woodbine, God does away with a world that is seemingly a human creation. Jonah wrongly thinks that his *logge* is all his own making, his safe and contained little *bour*, which he wishes were away from the foreign land and back "in his kyth" (462). There is significantly no sunlight in Jonah's false world, as, or so he thinks, there is no possibility of God's unwelcome mercy, which is threatening to the integrity and honor of a prophet. But Jonah can no more stay in this *bour* than he could in the little *hyrne* within the whale or in the corner he found on shipboard. He is again, figuratively this time, returned to the openended story of providential history. In those earlier instances we saw Jonah physically wrenched out of his hiding places, kicked ("frunt" — 187) and spewed ("sput" — 338), whereas now it is simply and purely God's voice that pulls Jonah out of his beloved *bour*.

In the Woodbine episode, Jonah's movement becomes less explicit and more figurative, just as the voice of God is less

[29]Compare Andrew and Waldron, who gloss *balteres* as "rolls around"; Anderson, who gives "capers"; and Vantuono, who has "hobbles." Vantuono's definition does not suggest the gaiety, but it works better for *balterande*, which is used to describe the cripples approaching Jesus in *Cleanness*, 103. See also *MED*, which gives the meaning "to move about clumsily." The word is rare and occurs first (so far as is known) in the Pearl poet's works, so its usage was probably not fixed. I think there can be little doubt that the poet intended the word (in *Cleanness* and *Patience*) to convey both clumsiness and gaiety.

physical than the whale's or sailors' actions. This difference corresponds to the changes in *Patience* from the mythic, highly visual sign to the subtler, often paradoxical, verbal sign. Each change contributes to the poem's development from the external, public history of Israel to the internal and private development of individuals in the poem's audience. When God breaks into Jonah's closed world with the destruction of the woodbine and with the voice of his unwelcome divine presence, he also breaks open both the end of Jonah's story and the frame of the poem, resulting in a conflation of speakers and voices in the last lines of *Patience*.

At the close of the poem, after reminding Jonah of the divine love for creation by comparing it to Jonah's fondness for his woodbine, God contrasts Jonah's "hastif" judgment (520) with God's "mercy" (523). Then follows:

> Be noȝt so gryndel, godman, bot go forth þy wayes,
> Be preue and be pacient in payne and in joye;
> For he þat is to rakel to renden his cloþez
> Mot efte site with more vnsounde to sewe hem togeder.
> (524–27)

These lines present problems for editors and readers, who wonder if this is still God speaking, and, if not, where his voice stops and the narrator's takes over. Andrew and Waldron give the best solution: while God is speaking up until this point (through line 523), the next four lines (the ones quoted above) form a "bridge" to the final lines of the poem, which are, as all agree, in the narrator's voice (206, note to line 524).[30] The voice that we hear in the poem's closing lines recalls the voice of the Prologue, with its personal application of the "*poynt*" of "*pacience*":

[30]Compare: Morris, who ends God's speech after line 524; Anderson, after line 523; Gollancz, after line 527. All of these editors have the narrator's voice pick up right after God stops speaking, wherever they make that be. I think Andrew and Waldron have clearly made the right choice about the respective voices, though I do not agree with them that the narrator's voice is "in the *persona* of a preacher" (italics theirs). This narrator has become a prophet, although

Forþy when pouerté me enprecez and paynez innoȝe
Ful softly with suffraunce saȝttel me bihouez;
Forþy penaunce and payne topreue hit in syȝt
Þat pacience is a nobel poynt, þaȝ hit displese ofte.
Amen. (528–31)

The "bridge," the lines in between the conclusion of God's speech and the beginning of the narrator's, is the prophetic voice that appears in Isaiah, Jeremiah, and in virtually all the prophets, including the Book of Jonah, the voice that puts God's Word in the mouth of the prophet and that is often introduced with the phrase, "Thus says the Lord."[31] The poet, by merging the narrator's voice with God's and by conflating historical past time with present poem time, does for his poem what is urged in the Prologue: he moves into present time and internalizes the Kingdom of God.

During the course of this, his shortest poem, the Pearl poet has effected a full revision—of history and of iconographic signs. He has converted his poem to a conversion poem; he has internalized and demythologized signs of God and his kingdom; he has recounted a story set in the past in order to bring us not to an end but to a beginning, and, more precisely, move us out of Old Testament history into the "present" time of the narrator and his audience; and finally he has merged his voice with God's, and thereby obediently and patiently merged his story, his *fayre forme*, into God's.

---

a prophet in the post-incarnation world of fourteenth-century England. Compare Hill and his thesis that *Patience* is a poem for and about preachers.

[31]In the Latin: "haec dicit Dominus Deus." See, for example, Isa. 7.7, when the Lord sends Isaiah to meet Ahaz. Even when the formula, in this or one of its variations, is not repeated, the Lord tends to speak directly (usually in the first person) through the mouth of his prophet. Thus, whereas Jonah's message to the Ninevites is very brief and there is no equivalent of the above formula, earlier God orders Jonah explicitly to speak the words God puts into his mouth—"quam ego loquor ad te" (Jon. 3.2); "Lo, My lore is in þe loke, lauce hit þerinne" (*Patience* 350).

FOUR

The *Fayre Formez* of *Pearl* and *Sir Gawain and the Green Knight*

WHILE *Cleanness* and *Patience*, the two of the Pearl poet's works that are set in the biblical past, are fittingly in the *formez* of sacred history, the other two poems, *Pearl* and *Sir Gawain and the Green Knight*, which are set in non-biblical, post-incarnation time, are structured according to the *formez* of dream vision and romance, the most "medieval" *formez* available to the poet. Although there has been much helpful work on both medieval romance and dream vision, I believe we can get a better sense of the Pearl poet's use of these genres by focusing on what the poems themselves say about their *formez*.

Each poem is both archetypal and atypical in its respective genre. *Pearl* combines the visionary and didactic qualities of apocalypse found in poems like *Piers Plowman* with the pleasure and desire of love lyric that characterize Guillaume de Lorris's *Roman de la Rose*.[1] *Sir Gawain and the Green Knight* narrates the adventures of a chivalric knight set in the Arthurian court, at once located as part of England's historical past and also imbued with the magic and otherworldliness of Celtic fairyland. In these respects, both poems are archetypes of their genres, as those

[1]While the didactic features of Pearl are never missed, the lyric qualities are seldom noted; see, for example, Andrew and Waldron's introductory remarks on this poem (esp. 29). Luttrell is the noteworthy exception; in his article, "The Introduction to the Dream in *Pearl*," he demonstrates "how the poem takes its starting point from the courtly world of love poetry" (279). Spearing, with his usual good sense and sensitivity, emphasizes the suggestions of *fine amour* in the poem's opening lines (138–39) and also discusses the ways in which *Pearl* draws on the the traditions of secular love visions (*Gawain-Poet* 118–23).

genres had evolved by the fourteenth century. At the same time, each is atypical: both are more courtly and more self-consciously crafted than is usually found in English examples of their genre (except, of course, for Chaucer); both poems are shorter and more rhetorically and tightly structured than most English and continental examples; and finally, both poems, unlike most English examples but more characteristic of twelfth-and-thirteenth-century French courtly literature, are at least in part about their respective *formez*. As *Pearl* explores the implications of dream vision genre, so *Gawain* examines the possibilities and limitations of romance; moreover, this self-consciousness about *formez* is reflected in the labels each poem uses for its respective genre.

Pearl—"So Swete a Sange"

In the second stanza of *Pearl*, the dreamer describes the emotional context of his dream and his poem:

> Syþen in þat spote hit fro me sprange,
> Ofte haf I wayted, wyschande þat wele
> Þat wont watz whyle deuoyde my wrange
> And heuen my happe and al my hele—
> Þat dotz bot þrych my hert þrange,
> My brest in bale bot bolne and bele.
> Ȝet þoȝt me neuer *so swete a sange*
> As stylle stounde let to me stele. (13–20; emphasis mine)

The dream comes in a "stylle stounde," a "moment of peace" in the midst of grief. The dreamer waits in pain, longing for the comfort of his pearl and to him comes "so swete a sange."

At the end of the poem, when the dreamer is awakened abruptly, he refers to his dream not as a "sange," but as an "avysyoun":

> A longeyng heuy me strok in swone,
> And rewfully þenne I con to reme:

> "O perle," quoþ I, "of rych renoun,
> So watz hit me dere þat þou con deme
> In þys *veray avysyoun*!" (1180–84; emphasis mine)

Returned to the mood of deep longing that has begun the poem, the dreamer now evaluates, interprets, and names his dream, moving from the doubt and remorse articulated in the above lines to the confidence expressed in the final stanza:

> Ouer þis hyul þis *lote* I laþte,
> For pyty of my perle enclyin,
> And syþen to God I hit bytaȝte,
> In Krystez dere blessyng and myn.
> (1205–1208; emphasis mine)

In this final stanza *lote* is now used to refer to the dream experience. Most editors gloss this word as "happening, chance"; although Andrew and Waldron (rightly I think) see a possible pun on the word for "speech, word" (110, note to 1205–10), and Gollancz defines *lot* as "vision" (from the Old Norse *lat*).[2] I think it probable that the poet seized on this word precisely because it could carry such a large and diverse cluster of meanings: *lote* refers first of all to the narrated experience, which includes the dream and also the discourse within the dream; second, *lote* stands for the poem itself, insofar as the poem can be viewed as something sent to the poet, not created by him. It is significant that by the last stanza the poet sees his poem as the experience it records, not just as the words the poet crafted and arranged. This is the only real progress the dreamer makes, the only conversion he experiences.

Pearl is about itself—itself as a lyric song and a vision and itself as the carefully crafted poem, the artifact created by its poet, the *juelere*. Most have noted that the story of *Pearl* is the

[2]For a summary of the various editorial positions on the word *lote*, see Vantuono (285, note to 1205).

story of the dreamer and his progress, or lack thereof.[3] This is in keeping with visionary and apocalyptic literature. What none have seen is that *Pearl* also tells the story of a poet trying to make a poem about his desire, a concern of many of the more sophisticated love lyrics. Not only does *Pearl* explicitly examine the dreamer's progress as a dreamer and as a Christian in need of consolation; it also implicitly draws attention to itself and to its making. In all the often tiresome discussions of what the pearl is or represents, virtually no one has acknowledged that the pearl is first and foremost simply the subject of the poem, and by extension also the poem itself, or more precisely the poem is the pearl placed in its setting.[4] What that setting should be and who makes and possesses the setting, God or the dreamer/poet, is central to the conflict of the poem.

The ultimate story of *Pearl*, its metafiction, is the combined story of the lyric poet and the visionary. At first, the dreamer sees his role as that of a lyric poet—or, in his terms, a *juelere*—who seeks to obtain the pearl and craft its setting, but who must learn that the pearl is not his nor is the pearl's proper setting one made by him. The *juelere* comes by stages to this knowledge—first, to an appreciation of the art of the one "quo formed . . . [her] fayre fygure" for her (747), and only at the poem's very end, to an acknowledgment of the true setting for that "fayre fygure." The poem begins in a mood of deep longing and desire, very close to the desire that impels the poet's song in lyrics like

[3]While many critics have traced some kind of progress, even finding the dreamer's attainment of mystical enlightenment, Aers, in his recent article, "Reflections on *Pearl*," argues persuasively for a "regression," one in which "the poet figures forth a movement that involves a failure to complete the work of mourning" (68).

[4]Cary Nelson, however, comes close to saying the pearl is the poem when he asserts that: "[The] figural verbal drama continues until the poem's entire form—its flawed circle yearning for completion—becomes itself a figure to be fulfilled in the perfect understanding achieved after death" (43); in the final paragraph of his chapter on *Pearl*, Nelson also says, "*Pearl* is a sphere dense with language" (49). However, as these two quotations indicate, it is the figure of the circle (or sphere) that Nelson identifies with the poem, not so much the pearl itself.

those of Bernart de Ventadorn;[5] in *Pearl* this desire is equivalent to the emotional crisis that precipitates apocalyptic vision.[6] However, as in many medieval love visions, the dreamer's desire is distinctly secular and nonspiritual, and the poem goes on to recount the effort at converting this secular human desire into something spiritual and Christian. *Pearl* is the story of the narrator who begins as a lyric poet making his poem about his beloved and then starts to develop into an apocalyptic visionary witnessing the celebration of God's kingdom.

However, because the change is not realized, the *forme* of *Pearl* is not a conversion *forme*, like the one in *Patience*; neither is it a pattern of judgment, like those in *Cleanness*, since it lacks the sense of an ending. The *forme* of *Pearl*, and by implication of the dream vision and lyric genres, is a conversion pattern suspended. While the desire for such conversion imbues the poem, and the possibility of conversion is tantalizingly ever present, the poem lacks actual history as action within time and can record only the transformation of words in puns and exegesis, not the transformation of itself or of its dreamer or of its maker. The dreamer's efforts to become an apocalyptic visionary fail; he stumbles in his spiritual development, and his vision is finally cut short by the rashness of his *luf-longyng*, the same *luf-longyng* that impels him to have the vision in the first place (and a desire that, were it transformed and converted, could save him, as it does Dante). Nonetheless, although he finally fails in his role as apocalyptic visionary, *Pearl*'s *juelere* does end his poem in a mode that is wholly Christian and has been freed from its earthly and romantic desires. This achievement is not without a price: there is a flatness and a distance to the resignation of the

[5]See, for example, Bernart's "Non es meravelha s'eu chan," which exalts the power of desire (Goldin no. 21; pp. 126–29); see also Cercamon's "Quant l'aura doussa s'amarzis" (Goldin no. 18; pp. 96–99), a lyric that calls the poet's lady a "precious jewel" ["joja . . . fina"] (13–14).

[6]See Chapter One (24); see also McGinn on the precipitating crisis in apocalypticism, where he cautions against a simplistic link between historical crises and apocalypticism (*Vision* 30–31).

last stanzas, wholly unlike the transcendent exaltation of the end of the *Divine Comedy*, for example.

To see how the transformation fails and why, it helps to examine closely the movement in the poem, to see where the dreamer begins, what happens to him in his dream, and where he ends. In the beginning, *Pearl* unmistakably establishes a lyric setting. The first stanza opens with a direct apostrophe to the pearl, in terms suited to a lady addressed by a poet-lover:

> Perle plesaunte to prynces paye,
> To clanly clos in golde so clere:
> Oute of oryent, I hardyly saye,
> Ne proued I neuer her precios pere.
> So rounde, so reken vche araye,
> So smal, so smoþe her sydez were. (1–6)[7]

The metaphor of the lady as a pearl uses the same jewel imagery found in many love lyrics. In the Middle English lyric, "Ichot a burde in a bour ase beryl so bright," the lady is compared to a

[7]I am using my own punctuation here, placing a comma after the first line, but not after "pleasaunte," so that the second line stands in apposition to the first, not as an infinitive completing "prynces paye." I believe "to clanly clos" is an adjectival phrase, describing the pearl, and *clos* should be translated as the participial adjective "enclosed," with "to" as an intensifier, not as a signal of the infinitive. My reasons for this reading, "very finely enclosed," are: 1) The poet's usual style is one with an unconstricted, though not uncomplicated, syntax. In *Pearl* especially, he, like many lyric poets, takes full advantage of the looser syntax in order to enrich and deepen meaning. Compare the function of the bobs in the stanzas of *Gawain*—their syntactical postion is usually difficult to determine, and one often cannot tell whether they complete the sentence of the preceding lines or begin that of the wheel. If the second line of *Pearl* is read as an infinitive, especially one that completes the first line, the effect is more controlled and more reflective than seems appropriate, particularly in view of the intensely emotional "Allas!" of line 9. 2) *Close(e)* as a verb and *closed* as a past participle are easily confused with *clos(e)* as adjective and adverb. All grammatical forms and spellings appear in Cotton Nero A.x. (see Kottler and Markman), and there is no consistent correlation between grammatical function and

long list of jewels, all emphasizing her worth and her bright beauty.[8] Other love lyrics use stock images of jewels, flowers, and fruits to exemplify the lady's desirablity.[9] In most of these poems there is no one jewel particularly favored as a figure for the Lady—coral, ruby, diamond, and others are all used. However, in one Middle English lyric (of considerably later date than *Pearl*) the Lady is also likened to a pearl:

> O excellent sovereigne, most semely to see,
> Both prudent and pure, like a perle of prise,
> Also fair of figure and oreant of bewtye,
> Both cumlye and gentil and goodly to advertise. (1–4)[10]

Both this poem and *Pearl* are obviously alluding to Matthew's brief Parable of the Pearl of Great Price (13.45–46), which gives to pearls a special value beyond the one they share with all jewels and precious metals.[11] However, *Pearl* goes beyond the

---

spelling. The adjective *clos* has a rich cluster of meanings, which are especially suited to the Pearl poet. Its appearances in *Pearl* and *Cleanness* are noteworthy; in the latter *clos* can mean "enclosed" or "wrapped up" (12) and also "private" or "intimate" (512; see also the gloss by Andrew and Waldron, p. 133).

Schless has an important short article on the phrase, "princes paye," which he argues (quite persuasively) comes from the Justinian legal maxim, " 'quod principi placet legis habet vigorem' . . . ['the prince's pleasure has the force of law']" (184). Schless's conviction that the final section of the poem is characterized by "pathos and yearning" (185) and also his comments about the problems with punctuating the first stanza fit well with my reading (although I'm not sure he would be any happier with my punctuation than he is with Andrew and Waldron's).

[8]This is one of the Harley lyrics. It can be found in Luria and Hoffman (no. 26, pp. 21–22).

[9]See, for example, "A wayle whit as whalles bon" in Luria and Hoffman (no. 31, pp. 28–30). See also the citations of jewel metaphors, found both in the Harley lyrics and in other Middle English love poetry, in Luttrell (27–28).

[10]This lyric, taken from Bod. 12653, an early sixteenth-century manuscript, is in Luria and Hoffman (no. 43, pp. 42–44).

[11]See Robertson, who views the Matthean parable as the key to the meaning of *Pearl* ("The Pearl as a Symbol").

above examples of lyrics employing jewel imagery, since it not only emphasizes the lady/pearl's beauty and value, but also describes her in distinctly sensual terms: "so rounde," "so smal," and "so smoþe her sydez were" (compare the similar, but less sensuous, "fair of figure" in "O excellent sovereign").

Furthermore, the jewel metaphor in *Pearl* has been extended to include the poet/lover's role as jeweller. It is the poet who admires the pearl and who values her beauty and who aspires to place her in a setting. Although less common than the jewel/lady figure, the figure of the poet as jeweller is implicit in certain texts. Dante, in one of his *rime*, uses the role of gold craftsman to describe his action as a poet/lover:

Per pruova di spaer com vale o quanto
lo maestro l'oro, adducelo a lo foco;
e, ciò faccendo, chiara e sa se poco,
amico, di pecunia vale o tanto.

[The jeweller who would try his gold and know
Its worth, if any, makes fire and puts it in
And doing so, can tell, when it runs thin,
Whether its price, dear friend, be high or low.][12]

Here Dante is focusing primarily on the artisan's action of choosing and evaluating, an important job for a jeweller, but seemingly rather odd for a lover. It reminds us, however, that the poet/lover's role as judge and appraiser is a crucial one. Arnaut Daniel uses a similar image, that of an artisan, or *obrador*, crafting his poem:

En cest sonet coind'e leri
fauc motz e capuig e doli,
que serant verai e cert
qan n'aurai passat la lima;

[12]This is one of Dante's early *rime*; it is in Diehl's ed. (no. 2), and the translation is Diehl's.

q'Amors marves plan'e daura
mon chantar, que de liei mou
qui pretz manten e governa.

[To this sweet and pretty air
I set words that I plane and finish;
and every word will fit well,
once I have passed the file there,
for at once Love polishes and aureates
my song, which proceeds from her,
ruler and guardian of merit.]
(Goldin, no. 39, 1-7; pp. 216-17)[13]

The poet as artisan is implicit in Matthew of Vendôme's *Poetria*, when he writes of poetry as jewels:

> Suquidem sicut in constitutione rei materialis ex appositione alicujus margaritae vel emblematis totum materialum elegantius elucescit, similiter sunt quaedam dictiones, *quae sunt quasi gemmarum vicariae*, ex quarum artificiosa positione totum metrum videbit festivari.(2.11; Faral ed., p. 154; emphasis mine)
>
> [So just as the addition of a pearl or an emblem to a worthy garment will make the whole costume seem more elegant, there are some expressions—*gems of diction*—whose artful use makes the whole composition seem more felicitous.] (Galyon 66; emphasis mine)

[13]Here, as in the other poems I take from his edition, the translation is Goldin's. The translation of *daura* as "aureates" seems right, if awkward—I assume the reference here is to the process of applying gold leaf, but maybe it is just another way of saying "polish" or "make shiny." Also, no doubt the topos of poetry-making as building, measuring out to make the parts fit, works here, as in Chaucer's *Troilus*, to emphasize the structural *forma* of a poem. I am grateful to Robert M. Stein for drawing my attention to this lyric of Arnaut Daniel's.

Here jewels are the rhetorical figures set in the poem by the poet, who once again is cast in the role of jeweller or artisan.

Pearl thus opens with the typical situation of a poet/lover, who is prizing and praising his lady and placing her in his setting. Once set, "to clanly close [very finely enclosed] in golde so cler,"[14] the pearl is fit for princes, a fine work of art. The dreamer's two actions of judging and setting his pearl are closely linked in the middle of the first stanza:

> Quersoeuer I jugged gemmez gaye
> I sette hyr sengeley in synglure. (7–8)

Up until this point we have had the ideal of the lyric poet/lover: the lady as the focus of a poem, and the crafted poem in turn inspired by her fairness and her nobility, and contributing to her fame. The eighth line, however, introduces an obtrusive note of possession: the "I" that begins the line has in this sentence replaced the pearl as subject. The poet/lover repeats the uniqueness ("sengely in synglure") of the setting, but now focuses on his own solipsistic actions, not on the beauty of the pearl. This change in subject also serves as the transition from praise of the pearl to complaint of her loss:

> Allas! I leste hyr in on erbere;
> Þurȝ gresse to grounde hit fro me yot.
> I dewyne, fordokked of luf-daungere
> Of þat pryuy perle withouten spot. (9–12)[15]

[14]See note 6 above on this phrase.

[15]I am following Gollancz's emendation of *fordolked* ("wounded") to *fordokked* ("robbed"), as does Luttrell. As Luttrell explains (in an argument I find totally convincing), there are three basic reasons for the emendation: 1) There is no verb *dolken*, only a noun *dolc*, and that no later than the mid-thirteenth century. 2) The verb *dokken* is common, meaning "cut short"; *fordokked* then would mean "cut off from" or "denied" or "robbed of." 3) Cotton Nero A.x. has several "instances where *k* and *h* appear as *l* through omission of the additional strokes" (Luttrell 275–76; see also Gollancz 116–17). Compare the facsimile (especially Intro., p. 12; and f. 39).

Breaking in with "Allas," the poet describes a fate not uncommon to the lyric lover—the loss of his beloved. When we follow Gollancz's emendation of *fordolked* ("wounded") to *fordokked* ("robbed"), we see that the *juelere* has not been wounded by his pearl's standoffishness or even by love's power, but rather he has been robbed of, or cut off from, love, most particularly from the obsessive power of human love.

The *juelere* thus is suffering because his pearl and the power of love have been taken from him, and he now languishes, waiting for her return in the spot where "hit fro me sprange" (13). This is like the situation of the poet with an *amor lonh*, and there are usually two possibilities open to him: either he can lapse into nothingness (no words and no poem), or he can be inspired to create an even finer and nobler poem, because it will be about his loyalty to the ideal and the humanly unattainable. Bernart de Ventadorn's *canzone* include examples of both alternatives. In "Can vei lauzeta mover," the poet complains of his unattainable love and the cruelty of his lady and ends by renouncing both her and his poetry:

> Tristans, ges no•n auretz de me,
> qu'eu m'en vau, chaitius, no sai on.
> De chanter me gic e•m recre,
> e de joi e d'amor m'escon.
>
> [Tristan, you will have nothing more from me,
> for I go away, a broken man, I know not where;
> I shall withdraw from singing, I renounce it,
> far from joy and love, I hide myself away.]
> (Goldin, no. 26, lines 57–60; pp. 148–49)[16]

[16]As Goldin points out, "Tristans" is a *senhal* (secret name) for the lady. The most famous poem about *amor lonh* and the one that uses the term as its refrain is Jaufré Rudel's "Lanquan li jorn son long en may" [When days are long in May] (Goldin, no. 20; pp. 104–07).

In the canso, "Tant ai mo cor ple de joya" ["My heart is so full of joy"], the poet boasts that he is better off away from his beloved and even hopes that she will keep him at a distance:

> De s'amistat me reciza!
> Mas be n'ai fiansa,
> que sivals eu n'ai conquiza
> la bela semblansa. (25–28)
>
> [Let her make me keep my distance from her love—
> there's still one thing I'm sure of:
> I have conquered nothing less
> than her beautiful image.]
> (Goldin no. 22, lines 25–28, pp. 130–31)

At its most sublime the noble inspiration of an *amor lonh* leads to a genuine spiritual conversion. Such is the case with Dante, whose pining love and grief for Beatrice, described at length in *Vita Nuova*, are transformed in the *Divine Comedy* into a pure *caritas*, which is completely different from the poet's earlier self-centered obsession. In *Pearl* there is a strong expectation that a similar transformation will take place; indeed the dreamer experiences a marked change in his condition immediately after he falls asleep. However, the poem neither fulfills the promise of a conversion like Dante's, nor does it exalt the distant, solipsistic condition of the poet/lover as troubadour poetry often does.

In addition to the way in which the poet addresses his lady and describes his condition, there are other generic signals in the opening of *Pearl* that mark it as courtly love poetry.[17] One of these is the garden setting. Beginning in the waking world, where it is but a place for the *juelere*'s lyric complaints, the garden is transformed in the dream into the traditional garden of love: filled with shimmering sunlight, bird song, and sweet

[17]As I explain in the Introduction (note 3), I am using "courtly" as an adjective to modify "love poetry," not "courtly love" as a term in itself.

aromas of fruit, flowers, and herbs. The landscape is not one of purely natural beauty, however, for the linking word of section two, *addubbement*, emphasizes the artistry of the dream garden, which is a surrogate for the poem, a created setting for the poet's pearl. Like the *totum metrum* in Matthew of Vendôme's passage on adorning poetry, *Pearl*'s garden is beautified by gems: "crystal klyffez" (74), and a "glemande glorye" (70) that surpass nature:

> Þe sunne bemez bot blo and blynde
> In respecte of þat adubbement. (83–84)

The supernatural beauty of the garden suggests paradise to the dreamer, although it is quite clear that he is thinking of the earthly paradise, not the heavenly one.[18]

The garden setting of *Pearl* is then at once "supernatural," because it is more than nature, and at the same time wholly of this world. Just how far *Pearl*'s garden is from the transcendent heavenly landscape envisioned by apocalyptic seers becomes clear in the third section of the poem, when the dreamer first comes to the river that separates him from the pearl's setting. This river, as we have seen in Chapter Two, is an uncrossable boundary, but the dreamer longs to cross it nonetheless:

> More and more, and ȝet wel mare,
> Me lyste to se þe broke byȝonde,

[18]For a discussion of the medieval garden of love and its relationships both to the earthly paradise tradition (which developed from Genesis) and also to the classical tradition, see Giamatti (esp. 48–67). Giamatti's thorough and very informative study makes it clear that the two traditions had become so intermingled by the Middle Ages that it was often impossible to separate the threads. The dreamer and the reader have every reason to think of the earthly paradise in *Pearl*, but the contradictory suggestions in the dream landscape—of a garden of love, an earthly paradise, and a heavenly paradise—are not resolved. Compare Spearing's statement about the religious and secular love language in the poem: "The tradition . . . is so complex that its rich confusion may have been a strength rather than a weakness to a medieval poet" (121); see also Howes on gardens (esp. Chapter One).

For if hit watz fayr þer I con fare,
Wel loueloker watz þe fyrre londe. (145–48)

The dreamer's longing here is not the appropriate one for heaven and the world beyond, but rather the obsessive and self-centered desire of earthly love. Instead of transcending this world, the dreamer's desire is subject to the whims of fortune:

As Fortune fares þeras ho fraynez,
Wheþer solace ho sende oþer ellez sore,
Þe wyȝ to wham his wylle ho waynez
Hyttez to haue ay more and more. (129–32)

The dreamer places himself at the center of his landscape as subject. The recounting of his movement through the landscape in section three is filled with first-person references, such as: "I bowed" (126); "I folȝed" (127); and "I couþe telle" (134). All is dominated by the dreamer's excessive joy and his overwhelming desire, the "more and more" that forms the linking phrase of this section: "And euer me longed ay more and more" (144). Even the dreamer's joy is excessive:

Doun after a strem þat dryȝly halez
I bowed in blys, bredful my braynez;
Þe fyrre I folȝed þose floty valez,
Þe more strenghþe of joye myn herte straynez. (125–28)

As the poem *Patience* makes clear, this kind of excessive joy is fallen and mortal, and very different from that of the blessed who sing God's praises in heaven.

The praise of his lady, the artistic beauty of the garden setting, the dreamer's excessive joy that follows his overwhelming grief, above all his human and obsessive longing—all establish *Pearl* as a courtly love vision. And like the best and most sophisticated of medieval love visions, *Pearl* begins essentially as a love lyric. From the love lyric openings, love visions usually go one of two ways (more often a bit of both): they can become allegorical narratives that recount the course of desire and its failures and successes; and/or they can turn into discourses, often represented as a debate or a dialogue, on the nature of human love. Guillaume de Lorris, for example, although he includes much advice and commentary, essentially provides a well-developed narrative of the dreamer's quest for his rose: from the entry into the garden, through his falling in love, to the struggle with *Daungier*. Jeun de Meun's portion of the poem, on the other hand, is much more discursive, with the frame narrative often buried and lost track of in the discourse on love, nature, and an encyclopedia of topics.

Much shorter than the typical French love vision, *Pearl* is also more tightly and clearly structured. It moves fairly quickly from its love lyric opening into a debate between the dreamer and the Pearl Maiden, a debate that is fairly one-sided and really more a teaching dialogue. In this, the Pearl Maiden is like Philosophia in Boethius's *Consolation*, Vergil in *Inferno* and *Purgatorio*, and Beatrice in *Paradiso*: Pearl is the authority figure who guides the dreamer, mentally and emotionally, through the issues of mortal and divine values, as Philosophia does Boethius and Beatrice does Dante (although, of course, in Dante's case the spiritual movement is reflected in a physical one).[19]

It is this aspect, among others, that medieval dream vision shares with apocalypses; this is "the great discourse" generally

[19]Kean discusses the ways in which the Pearl Maiden functions as a guide and compares her to Boethius's Lady Philosophy and Dante's Beatrice, among others (114–31), but the focus of Kean's interest is whether or not the pearl is a "straightforward allegorical figure" (115), a question I find distracting and misplaced, although Kean does acknowledge the complication of having an authority figure who is partly a "personification of an idea," like Philosophy and Nature (115), but more a figure that is "part allegorical, part humanly individual," like Beatrice and Matilda in the *Divine Comedy* (120). Piehler makes the most sense on this issue. Using his term "*potentia animae*" (initially defined on pp. 19–20), Piehler says that "on the one hand the maiden partakes of the nature of the *potentia animae,* the mistress of dialogue, such as Boethius's Lady Philosophy" and "on the other hand, like Beatrice, she has specifically human dimensions" (156).

viewed as a feature of apocalyptic literature.[20] However, in *Pearl*, as in similar texts like the *Consolation* and *Purgatorio*, the discourse is not so much revelatory as it is polemic. Using a variation of dialectic, the Pearl Maiden works to change the dreamer from his selfish earthly views, so that he can gain true understanding. This process occupies the poem's central passages—from Section Three, when the Pearl Maiden first greets the dreamer, through to Section Seventeen, when the vision of the New Jerusalem begins.

The purpose of the central discourse in *Pearl* is then none other than conversion, the purpose of all preaching and of apocalyptic literature in particular. In apocalypses the visions of joy that are available to the saved, together with those of disaster and punishment that will be inflicted upon the damned, are meant to convert the readers. As noted earlier, apocalyptic texts, while part of a conversion pattern, do not generally contain a conversion *forme*. However, some medieval visionary literature does, notably Boethius and Dante. *Pearl* too, potentially at least, could contain a conversion *forme*, taking the dreamer through a development much like Jonah's in *Patience*. The dreamer could either end so converted to enlightenment that his voice would merge with the authority figure's, as Boethius's does, and/or he could physically arrive at a spatial and visual equivalent of enlightenment, as Dante does in *Paradiso*. Neither of these conclusions is realized in *Pearl*, however. Although in *Pearl* the dreamer does obtain a visual reward, the vision of the Lamb and his *meyny* in the New Jerusalem, he remains separated from that vision. Furthermore, right up through the end of his dialogue with the Pearl Maiden, he continues to speak as a mortal bound to earthly place, mortal time, and human desire. It is through his responses, first to the Pearl Maiden's teaching and later to the vision that follows, that we see how the dreamer falls short of a completed conversion and how therefore

[20]See Chapter One, esp. pp. 23–25, for this and other features of apocalyptic literature.

his story, the story of his quest within a dream, is not one of conversion.

The methods of conversion employed by the Pearl Maiden are primarily those of medieval exegetes and preachers. The issues the Pearl Maiden addresses are: the nature of salvation and divine justice; the differences between earthly time and space and heavenly time and space; and finally, the differences between mortal love and divine love. Beginning with a retelling of Matthew's Parable of the Vineyard, the Pearl Maiden goes on to quote freely from other passages in the Bible. Her teaching uses various rhetorical tools common in exegesis, including explication, illustration, and wordplay. Of these, her most dazzling technique is wordplay: punning with words, stretching their literal meanings, multiplying their metaphorical implications, making explicit the inherent paradoxes and contradictions, and sometimes indulging in that favorite medieval word game of false etymology.

Three words that *Pearl* puns on—*date*, *more* (along with its close relatives, *gret inoghe* and *neuer þe lasse)*, and *mote*—are especially important because they illustrate the nature of dimensions in heaven, so different from their counterparts on earth. *Date* is first of all "limit," especially in time. As the linking word of section nine, *date* emphasizes the limits of earthly time, thereby drawing attention to the eschaton. The working day in the vineyard, like human life on earth, like the created world itself, is finite—the day's end looms over all. The vineyard owner says to the workers:

> "Why stande ʒe ydel?" he sayde to þos;
> "Ne knawe ʒe of þis day no *date*?"
> (515–16; emphasis mine)

Later the owner brings more workers in as the end approaches:

> And nw men to hys vyne he broʒte
> Welneʒ wyl day watz passed *date*.
> (527–28; emphasis mine)

Date refers not just to limits in time but also to limits in happiness and reward. *Date* is the reward enjoyed by the Pearl Maiden, a reward that is too high a rank, according to the *juelere*, who cries: "Bot a quene!—hit is to dere a *date*" (492; emphasis mine). As a human term and concept, *date* is inappropriate for divine justice, for, as the Pearl Maiden tells the dreamer: "Þer is no *date* of Hys godnesse" (493; emphasis mine). The pun on *date* thus teaches the same lessons that the parable itself does: on the one hand, time is limited and the end is coming, so God's laborers must work hard to earn their reward; on the other hand, there is no limit to God's goodness, and his divine justice is not constrained by human values.

A similar point is made by the link words of the following sections: *more* and *gret innoȝe*. *More* is primarily a human term, one that signals human desire. The linking phrase of section three, *more and more*, describes the dreamer's delight in his love garden and his beloved and his very human longing to increase that pleasure. In section ten, which retells the Parable of the Vineyard, *more* refers to another kind of *cupiditas*, the ambition for material reward and particularly for more payment than one's fellows. The point of the parable, however, is that heavenly rewards do not work according to human desire and ambition. As the linking phrase of section eleven puts it: "For þe grace of God is gret inoghe" (610, 624, 636, 660). What is remarkable is that in this section, unlike any other, the linking phrase is an entire line, repeated exactly verbatim at the end of every stanza, except one, in which "wex" replaces "is"—a case of substituting "becoming" for "being." By this ploy the Pearl Maiden draws attention to the paradox of sufficiency in increasing abundance, since having repeated that grace is enough, she now insists (in the second-to-last stanza of the section) that the grace will *grow* to be enough. Furthermore, since this variation concludes the stanza that describes the saving actions of Christ's Passion, *Pearl* is able to have it both ways: God's mercy is always sufficient, but, with the historical events of Christ's life, it has become, in time, more sufficient (a contradiction in terms, of course).

Another bit of wordplay involves the same paradox of sufficiency in abundance. The closing line of section ten reads: "And euer þe lenger the lasse þe more" (600). Translated, this line does not make a lot of sense; some possibilities are: "However much less so much the more" (Andrew and Waldron); "And increasingly, the less [they do], the more [they receive]" (Vantuono); or, better than either I think: "And the greater the lessening, still the more [there is]" (mine). While Vantuono translates the line so that it specifically refers to the laborers' work (and it does indeed complete the preceding line ["Þenne the lasse in werke to take more able"]), such a reading ignores the fact that the specific line's ellipsis of all references to agents or actions allows it to become more abstract and to refer simultaneously to the literal story of a vineyard and also to the figurative story of salvation. What is striking, moreover, is that now the human word and concept, *more*, is used for divine reward. Through wordplay and paradox, *more* has been transformed from *cupiditas* to *caritas*, from human desire to divine love and mercy. This transformation is rendered in verse, since the next stanza, the first one in section eleven, begins: " 'Of more and lasse in Godez ryche,' / Þat gentyl sayde, 'lys no joparde' " (601–02)"; and then ends "For þe grace of God is gret inoghe" (612). God's kingdom is both *more* and *lasse*—it is sufficient.

A similar transformation of a word from human to divine occurs with *mote*. While *date* and *more* are primarily concerned with the limits of time and reward, the puns on *mote* draw attention to the physical dimensions of space. The dreamer first uses *mote* to mean "castle," the earthly, physical place he expects to find within his dream garden:

> Byȝonde þe broke, by slente oþer slade,
> I hoped þat *mote* merked wore. (141–42; emphasis mine)

Later, the poet uses *mote* as the link word in section sixteen. Here, as Andrew and Waldron point out, the punning is on what are actually two different words: *mote* as "blemish," and *mote* as "city" (97–98, note to lines 913–72).[21] The *juelere* asserts that the pearl's "wonez schulde be wythouten *mote*" (924; emphasis mine), meaning not that her home should be without walls, but rather without blemish; but, of course, the pearl's home is without either. The Pearl Maiden's retort, "So is Hys *mote* withouten *moote*" (948; emphasis mine), intentionally speaks to both meanings of *mote*, as had the dreamer, albeit unwittingly. Having thus asserted that the New Jerusalem is not limited to one place, as is its earthly counterpart, the Pearl Maiden tells the dreamer that it *is* a place—it is "Hys mote." Like the reward of God's kingdom, which is both "more" in a transformed sense and not at all "more" in its earthly sense, the place of God's kingdom is, and is not, a *mote*.

While the wordplay of the Pearl Maiden's lesson demonstrates both the earthliness of human signs and the transcendence of divine truth, the objects and spaces visualized within the dream stress the radical difference between earthly and heavenly spaces and bodies. The earthly paradise on the dreamer's side of the river is contrasted with the heavenly one on the Pearl Maiden's side, which in turn corresponds to the differences between the old Jerusalem and the new and between the pearl that the dreamer lost and the pearl who is saved. Thus, unlike *Pearl*'s vocabulary lessons, which suggest the ontological transformation of human things to divine reality, a transformation which the Pearl Maiden has undergone, the physical and spatial features of the poem make explicit the essential separation between the earthly and the heavenly, a separation that the dreamer must experience as well as see. Epitomized in the river, which so dominates the illustrations to *Pearl* in the manuscript,[22] the barrier to conversion is never removed for the dreamer. [Figure 10] If the barrier were surmounted, we would have: a

[21]Note that we have the same pun available in "spot."

[22]For the dominance of the river in the illustrations of *Pearl*, see folios 41, 41b, 42, 42b of Cotton Nero A.x. (one of which I include in Figure 10), reproduced in the facsimile edition of Gollancz and also in Vantuono's edition. In "Limit," Hanning discusses *Pearl*'s river as a boundary.

poem that is an apocalyptic vision, a dreamer who is a visionary blessed with the beatific vision, and a *juelere* who, instead of making earthly settings for his pearl, joins with her in the *nwe songe* of the 144,000 praising their *Juele*, the Lamb. In each of these respects, the poem puts before us the heavenly counterpart, while at the same time stressing its own earthliness.

The dreamer, for example, asks for and is granted a sight of the New Jerusalem, which is sent from the Lamb, through the Pearl Maiden:

> "Motelez may so meke and mylde,"
> Þen sayde I to þat lufly flor,
> "Bryng me to þat bygly bylde
> And let me se þy blysful bor."
> Þat schene sayde: "Þat God wyl schylde;
> Þou may not enter withinne Hys tor;
> Bot of þe Lombe I haue þe aquylde
> For a syȝt þerof þurȝ gret fauor. (961–68)

The important qualification to this vision is that the dreamer may only see, but he may not enter, the New Jerusalem. The limits and prohibitions of this gift of *syȝt* frame and dominate the Pearl Maiden's speech, so that the opportunity is almost buried in the middle of an adversative clause. Her immediate answer to the dreamer's plea is essentially "no." Furthermore, the dreamer's inadequacy is obvious in the very way he asks to come to the Pearl Maiden's side of the river—not as a Christian praying for the beatific vision, or for salvation, or for entry into the New Jerusalem, but as a lover seeking a welcome into his beloved's bower.

The *juelere*'s *luf-longyng* is still strongly human, even at this turning point, as he is about to receive the climactic vision of his dream. Human desire continues to overwhelm him and two sections later is directly contrasted with the joy of the 144,000. Using the linking phrase "*gret delyt*," this penultimate section of the poem provides the climax (and nadir) of the dream. The section's first three stanzas are a brilliant rendering of the *nwe songe*, which follows upon, respectively, the visions of the New Jerusalem in section seventeen and of the Lamb and Throne in section eighteen. The *gret delyt* in section nineteen is precisely the delight of the Lamb's followers, a delight past human recounting:

> So droȝ þay forth with *gret delyt*.
>
> *Delyt* þat Hys come encroched
> To much hit were of for to melle.
> (1116–18; emphasis mine)

The would-be climax of the dream, when the *juelere* almost joins in the *nwe songe*, comes at the end of the third stanza of this section:

> To loue þe Lombe His meyny inmelle
> Iwysse I laȝt a *gret delyt*. (1127–28; emphasis mine)

But it is not to be. This dreamer is still earthbound. For one thing, he is undone by his lack of comprehension. When, in the next stanza, he sees and describes the Lamb, he speaks of the wounds not as the saving instruments of the divine comedy, but as a terrible tragedy:

> Bot a wounde ful wyde and weete con wyse
> Anende Hys hert, þurȝ hyde torente.
> Of Hys quyte syde His blod outsprent.
> Alas, þoȝt I, who did þat spyt?
> Ani breste for bale aȝt haf forbrent
> Er he þerto hade had *delyt*. (1135–40; emphasis mine)

The narrator explicitly contrasts *delyt* with the grief inspired by the Lamb's wound, when in fact the *gret delyt* of the saved is ultimately brought about by that wound. The *juelere* is not one of the blessed singing the *nwe songe*, but rather a mortal poet, complaining of the Lamb's blood as a mourner would grieve for a wounded beloved. The dreamer can see that this wound does not cause pain nor lessen the Lamb's *delyt*, since always are "His glentez gloryous glade" (1144), yet the dreamer delights not in the Lamb's wounds nor for long even in the Lamb.

As soon as the dreamer catches sight of the Pearl Maiden, he reverts completely to the possessive and obsessive desire of a human lover:

> Þen saȝ *I* þer *my* lyttel quene
> Þat *I* wende had standen by *me* in sclade.
> Lorde, much of mirþe watz þat ho made
> Among her ferez þat watz so quyt!
> Þat syȝt *me* gart to þenk to wade
> For *luf-longyng* in gret delyt. (1147–52; emphasis mine)[23]

This human desire, which drives the *juelere* to cross the stream, is the madness of human passion and is characterized by selfish, human willfulness:

> Delyt me drof in yȝe and ere,
> *My manez mynde* to maddyng malte;
> Quen *I* seȝ *my* frely, *I wolde* be þere,
> Byȝonde þe water þaȝ ho were walte.
> (1153–56; emphasis mine)

The willfulness of the *juelere*'s passion is contrasted to the will of God: "Hit watz not at my Pryncez paye" (1163).

Once returned to his wakening state, the dreamer can recognize his error, but that recognition is couched in remorse and excessive sorrow:

> I raxled, and fel in gret affray,
> And, sykyng, to myself I sayd:
> "Now al be to þat Pryncez paye." (1174–76)

[23]Aers notes that the "possessive pronoun and the adjectival dinimutive in 'my lyttel quene' are, "in the contexts established by the poem, . . . expressions of [the dreamer's] will to control her form of life" (67).

As many critics have pointed out, there is resignation in this sorrow and some new awareness, but these are primarily a resignation and an awareness that are based on the differences between God's kingdom and this world. This new consciousness lacks the certitude and the immediacy of a full conversion. The dreamer in one line can refer to his experience as "þys veray avysyoun" (1184), and in the next wonder "*if* hit be ueray and soth sermoun" (1185; emphasis mine) that his pearl is in heaven. The dreamer remains in "þys doel-doungoun" (1187), while the Pearl Maiden enjoys the bliss of heaven.

The doubts about his dream seem to extend to the entire experience. Presumably, the dreamer does not question the "truth" of the vision of the New Jerusalem and the 144,000, but this is not really his vision—it is the Apostle John's. As the narrator reminds us repeatedly, he is reporting not his vision, but John's, not in his words, but in John's. In the first section devoted to the dreamer's vision of the New Jerusalem, section seventeen, the linking phrase is "þe apostel John" (984 and *passim*). The dreamer describes the city "as deuysez hit þe apostel John" (984); he sees it "as John þe apostel hit syȝ with syȝt" (985); he names the jewels "as John þise stonez in writ con nemme" (997); he recognizes the *rybé* because John "con hit wale" (1007); in short, the dreamer knows it all "by his deuysement / In þe Apocalyppez, þe apostel John" (1019–20).[24] The *juelere* then is both the love poet, who like all courtly lyric poets makes poems that are settings for his beloved and his desire, and at the same time the poet who, as the author of *Cleanness* and *Patience*, accords to the divine words of the Bible a primacy over all human literary creations.

The *juelere*'s setting is a wondrous artifact. *Pearl* is dazzling in its artistry; moreover, its intricate versification and its brilliant wordplay are not just brilliant in themselves, but work together in the metafictions of the poem and the poet. The rhyme

[24]As I explain in Chapter One, despite editors' careful glossing of the names for these stones, I think the poet was less interested in the identity of each stone than in transliterating John's text (see p. 48, and note 18).

scheme—twelve lines, divided into three quatrains, two rhyming *abab* and a third rhyming *bcbc*, with therefore only three rhymes per stanza—is demanding enough, but then are added the limitations of the concatenation, so that the "c" rhyme often includes the linking word and therefore must be constant throughout a given section. On top of all this is alliteration, although in this poem less than in the usual alliterative line (of this poet's and of others'), since many lines alliterate only two of the four stresses, some none (for example: 966, 834, 764).

Finally, *Pearl* is constructed around an elaborate number scheme: 101 stanzas; twenty sections of five stanzas each (with one exception, of which more later);[25] and twelve-line stanzas in a poem of 1212 lines. Several critics have written extensively on the number symbolism, others on the patterns in the stanza groupings, and, while a few of their suggestions may be somewhat strained, most of the patterns and meanings found are probably legitimate.[26] At the very least, there is a balancing of an opening section, set in the waking world, with the closing section that returns to this world. Equally certain is the significance of the number twelve in Judeo-Christian tradition and in John's Apocalypse in particular: twelve is the number of Israel's sons and twelve the number of her tribes, twelve the gates to the New Jerusalem, and twelve times twelve thousand the number of followers of the Lamb. In short, twelve is the number for fullness, plenitude, and completion in God's kingdom. All in all there is probably no early poem in English that is so complex in its craft as is *Pearl*, and all this craft works around a "heavy" message, itself conveyed in language games that rival the num-

[25]I am assuming, with most editors, that a line has been lost in the last stanza of section eight (what would be line 472), although this may be an intentional imperfection, like the "otiose" stanza of section fifteen. See Vantuono (247) and Andrew and Waldron (76). Cary Nelson, for one, thinks the missing line is an intentional move on the poet's part, in order to make the poem in "the form of a pearl deliberately flawed" (33).

[26]Of the several discussions of the poem's numerical discussion, among the best are Hieatt's ("Numerical Structure") and Bishop's (28–29); see also Chapman.

ber games of the versification. *Pearl* is truly "a jewel of a poem"—a bejewelled work of art, a garland and a crown, the artful setting for the *juelere*'s pearl.

However, *Pearl* is not a perfect poem. It has one striking flaw in its versification: an extra stanza in section fifteen (and possibly another flaw if the poet, not a scribe, omitted line 472). For some time, editors assumed a mistake had been made in the manuscript transmission of section fifteen, although a scribal error that adds an entire stanza begins to look like a poet's error (the first poet or another). Furthermore, no stanza in the section stands out as obviously unfit; a few editors single out the second stanza (853–64), Gordon the last (901–12), but increasingly there has been a tendency not to find a spurious stanza (indeed from the first Gollancz at least was reluctant to do so).[27] As has been pointed out, not only does the "extra" stanza yield the significant 1212 number of lines (though without the stanza, we would get a still significant number of 1200), but the total number of stanzas, 101, is the same as that in *Sir Gawain and the Green Knight*. What is most compelling, though acknowledged by far fewer critics, is that 101 is an imperfect number. One hundred, the number of cantos in Dante's *Divine Comedy*, is perfect, but adding to perfection is to make it imperfect, to give the circle a bump as it were.[28] The extra stanza in *Pearl* is just one more sign of the poem's humanness. As a setting, the poem is more than perfect, unlike the divine setting, the Kingdom of God, which is simply and purely perfection, which is *gret enoȝ*.

Pearl then does not achieve perfection, the *juelere* does not arrive at the New Jerusalem, and the poem does not effect a conversion. There is some progress, however, though of a very limited kind. This progress does not involve converting a lyric poem to an apocalyptic vision or converting a poet/lover to a

[27]See Andrew and Waldron (94) and also Vantuono (271) for a summary of the editorial positions on the question of the extra stanza.

[28]Nelson has probably the best discussion of the poem as an imperfect circle, but he is focusing on the missing line at 472 (33; see note 24 above) and does not mention the imperfection of a more-than-complete circle as well as a less-than-complete one.

seer, but rather moving from the dream world and time to the similar, but holier, world and time of sacrament, a complete shift in mode:

> And syþen to God I hit bytaȝte,
> In Krystez dere blessyng and myn,
> Þat in þe forme of bred and wyn
> Þe preste vus schewez vch a daye.
> He gef vus to be His homly hyne
> Ande precious perlez vnto His pay.
> Amen. Amen. (1207–12)

Although not John the Apostle, or any other visionary, the dreamer is now quite clearly no longer the *juelere*. He identifies himself simply as a Christian, one who, although not yet singing the *nwe songe*, looks to do so someday. He has released his possessive desire, as he bids farewell to his pearl. He no longer speaks of making a setting for the pearl or of singling her out in an individual way, as in the opening stanza and again as late as the final part of the vision. In the final stanza the Pearl Maiden has merged into a community, a whole group of "precious perlez," who are Christ's "homly hyne," a group that the dreamer prays to be allowed to join.

As the dreamer and his pearl have changed to *perlez*, the mode of the poem has changed from a record of a loss and of a dream to a prayer for future happiness, a prayer that is signalled with the words, "He gef" ("May he give").[29] Both the prayer that concludes the poem and the eucharist invoked in the final

[29]*Gef* in 1211 can either be a present subjunctive or a preterite, most editors taking it for the preterite. I believe that since the narrator has moved into prayer (especially with the line saying he has committed his pearl to Christ), *"He gef"* is a subjunctive and should be translated "may He grant" (the alternative suggested by Andrew and Waldron [110, note to 1211f]). Of course, given this poet's habits, it is possible that the verb is both past indicative, referring to the saving events of Christ's life and death, and also present subjunctive, looking to the future restoration while acknowledging the present possibility within the sacraments.

stanza belong to sacramental time and space. Like apocalyptic vision and much love lyric, the sacramental mode does not take place in earthly space, and it does not occur in earthly time. But sacramental time and space, if less immediate than the visions enjoyed by saints like the Apostle John, or by poets like Dante, is also more "real" and certainly fairer than the beauty and joy of love vision or love lyric. *Pearl*'s final word on apocalyptic vision is to turn to prayer and sacrament, the fairest *forme* available in this world, the one that in the *forme* of bread and wine reveals the divine to Christians every day.

Sir Gawain and the Green Knight— "An Aunter in Erde"

As in *Pearl*, the poet tells us early in *Sir Gawain and the Green Knight* what kind of poem we are reading: it is an "aunter in erde" (27); "a selly in siȝt" (28); "an outtrage awenture of Arthurez wonderez" (29); and finally, simply a "laye" (30); that is, it is a "happening"—both an event and its story; a story that is wondrous and almost unbelievable (wondrous in a mortal sense, not in a divinely miraculous one, since it takes place "in erde"); and a lay, a simple story told or sung, probably to a courtly audience, as opposed to an event recorded in writing. Such a narrative is thus a far cry from the divinely guided stories of Abraham or Noah or Jonah, and its form and source are very different from the biblical record that provides the dreamer with the very words, as well as the *formez*, with which to describe his vision in *Pearl*.

Much more has been written on medieval romance than on dream vision and even more on *Gawain* than on *Pearl*. However, few of the critics writing about *Gawain*'s genre consider it in its own terms—as an *aunter* or *laye*—even fewer in the context of history or sacred history; while virtually none of them (even those writing about all four poems) analyze the poem's narrative form in light of the other two narratives of the manuscript, *Patience* and *Cleanness*. But if *Gawain* invites comparison with other romances, surely it does so in terms of its own labels and also with its own manuscript context in mind, and reading *Gawain* in terms of the other poems in Cotton Nero A.x. involves considering its relationship to sacred history—if we are asked not by the poet to do this, we are at least by the scribe or compiler or whoever put all four poems together.

It is clear by its own labels that *Sir Gawain and the Green Knight* is unlike the narrative poems that precede it in the manuscript, neither of which uses any of these terms for its respective *forme*. Even without the labels, however, two aspects of the narrative in *Gawain* distinguish it. First, because the story is not part of recorded sacred history, its place in the providential scheme is unclear. Moreover, the divine plotter who controls the narrative *forme* in *Patience* and *Cleanness* is absent in *Gawain* and has left no obvious surrogate. Second, *Gawain* fits neither of the *formez* used in the other two poems: it is neither a judgment narrative, like those in *Cleanness*, nor a conversion narrative, like the story of Jonah in *Patience*. Nonetheless, the narrative in *Gawain* seems at times to be tantalizingly like one or the other of these important *formez* of sacred history. On the one hand, much of the patterning of the story of *Gawain* suggests a judgment narrative, especially in the way the two contests are set up—each looking to a conclusion, an end that will provide judgment, either as reward, as in the Exchange-of-Winnings game, or as apocalyptic punishment, as in the Beheading game. At the same time, the allusions to penance and guilt, especially in the last fitt of *Gawain*, would seem to indicate a conversion story. The openendedness of the story, the sense that the various judgments given are not final, is a further sign that we have in *Sir Gawain and the Green Knight* the kind of narrative found in *Patience*.

The very secular nature of *Gawain* and other Arthurian romances might seem to preclude viewing them as sacred history. In fact, however, Arthurian verse narratives, while they may be *layes* (if that means short narrative poems) or *aventures* (presumably the stories of knightly adventures), are often judgment or conversion narratives as well. Certain Arthurian texts, notably the *Alliterative Morte Arthure*, and to a large extent even Geoffrey of Monmouth's *Historia*, are strongly judgmental in their tone and narrative structure.[30] Other Arthurian romances follow what looks like a conversion *forme*, tracing the adventures and development of a protagonist, who in the end wins honor, love, and, according to Hanning, fulfillment.[31]

One way of viewing the two kinds of narrative—judgment and conversion—as they appear in Arthurian romance is in terms of their respective subjects. A judgment pattern aims at the conversion of the reader/audience. As in most apocalypses, the conversion is outside the frame of the narrative, and ultimately so is the subject, since the reader is the one who is supposed to be converted. The *Alliterative Morte Arthure*, for example, ends with the battle and the brief denouement of Arthur's translation to Avalon and burial. Here the conversion of the society lies outside the time frame—it belongs to the "futurus" king and his people; likewise, the subject of the conversion falls outside the narrative frame, with the (presumably British) audience. Other Arthurian romances, Chrétien's, for example, or the *Stanzaic Morte Arthure*, focus on a subject within the romance, on the protagonist, the knight of Arthur's court whose words and deeds are the focus of the narrative. By including the story of Lancelot's end at the conclusion of the poem, the *Stanzaic* places the converted subject within the narrative frame—Lancelot's beatification follows the apocalyptic judgment of the fatal battle on Salisbury Plain.

The differences among Arthurian narratives, between a

[30]British histories in general are strongly judgmental, none more so probably than Gildas. For the best discussion of these texts, see Hanning, *A Vision of History in Early Britain*.

[31]Although Hanning has somewhat revised this view since the publication of *The Individual in Twelfth-Century Romance*, and while I have certainly grossly oversimplified a fascinating study in this brief allusion, I still think it valid to see the internal growth of the hero as producing a different narrative *forme* from the public story of a society that failed. While Hanning primarily discusses the romance in terms of the hero and his development, I hope the position I am taking here, in terms of the narrative *forme*, is not inconsistent with his analysis.

judgment narrative and a conversion narrative, correspond to the differences between chanson de geste and history, on the one hand, and romance and saints' lives, on the other. All of these differences are exploited in *Sir Gawain and the Green Knight*, a poem which, more than any of the other three in the *Pearl* manuscript, is about itself—its genre, its making, and its reading. For, in *Sir Gawain and the Green Knight*, the poet implicitly makes Arthurian romance and its disparate *formez* the subject of the poem. As Hanning has argued in "Red Herring," this poem is about reading and interpretation, and, I would add, it is also about the making of romance, a making not so much the self-conscious creation of an individual poet, as it would be in lyric and dream vision (the making that is the subject of *Pearl*), but rather a making that is (at least fictionally) the product of a tradition and a culture.

The *aunter* that the narrator proposes to tell is an "outtrage awenture of Arthurez wonderez" (29), not apparently a story about Gawain, but an account of something wondrous and unbelievable that happened in King Arthur's court. For all that Gawain is the protagonist of this poem, he is not finally the poem's subject. Unlike Chrétien's Yvain and Lancelot, the figure of Gawain is not central to the plotting of this romance. Gawain is but the self-chosen representative of the court, which is the stated object of the Green Knight's challenge and Morgan's revenge. It may be that, as Sheila Fisher argues, Morgan and Guinevere are actually the real players, who, however, have been displaced by the Green Knight and Gawain, but, in any event, Gawain in turn is displaced by King Arthur and his court. For, as Gawain steps forward in the beginning to represent the court, so too in the end the court takes back, in the *forme* of Gawain's prize girdle, the story of failure and success, sin and penance, that was Gawain's, thereby making the poem's story about Britain and its people in Arthur's time.

Added to the larger Arthurian setting for Gawain's adventures is the similar courtly setting evoked by the fictional poet, who proposes to tell his audience a *laye* he "in toun herde" (30). With this introduction the poet not only creates the sense of immediacy and a present audience that are a part of fictional orality;[32] he also has his audience share in the making of the poem and in the interpretation of it. In this respect, the poem comes close to the immediacy and involvement and openendedness of the prophetic books of the Bible, which are marked by direct and apparently oral addresses to the audience.

The history of Britain evoked in *Sir Gawain and the Green Knight*'s first and last stanzas stands in contrast to the romance setting of the second stanza.[33] Whereas the latter is oral and in romance time, the former is public and written, a narrative to which "þe Brutus bokez þerof beres wyttenesse" (2523). The chronological frame, like the genealogies in chansons de geste and in histories (including Israel's history in Genesis), not only establishes the story of *Gawain* as a public one, belonging to written history; it also creates an expectation of linear historical development. From "Ennias þe athel and his highe kynde" (5) to "riche Romulus" (8), and finally to "Felix Brutus" (13), the kings of Britain have descended, one following another in linear sequentiality. Although this chronological linearity is suspended or aborted in the poem's second stanza, with the switch to romance time and place, the public, historical, and patrilinear mood of the opening stanza returns in the poem's conclusion. Thus, there is a strong sense, in the poem's frame at least, of a linear, historical movement to the "present" time, the time, that is, of the poem's making and reciting.

The sense that the poem moves toward an ending is made

[32]I think we have to call it "fictional" because in fact we only know this poem as a written text in a manuscript. Nonetheless, the sense of orality is an important, if only occasional, feature of the poem. For two of the best discussions of this sense of orality, see William Nelson's historical survey and Burrow on the addresses to the audience in the Pearl poet's work, "features of style which belong to the newer, baser art of the 'geestour' "(*Ricardian Poetry* 25).

[33]Cf. Burrow, who distinguishes between the "sense of historical time" of the prologue and the epilogue and the lack of a sense of a past in the rest of the poem (*Gawain* 174), a lack Burrow attributes not so much to romance as to the poet's interest in "cyclic time or the time of nature" (175). See also Bercovitch on *Gawain*'s elements of "romance and anti-romance."

even stronger by the two main actions of the poem: the Beheading Game and the Exchange-of-Winnings Game. Both games are outstanding plot structures for a judgment narrative, since they are linear and closed: their beginnings are clearly marked, as are their ends, and their promised ends are suitably apocalyptic—in the one a fatal beheading with an axe, in the other an earned reward. As the Beheading Game evokes the catastrophic disasters of the Last Days, so the Exchange-of-Winnings Game could be seen as a playful romance version of the rewards and punishments that will be meted out by Christ the Judge on the day of judgment. Of course, the playfulness undercuts much of the apocalyptic sense and reduces both of these plots to what they are, or claim to be—exciting games in a story-telling and feast-making setting. Indeed, the Green Knight labels the Beheading Game a "Crystemas gomen" (282) when he first introduces it. And, although the Beheading Game may not be too much fun for Gawain, it is treated playfully by the court and King Arthur, as well as by the narrator, who promises us the *outtrage awenture*.[34] Oddly enough, the Exchange-of-Winnings Game is never precisely called a *gomen*, even though it would appear to be more fun and better suited to the holiday spirit than the literally deadly serious Beheading Game. In keeping with the slippery language that characterizes this poem, the Exchange-of-Winnings Game is treated to formal, legal, commercial language, all of which undercut the festive gaiety that one would expect from hunting, flirting, and gift-giving.[35]

It is not just the language of the games that is misleading, but

[34]See Stevens for an excellent discussion of the "Laughter and Game" in this poem. At the time this article first appeared, it served as an important and necessary corrective to the over-moralizing readings that were then so prevalent. (Our currect moralization takes a different form, focusing on the society's ills instead of the hero's immortal soul—a good dose of humor and irony and a reminder of how much they figure in the poem is needed again, I think.)

[35]Shoaf's book-length study of the commercial vocabulary in *Sir Gawain and the Green Knight: The Poem as Green Girdle*, is valuable and thought-provoking, although finally perhaps a bit strained and heavyhanded.

also their narrative *formez*, which turn out to be neither as linear nor as closed as first expected. In part, this is owing to the change or delay in the promised ends, in part to the various non-linear patterns introduced by the Exchange-of-Winnings Game, and in part to the time settings of the events in the poem. The Exchange-of-Winnings Game, with its repetitive and parallel structures, is especially effective in at once suggesting progressive linearity and simultaneously undercutting those suggestions. The pattern of three days of hunting and *luf-talkyng*, three separate narratives within a larger story, bears many resemblances to the three major narratives recounted in *Cleanness*. In both cases, a pattern or small narrative *forme* is established: in *Cleanness* an apocalyptic warning that looks to a punishing catastrophe, in *Sir Gawain and the Green Knight* a *forward* made that promises a reward and a gift. However, the respective contexts for these smaller *formez* in the two poems differ. In *Cleanness*, the three repeated *formez* combine to make a linear progression, or more precisely a regression, both in God's relationship to humanity and also in the scope of divine action. In *Gawain*, on the other hand, while the three separate days are brought together in a narrative frame, the pattern of this larger *forme* is not at all clear, but rather subject to contradictory interpretations, both within and without the poem. Furthermore, since each day includes not one series of events, but two, Bertilak's hunting and Gawain's *luf-talkyng*, within each of the smaller *formez* we have two parallel stories. Though these two narrative units look to the evening's exchange, one end that will join them and make of them one story, the joining is weak and tenuous at best. What in fact the rules of the Exchange-of-Winnings Game demand is that one narrative unit, Bertilak's deer-hunting for example, switch ends (the *prys* of venison for a kiss) with a separate narrative unit, Gawain's flirtations with the Lady.

There are thus several patterns, or structural *formez*, at work in the third fitt of *Sir Gawain and the Green Knight*: the linear pattern from daybreak to dusk, the cyclical pattern from day to day, the parallel pattern of the two activities, and finally the cross pattern of one episode with the other (because they trade endings and because they are alternated and intermingled in the narration). Since most of these patterns have been examined (some quite exhaustively) by various critics,[36] I would like simply to focus on the way the multitude of smaller *formez* combine to make the extraordinarily complex *forme* the poet has constructed for the central action in *Gawain*.

The hunt is one of the most linear of human activities, both temporally and spatially. Bertilak begins his hunting day early in the morning: "Bi þat þe coke hade crowen and cakled bot þryse, / Þe lorde watz lopen of his bedde" (1412–13). Bertilak rides out from his castle, chases the game through the countryside, kills the prey, and ends the day with a prize of meat or hide. The hunt begins in one place at daybreak and ends in another at day's end. However, the spatial linearity is somewhat undercut by the return to the castle, while the temporal linearity is even more tenuous, since each day's end both concludes one hunt and looks to the beginning of the next:

> And efte in her bourdyng þay bayþen in þe morn
> To fylle þe same forwardez þat þay byfore maden:
> Wat chaunce so bytydez hor cheuysaunce to chaunge,
> What nwez so þay nome, at naȝt quen þay metten.
> (1404–07)

As is true with the succession of apocalyptic stories in *Cleanness*, the pattern of repetition in the third fitt of *Sir Gawain and the Green Knight* imposes circularity on the smaller linear *formez*. However, while in *Cleanness* a development from one narrative to the next can be discerned, in *Gawain* such a development is harder to discover. Certainly, there is no progress from one of Bertilak's hunts to the next. The first hunt is for deer, but it is not what the hunting manuals consider the noblest game, the

[36]One of the best discussions is still Howard's "Structure and Symmetry in *Sir Gawain and the Green Knight*." Howard concludes: "The poem's elaborate parallelism, with its multiple contrasts, helps produce the gamelike, ironic tone of *Sir Gawain*" (173).

chase of the red stag on horseback ("to slee the hart with strengthe" or "prendre le cerf a force").[37] Instead, Bertilak is hunting female deer (it is "fermysoun tyme" for all male deer—1156) and doing it in a mass round-up, by driving a herd of deer into an ambush of arrows, rather than pursuing one hart with hounds till it comes to bay and is dispatched by the master huntsman.

The second day's hunt is certainly more exciting than the first, and it constitutes what would have been considered a nobler sport than the deer ambush. Although for a boar (not the best *prys*, but still first among the *bestes noires* in the French hunting manual, *Les Livres du Roy Modus et de la Royne Ratio*), Bertilak's hunt the second day is conducted on horseback with hounds, which climaxes with an exciting confrontation between hunted and hunting. While the second day's chase is thus an improvement over the first day's, at least in excitement and demonstration of skill, there is no doubt that the *prys* has lessened, in both number (from "such a sowme" [1321] of deer to one boar) and quality (a barely digestible wild pig instead of tasty, fat venison).

The third day's hunt includes an exciting, but hardly ennobling, chase and a distinctly inferior *prys*.[38] However, whereas according to the hunting manuals foxes were usually hunted by

[37]The hart, the male of the large red deer, was, according to all the French hunting manuals and the later English ones, the noblest *prys*, and the noblest hunt was to chase the hart on horseback. No weapons were used, except the dogs, until the very end, when a hunter drew forth his sword and used it to kill the hart (an action euphemistically termed "*servir le cerf*" in French). On the medieval hunt, see Thiébaux ("Mediaeval Hunt" and *Stag of Love*) and, for a fuller discussion of Bertilak's hunts, Prior ("Poet of the Word," 257–60 and "*Gomens* and *Hert-Huntyng*").

[38]The hunting manuals make clear the lowliness of the fox as a *prys*, mostly by their lack of interest in hunting it; see Savage's discussion of this (33–35), in a study that is otherwise marred by its overly allegorial reading, as well as by its reliance upon a sixteenth-century hunting manual as a source. The Morgan manuscript of the fourteenth-century hunting treatise *Les Livres du Roy Modus and de la Royne Ratio* has an amusing illustration of the fox being hunted by men with staves (clearly not noblemen) and dogs (MS.M820 fol. 29v).

men on foot with dogs and staves (the latter for poking into the dens), Bertilak pursues his fox on horseback (in a remarkable anticipation of foxhunting in post-Renaissance England) and thereby elevates this day's sport somewhat. At least in excitement and in climactic suspense, Bertilak's fox hunt is superior to his deer slaughter on the first day. Nonetheless, because of the fox's proverbial deceit and its role as vermin, it is not a worthy opponent nor a test of the hunter's bravery. Moreover, its flesh is inedible, and its unpleasant smell lessens its value as a *prys*—as Edward of York remarks in his hunting manual: "Þe foxes skynnes been wonder hoote for to make cuffes or furres and ȝit þie stynke evere more but if thei be wel tawed. . . ."[39]

There is thus no clear overall pattern in the three days of hunting, no obvious progression or regression from one day to the next, either in the *prys* or in the chase itself. Indeed, within the text itself, there are only implicit suggestions that we compare one day to the next, when on the eve of the second day, Bertilak says to Gawain: "Ȝe ben ryche in a whyle, / Such chaffer and ȝe drowe" (1646–47); and later, "For I haf fraysted þe twys and faythful I fynde þe. / Now 'þrid tyme, þrowe best' þenk on þe morne" (1679–80).

What the text and the terms of Bertilak's game explicitly invite us to compare are the respective winnings earned on each day: Bertilak's hunting *prys* to the gains from Gawain's lovemaking. In this, as in the narration of each day's activities, the pattern is unmistakably parallel, not linear. Of course, there is something odd about this comparison insisted on by Bertilak and the text. Bertilak's winnings will be the *prys* of his hunting, or, as he puts it: "Quatsoeuer I wynne in þe wod hit worþez to yourez" (1106). What Gawain's winnings will be is much vaguer—some chance gain of fortune, as Bertilak says to Gawain: "And quat chek so ȝe acheue chaunge me þerforne" (1107). Typically, Gawain does not seem concerned about this

[39]Edward of York's *Master of Game* is a generation or so later than the most likely date for *Gawain*, but, as I note above, the earlier treatise, *Les Livres du Roy Modus*, also clearly shows the lowliness of foxhunting.

discrepancy and readily agrees to give over his future, not-to-be-guessed-at, winnings. But those turn out to be the sexual favors of the Lady, and how does one turn over kisses, which are not a commodity, but a service?[40] Being kissed by Gawain is surely not the same as being kissed by Bertilak's Lady. In one respect, the illogic and improbability are all part of the fun and merriment—they make for an *outtrage awenture*—but the serious flaw in the game is nonetheless there and creates an unbalanced effect.

The most explicit comparison of the winnings is made on the last day. According to Bertilak, he and Gawain are exchanging remarkably unequal gifts, for, after receiving three kisses, Bertilak speaks of his own catch with scorn and even anger:

> "Mary," quoþ þat oþer mon, "myn is bihynde,
> For I haf hunted al þis day and noȝt haf I geten
> Bot þis foule fox felle—þe Fende haf þe godez!—
> And þat is ful pore for to pay for suche prys þinges
> As ȝe haf þryȝt me here þro, such þre cosses
> So gode."
>
> (1942–47)

Bertilak's speech here goes well beyond a judicious comparison of the respective winnings, for the scorn of his foxskin *prys* and the syntactical interruption consigning it to the devil have nothing of gaiety or playfulness in them—we seem far from the spirit of Christmas *gomen* and fairy-tale adventures, even from the playful horror of war games. Gawain indeed has to break into Bertilak's diatribe, so that they can proceed to an account of the hunt itself. The exchange would, of course, be still more uneven if Gawain were keeping the rules, for then he would be offering

[40]Furthermore, Andrew and Waldron point out that, as Gawain may realize, the Lady's kisses already in a sense belong to her husband (259, note to 1396f). There is, however, a precedent, especially in fabliaux, for speaking of sexual favors as an exchangeable commodity. Cf. Chaucer's version of such a situation in The Shipman's Tale; see also Burrow's discussion of the fabliaux elements in the third fitt of *Gawain* (*Gawain* 77).

three kisses and one magical girdle in exchange for one stinking foxskin.

In one respect then, we must see the exchange as emphasizing the inequality of the gifts. Bertilak's earnings decrease in value—from hundreds of tasty deer, to one tough boar, to one inedible animal's smelly pelt, while Gawain's winnings progressively increase in number and value. On the other hand, on the last day there are several hints that, were the rules to be kept, an exchange of remarkably similar gifts would be made. Both girdle and fox pelt are external coverings to be lapped around one's garments; both are associated with guile and trickery. Nonetheless, the girdle has finally to be seen as worth more than the foxskin, especially since it is accompanied by three kisses, which by themselves Bertilak rates higher than the hunting *prys*.

At the same time that Bertilak in his Exchange-of-Winnings Game keeps insisting on judgment and evaluation, and an evaluation that, as Shoaf points out, is commercial and mercantile, the process of evaluation becomes harder and harder to do. Human activities, more precisely chivalric and courtly activities—such as hunting, flirting, feasting—are difficult to evaluate in concrete and commercial terms, especially if they are all part of Arthur's *aventures* and recited in a *laye*. If we reduce an activity, a process, to its end-result, that is, to its product or its *prys*, we would expect the comparison to be simpler. Such, however, is not the case, as the Exchange-of-Winnings Game demonstrates. Hidden factors (the unexchanged girdle), inherent inequalities (actions like kisses to things like venison), and a lack of clear standards—all make the judgments tricky and inconclusive. And yet we are repeatedly and insistently invited to judge. It turns out, of course, that we are meant to judge Gawain's behavior, not the prizes he wins himself, nor those he gains in exchange. In other words, it is the activity, the process and not the product, that is to be evaluated; and moreover it is only Gawain's luf-talking activity that is under scrutiny, not Bertilak's hunting.

Similar contradictions between the explicit and implicit exist in the poem's other game, the Beheading Game. Ostensibly, the terms and conditions are simple and clear. The Green Knight must endure one blow of the axe from Gawain, and one year later Gawain must submit to the same from the Green Knight. It is a test of courage and skill—the courage of the struck and the skill of the striker. Of course, as Gawain petulantly points out in the scene at the Green Chapel, the terms are not so simple and the exchange is not an exchange. The Green Knight needs no courage since he is impervious to mortal blows. Gawain, however faces near certain death, because, as he puts it: "Þaȝ my hede falle on þe stonez / I con not hit restore" (2282–83). Not only is the Beheading Game no test of the Green Knight's courage, it is also not actually a test of Gawain's skill. For, although Gawain administers the best blow possible, one that completely decapitates the Green Knight, he still must make the unwelcome journey to the Green Chapel to receive the return blow. This result is in direct refutation of the assurance King Arthur gives Gawain, with studied understatement, an assurance that at the time seems perfectly reasonable:

> "And if þou redez hym ryȝt, redly I trowe
> Þat þou schal byden þe bur þat he schal bede after."
> (373–74)

The Beheading Game is thus not at all an equal exchange, but it may be, at least in its tone and setting, a "Crystmas gomen" of holiday fun. The repeated irony, which mocks both King Arthur's confidence in Gawain's skill and Gawain's sense of fair play, invites the audience to smile indulgently at the hero, just as the Green Knight does in the last fitt (2335–36).[41] I doubt, however, that the audience is as ready as the Green Knight to find Gawain "on the fautlest freke þat euer on fote

[41]The text does not explicitly say that the Green Knight smiles, but I think it fair to assume that he is smiling, maybe even chuckling. What the text has is: ". . . in hert hit hym lykez. / Þenn he melez muryly wyth a much steuen / And, wyth a rynkande rurde, he to þe renk sayde" (2335–37). I would translate "melez muryly" as "speaks smilingly/laughingly"—cf. Borroff's translation, which has "gaily . . .calls" and Vantuono: "speaks merrily."

ȝede" (2363), any more than they are ready to condemn him in the same strongly censorious terms he uses on himself. However, while the poem is ambiguous about the final judgment regarding Gawain's behavior, it continues to focus on the need for judgment. Ever since the end of Fitt I, the game has been viewed largely as a test of Gawain's courage and honor, or specifically of his *trawþe*, as Burrow argues (*Gawain*, esp. 42–50).[42] While the importance of Gawain's experience is never wholly ridiculed, laughter undercuts the ostensible seriousness of the Beheading Game, which turns out not to be a mortal contest anyway.

However, the Beheading Game goes through another change even more radical, and this one is virtually unacknowledged by previous critics. In Fitt IV, when Gawain finally keeps his appointment at the Green Chapel, he learns that, although in some respects his *trawþe* is being tested, it is not tested so much in his pledge to the Green Knight as in his *forward* with Bertilak, just as it is not so much his courage to face the Green Knight but his courage to do so unaided that is in question. By revising the terms of the test in this way, the Green Knight has shifted the test from the Green Chapel back to the castle—backwards in the story, backwards in time, and backwards in space.

In addition, by shifting the test, from the Beheading Game to the Exchange-of-Winnings Game, the Green Knight and the poet have changed the Beheading Game from a test to a judgment, though not to a final judgment. Gawain arrives at the Green Chapel prepared, with a little help, to face an ordeal of testing; instead he endures an ordeal of judgment and penance. Furthermore, this revision of a test and final judgment to penance and equivocal judgment is directly linked to the poem's narrative *forme*: the poem begins with the chronological linearity of "Brutus bokez"; then promises a simple—that is a single—story; next changes that story by adding and imbedding a second story, which itself is cyclic and parallel, not linear; and then

[42]Compare Spearing, who thinks Burrow "exaggerates the centrality of *trawþe*" (*Gawain-Poet* 206–08).

finally delivers an ending that is not conclusive and closed, but ambiguous and open.

As A. Kent Hieatt has pointed out, this narrative tactic of "an unexpected but appropriate and organically developed second part of a story is practised" in both *Patience* and *Sir Gawain and the Green Knight* (*Patterns* 138). In both poems, the change in narrative patterns could be read as a metonymy of Providence. The respective stories do not end because history has not ended; the judgments are not final because history's is not. Penance—including remorse, forgiveness, and the promise of change—postpones the conclusion.[43]

However, whereas the stories in *Patience* are fully conversion *formez*, those in *Sir Gawain and the Green Knight* are not. For, although the linearity and conclusiveness of a judgment narrative are denied in *Gawain*, they are not replaced by the change of heart, much less the full open-endedness, that can be found in *Patience*. This, indeed, is the single most important difference between the secular *laye* and the sacred conversion story. Because *Sir Gawain and the Green Knight* is a *laye*, its *aventures* are not divine revelations, and its conversions and its calls for penance are equivocal for both its characters and its audience. Just as the judgment of Gawain's actions and of the Arthurian court is ambiguous and playful, so the change of heart is left unfulfilled, while the possibility of conversion in the present audience is closed off. To invite a courtly audience to "lysten . . . bot on littel quile" (30) is radically different from "Hear, O Israel," the traditional call to God's people found in the prophets. *Layes* are bits of entertainment. Even when about serious events, they are not serious, because they are only hearsay. Whether "in toun herde" (31) or recorded in the non-sacred "Brutus bokez," *layes* can be delightful exercises in storytelling and versification, and

[43]Cf. Braswell, who, in arguing for the importance of penance in the poet's characterizations, states that the Pearl poet has used "penance as character analysis" (100) in all four poems, but especially in *Gawain*. I have no doubt that the penitential tradition is important for the Pearl poet, as for his audience, though I am not sure it is as central as Braswell makes it.

even intriguing language games, yet they remain unreliable and ambiguous. *Layes* lack both the certainty of the closed and paradigmatic stories of *Cleanness* and also the authority of the voice of God, who speaks directly to Jonah in *Patience* and to Noah in *Cleanness*.

It could be otherwise; certainly some of the Pearl poet's contemporaries and predecessors in Arthurian literature moralized their tales and made them serious lessons with clear messages. That the poet who wrote so seriously, though not always without laughter, in three of his four surviving poems should choose to treat Arthurian *aventures* as pleasant tales—at best ones with ambiguous messages, at worst mere jokes—tells us much about his view of poetic *formez*. On the one hand, God's story, providential history, contains a variety of *formez*—narrative patterns, images, rhetorical structures, signs—some more complex than others, but all with an inner order and clarity, a match of form and content. On the other hand, a knight's story, a story from Arthur's time, can also take different *formez*, but the structure is not clear, and neither is the meaning. Moreover, just as in *Pearl* the *juelere's* setting for his pearl is brilliant but flawed, so the narrator's *laye* of *Sir Gawain and the Green Knight*, the "aunter in erde," is exciting but nonetheless anticlimactic and inconclusive. This inconclusiveness, this let-down and falling-off, is characteristic of a human poet's *formez*, and one feature that distinguishes them from God's *formez*. In *Gawain*, when the *laye* ends with a variety of audience responses within the text (the Green Knight's, Gawain's, the court's, even implicitly the narrator's, which seems closest to the Green Knight's), it is because the *laye*—including its events, its *formez*, and its meaning(s)—is a human creation. The Pearl poet does not conclude his Arthurian *aunter* with a final judgment (like those in *Cleanness*) or with an openended conversion (like the one in *Patience*) because his story is not God's, just as his dream in *Pearl* is not an apocalyptic vision, and his poem of *Pearl* is far from the divine setting for *perlez*.

It is important that we note the differences between the inconclusiveness of *Patience* and the ambiguous ending of *Sir Ga-*

wain and the Green Knight. Whereas *Patience* is a retelling of a divine story from the Bible, *Gawain* narrates a human *aunter* from tradition and the "Brutus bokez" (2523). The overall *forme* of sacred history is not finished for us living in it, but its unfinishedness is not an imperfection, as an interrupted human tale would be—it is part of its final perfection. From the maker's point of view, the *forme* of Providence is perfect, a complete circle that returns his creatures to their rightful home. The only human *formez* that approach this perfection, this marriage of meaning and message, are those borrowed, paraphrased, or translated from the human rendering of the divine story. The Bible, because it records sacred history, the story created by God and written under divine inspiration, provides the Pearl poet with his clearest and fairest *formez* as patterns. Only by reading *Sir Gawain and the Green Knight* in light of the poet's renderings of sacred history in *Cleanness* and *Patience* can we see the full extent and import of the celebrated ambiguities and ironies of this, his best-known and most-loved poem.[44]

Similarly, the poet's equally brilliant, if less celebrated, crafts of versification and language, so dazzingly displayed in *Pearl*, are best appreciated and understood when viewed in light of their context, both within *Pearl* itself and also within the manuscript as a whole. It is through the narrative frame of *Pearl*, the story of the dreamer's failed attempt to transform himself and his dream poem into a seer and his apocalyptic vision, that we are made to see the imperfection of human signs and visions as compared to divine ones. For, as *Cleanness* goes on to demon-

[44]Dane argues that irony in medieval literature lies mostly in the critics' readings, not in the texts themselves (4–5). This is surely often the case, and Dane's examples are compelling, but I would disagree in the case of *Gawain*. Here the paradoxes, contradictions, and discrepancies are definitely imbedded in the text, as they are not in the poet's other three poems (where any contradictions are either revealing paradoxes or attributable to the erroneous perceptions of the human mind—the entire lesson and exegesis of the Parable of the Vineyard in *Pearl* is the fullest example of both). This is just one of the many ways that reading *Gawain* in the light of the poet's other poems leads to a fuller appreciation of all four texts.

strate, humanity in the "middest," between the first and second comings, lacks the divine *formez* found in biblical history—the simple, direct words of God to his creatures. With few exceptions, most Christians can only partake secondhand in divinely sent visions of the kind recorded by John in the Apocalypse. What is instead available to the Pearl poet and his Christian audience are the *fayre formez* available through the sacraments; these, however, are visual and verbal signs that, like the verbal signs of the written record of the Bible, lack the immediacy of the presence of God enjoyed by patriarchs like Noah and prophets like Jonah, or by those privileged to live during Jesus's ministry. While the effects of the sacraments are to make Christians worthy to be with God, their visual and verbal signs serve primarily as reminders of the divine presence enjoyed in the historical past and as promises of the beatific vision to come. Still, sacramental *formez* far surpass the creations of a medieval poet. Neither the court of the best king ever nor the secondhand dream vision of a would-be seer can approach the fairness of the divine *formez* of biblical history and of the sacraments, the fairest *formez* available in this world and time.

WORKS CITED

Aers, David. "The Self Mourning: Reflections on *Pearl*." *Speculum* 68 (1993): 54–73.

Alter, Robert and Frank Kermode, eds. *The Literary Guide to the Bible*. Cambridge: Harvard University Press, 1987.

Anderson, J. J., ed. *Cleanness*. New York: Barnes and Noble, 1977.

______, ed. *Patience*. New York: Barnes and Noble, 1969.

Andrew, Malcolm. "Jonah and Christ." *Modern Philology* 70 (1972–73): 230–33.

______ and Ronald Waldron. *The Poems of the Pearl Manuscript: Pearl, Cleanness, Patience, Sir Gawain and the Green Knight*. Berkeley: University of California Press, 1979.

Augustini, S. Aurelii. Sermon 59. *Textus Eucharistici Selecti*. Florilegium Patristicum 35, p. 7. Ed. Hugo Lang. Bonn: Peter Hanstein, 1933.

______. *The City of God*. Trans. Marcus Dods. New York: Modern Library, 1950.

______. *St. Augustine's Confessions*. Ed. W. H. D. Rouse. Trans. William Watts (1612). 2 vols. London: Heinemann, 1912; New York: Putnam's, 1912 (vol. 1) and Cambridge: Harvard University Press, 1912 (vol. 2).

______. *Quaestionum in Heptateuchum*. Corpus Christianorum, Series Latina 33, part 5. Turnholt: Brepols, 1958.

Barthes, Roland. "The Death of the Author." *Image, Music, Text*. Ed. and trans. Stephen Heath. New York: Hill and Wang, 1977. 142–48.

Baswell, Christopher and William Sharpe, eds. *The Passing of Arthur: New Essays in Arthurian Tradition*. Garland Reference Library of Humanities 78. New York: Garland, 1988.

Beckwith, John. *Early Christian and Byzantine Art*. 2nd edition. New York: Penguin, 1979.

Bellosi, Luciano. *Giotto*. Florence: Becocci editore, 1981.

Benson, Larry D. *Art and Tradition in Sir Gawain and the Green Knight*. New Brunswick, New Jersey: Rutgers University Press, 1965.

______. "The Literary Character of Anglo-Saxon Formulaic Poetry." *PMLA* 81 (1966): 334–41.

Bercovitch, Sacvan. "Romance and Anti-Romance in *Sir Gawain and the Green Knight*." *Philological Quarterly* 44 (1965): 30–37. Rpt. in Howard and Zacher. 257–66.

Bernard of Clairvaux. *On the Song of Songs*. Trans. Kilian Walsh. 3 vols. Kalamazoo: Cistercian Publications, 1976–79.

Bishop, Ian. Pearl in *Its Setting: A Critical Study of the Structure and Meaning of the Middle English Poem*. Oxford: Blackwell; New York: Barnes and Noble, 1968.

Bloomfield, Morton. *Piers Plowman as a Fourteenth-Century Apocalypse*. New Brunswick: Rutgers University Press, 1961.

Boethius. *The Consolation of Philosophy*. Trans. S. J. Tester. *Tractates, De Consolatione philosophiae*. Loeb Classical Library. Cambridge: Harvard University Press, 1973.

Bogdanos, Theodore. *Pearl: Image of the Ineffable*. University Park: Pennsylvania State University Press, 1983.

Borroff, Marie. *Pearl: A New Verse Translation*. New York: Norton, 1977.

______. *Sir Gawain and the Green Knight: A New Verse Translation*. New York: Norton, 1967.

______. "*Sir Gawain and the Green Knight*: The Passing of Judgment." Baswell and Sharpe. 105–28.

______. *Sir Gawain and the Green Knight: A Stylistic and Metrical Study*. New Haven: Yale University Press, 1962.

Braswell, Mary Flowers. *The Medieval Sinner: Characterization and Confession in the Literature of the English Middle Ages*. Rutherford, NJ: Fairleigh Dickinson University Press, 1983.

Brewer, Derek S. "Courtesy and the Gawain-Poet." *Patterns of Love and Courtesy, Essays in Memory of C. S. Lewis*. Ed. John Lawlor. London: Arnold, 1966. 54–85.

Burrow, John A. *A Reading of* Sir Gawain and the Green Knight. New York: Barnes and Noble, 1966.

______. *Ricardian Poetry: Chaucer, Gower, Langland and the 'Gawain' Poet.* London: Routledge and Kegan Paul, 1971.

Carruthers, Mary. *The Book of Memory.* New York: Cambridge University Press, 1990.

Chapman, C. O. "Numerical Symbolism in Dante and The Pearl." *Modern Language Notes* 54 (1939): 256–59.

Chaucer, Geoffrey. *The Riverside Chaucer.* Gen. ed. Larry D. Benson. Boston: Houghton Mifflin, 1987.

Chaytor, H[enry] J. *From Script to Print: An Introduction to Medieval Vernacular Literature.* Cambridge: Heffer, 1945. Rpt. London: Sidgwick & Jackson, 1966.

Cheetham, Francis. *English Medieval Alabasters.* Oxford: Phaidon, Christie's, 1984.

Chrétien de Troyes. *Erec and Enide.* Ed. and trans. Carleton W. Carroll. Garland Library of Medieval Literature, Series A, vol. 25. New York: Garland, 1987.

______. *The Knight with the Lion or Yvain* (Le Chevalier au Lion). Ed. and trans. William W. Kibler. Garland Library of Medieval Literature, series A, vol. 1. New York: Garland, 1985.

______. *Lancelot, or the Knight of the Cart.* Ed. and trans. William W. Kibler. Garland Library of Medieval Literature, series A, vol. 1. New York: Garland, 1984.

Christe, Yves. *Les Grands Portails Romains.* Geneva: Droz, 1969.

The Cloisters Apocalypse (facsimile). New York: Metropolitan Museum of Art, 1971.

Collins, John J. *The Apocalyptic Imagination: An Introduction to the Jewish Matrix of Christianity.* New York: Crossroad, 1984.

Conley, John, ed. *The Middle English* Pearl: *Critical Essays.* Notre Dame: University of Notre Dame Press, 1970.

Cuffe, E. D. "An Interpretation of *Patience*, *Cleanness* and the *Pearl* from the Viewpoint of Imagery." Diss. University of North Carolina, 1951.

Dane, Joseph A. *The Critical Mythology of Irony.* Athens: The University of Georgia Press, 1991.

Dante Alighieri. *The Divine Comedy.* 6 vols. Ed. and trans.

Charles S. Singleton. Bollingen Series 80. Princeton: Princeton University Press, 1970–75.

———. *Dante's Rime*. Trans. Patrick S. Diehl. Princeton: Princeton University Press, 1979.

Davenport, W. A. *The Art of the Gawain-Poet*. London: Athlone, 1978.

D'Aragon, Jean-Louis, S.J. "The Apocalypse." *The Jerome Biblical Commentary*. 2: 467–93.

Derrida, Jacques. "Of an Apocalyptic Tone recently adopted in Philosophy." Trans. John P. Leavey, Jr. *Derrida and Biblical Studies*. Ed. Robert Detweiler. Special issue of *Semeia: an experimental journal for biblical criticism* 23 (1982). 61–97.

———. *Of Grammatology*. Trans. Gayatri Chakravorty Spivak. Baltimore: Johns Hopkins University Press, 1974.

Derrida and Biblical Studies. Ed. Robert Detweiler. Special issue of *Semeia: an experimental journal for biblical criticism* 23 (1982).

Diekstra, F. N. M. "Jonah and *Patience*: The Psychology of a Prophet." *English Studies* 55 (1974): 205–17.

Dodd, Charles H. *The Parables of the Kingdom*. New York: Scribner, 1961.

Doob, Penelope B. R. *Nebuchadnezzar's Children: Conventions of Madness in Middle English Literature*. New Haven: Yale University Press, 1974.

Economou, George D. and Joan M. Ferrante, eds. *In Pursuit of Perfection: Courtly Love in Medieval Literature*. Port Washington, NY: Kennikat, 1975.

Edward of Norwich, Second Duke of York. *The Master of Game*. Ed. William and F. Baillie-Grohman. London: Ballatyne, Hanson, 1904.

Emmerson, Richard Kenneth. *Antichrist in the Middle Ages: A Study of Medieval Apocalypticism, Art, and Literature*. Seattle: University of Washington Press, 1981.

Fisher, Sheila. "Leaving Morgan Aside: Women, History, and Revisionism in *Sir Gawain and the Green Knight*." Baswell and Sharpe. 129–51.

Fleischman, Suzanne. "Philology, Linguistics, and the Discourse of the Medieval Text." *The New Philology*. Special issue of *Speculum* 65 (1990). Ed. Stephen G. Nichols, Jr. 19–37.

Gager, John G. "The Attainment of Millennial Bliss Through Myth: The Book of Revelation." *Kingdom and Community*. Englewood Cliffs, NJ: Prentice-Hall, 1975. 49–57, 64–65 (notes). Rpt. in Hanson 146–55.

Ganim, John. *Style and Consciousness in Middle English Literature*. Princeton: Princeton University Press, 1983.

Genette, Gérard. *Figures of Literary Discourse*. Trans. Alan Sheridan. New York: Columbia University Press, 1982.

Giamatti, A. Bartlett. *The Earthly Paradise and the Renaissance Epic*. Princeton: Princeton University Press, 1966.

Goldin, Frederick, ed. and trans. *Lyrics of the Troubadours and Trouvères*. Garden City, NY: Anchor, 1973.

Gollancz, Sir Israel, ed. Cleanness. 2 vols. Vols. 7 and 9 of *Select Early English Poems*. London: Oxford University Press, 1921, 1933. Rpt. in one vol., with trans. by D. S. Brewer, Cambridge and Totowa: Rowman and Littlefield, 1974.

______, ed. *Facsimile Reproduction of Cotton Nero A.x. in the British Museum*. EETS 162. London: Oxford University Press, 1923.

______, ed. *Patience: An Alliterative Version of Jonah by the Poet of Pearl*. Vol. 1 of *Select Early English Poems*. 2nd edition. London: Oxford University Press, 1924.

______, ed. and trans. *Pearl*. London, 1891; rev. ed. 1897; 2nd ed. with Boccaccio's *Olympia*, 1921.

______, ed. *Sir Gawain and the Green Knight*. Introductory essays by Mabel and Mary S. Serjeantson. EETS 210. London: Oxford University Press, 1940.

Gordon, E.V., ed. *Pearl*. Oxford: Clarendon, 1953.

Gospel of Nicodemus, The. Acts of Pilate and Christ's Descent into Hell. Ed. and trans. F. Scheiderweiler. *Gospels and Related Writings*. Vol. 1 of *New Testament Apocrypha*. 3rd ed. Ed. Edgar Hennecke and Wilhelm Schneemelcher. Ed. (for English trans.) R. McL. Wilson. Philadelphia: Westminster, 1963. 444–84.

Grabar, André. *Christian Iconography: A Study of Its Origins*. Bolingen Series 35.10. Princeton: Princeton University Press, 1968.

Hanning, Robert W. *The Individual in Twelfth-Century Romance.* New Haven: Yale University Press, 1977.

______. " 'Mony Turned Tyme': The Cycle of the Year as a Religious Symbol in Two Medieval Texts." *Saints, Scholars, and Heroes*. Ed. Margot H. King and Wesley M. Stevens. Collegeville, MN: Hill Monastic Manuscript and Library, 1979. 281–98.

______. "Setting a Limit: Loss, Landscape, and Language in *Pearl*." Paper, Division on Middle English Literature, excluding Chaucer, MLA Convention. Chicago, 29 December, 1985.

______. "Sir Gawain and the Red Herring." *Acts of Interpretation: The Text in its Context—Essays in Honor of E. Talbot Donaldson*. Ed. Mary J. Carruthers and Elizabeth D. Kirk. Norman, OK: Pilgrim, 1982.

______. *The Vision of History in Early Britain: From Gildas to Geoffrey of Monmouth.* New York: Columbia University Press, 1966.

Hanson, Paul D., ed. *Visionaries and their Apocalypses*. Philadelphia: Fortress, 1983.

Happé, Peter, ed. *English Mystery Plays*. Baltimore: Penguin, 1975.

Harrison, F. *Stained Glass of York Minster*. London: Studio, n.d.

Harwood, Britton J. "*Gawain* and the Gift." *PMLA* 106 (1991): 483–99.

Hearn, M. F. *Romanesque Sculpture*. Ithaca: Cornell University Press, 1981.

Henderson, George. "English Manuscript Illumination, Part II: The English Apocalypse." *Journal of the Warburg and Courtauld Institutes* 30 (1967): 104–37.

Heng, Geraldine. "Feminine Knots and the Other *Sir Gawain and the Green Knight*." PMLA 106 (1991): 500–14.

Hieatt, A. Kent. "*Sir Gawain*: Pentangle, *Luf-Lace*, Numerical Structure." *Papers on Language and Literature* 4 (1968): 339–59.

______. "Symbolic and Narrative Patterns in *Pearl*, *Cleanness*, *Patience*, and *Gawain*." *English Studies in Canada* 2 (1976): 125–43.

Hill, Ordelle G. "The Audience of Patience." *Modern Philology* 66 (1968): 103–09.

Howard, Donald R. and Christian K. Zacher, ed. *Critical Studies of* Sir Gawain and the Green Knight. Notre Dame: University of Notre Dame Press, 1968.

______. "Structure and Symmetry in *Sir Gawain*." Speculum 39 (1964): 425–33. Rpt. in Howard and Zacher 159–63.

Howes, Laura. "Chaucer's Gardens: The Language of Convention." Diss. Columbia University, 1991.

The Jerome Biblical Commentary. Ed. Raymond E. Brown, Joseph A. Fitzmyer, and Roland E. Murphy. 2 vols. Englewood Cliffs, NJ: Prentice-Hall, 1968.

Johnson, Barbara. Introduction. *Dissemination*. By Jacques Derrida. Chicago: University of Chicago Press, 1981.

Johnson, Lynn Staley. *The Voice of the Gawain-Poet*. Madison: University of Wisconsin Press, 1984.

Johnson, Wendell Stacey. "The Imagery and Diction of *The Pearl*: Toward an Interpretation." *ELH* 20 (1953): 161–80. Rpt. in Conley 93–115.

Jonassen, Frederick B. "Elements from the Traditional Drama of England in *Sir Gawain and the Green Knight*." *Viator* 17 (1986): 221–54.

Jordan, Robert M. *Chaucer's Poetics and the Modern Reader*. Berkeley: University of California Press, 1987.

Kean, P. M. *The Pearl: An Interpretation*. London: Routledge and Kegan Paul, 1967.

Kelly, T. D. and John T. Irwin. "The Meaning of *Cleanness*: Parable as Effective Sign." *Mediaeval Studies* 35 (1973): 232–60.

Kermode, Frank. *The Sense of an Ending: Studies in the Theory of Fiction*. New York: Oxford University Press, 1967.

Kirk, Elizabeth. " 'Who Suffreth More Than God?' Narrative Redefinition of Patience in *Patience* and *Piers Plowman*." *The*

Triumph of Patience. Ed. Gerald J. Schiffhorst. Orlando, Fla.: University Presses of Florida, 1978. Pp. 88–104.

Kittendorf, Doris E. "*Cleanness* and the Fourteenth Century *Artes Praedicandi*." *Michigan Academician* 11 (1979): 319–30.

Koch, Klaus. "What is Apocalyptic? An Attempt at a Preliminary Definition." *The Rediscovery of Apocalyptic*. Trans. M. Kohl. London: SCM Press, 1972. 16–36, 132–38 (notes). Rpt. in Hanson 16–36.

Kottler, Barnet and Alan M. Markman, ed. *A Concordance to Five Middle English Poems*. Pittsburgh: University of Pittsburgh Press, 1966.

Landes, George. "The Kerygma of the Book of Jonah." *Interpretation* 21 (1967): 3–39.

[*Les Livres du Roy Modus et de la Royne Ratio*.] MS. M820. Morgan Library, New York.

Les Livres du Roy Modus et de la Royne Ratio. Ed. Gunnar Tilander. Paris: Société des anciens textes français, 1932.

Lewis, C. S. *The Allegory of Love*. New York: Oxford University Press, 1958.

Loomis, Laura Hibbard. "*Gawain and the Green Knight*." Arthurian *Literature in the Middle Ages: A Collaborative History*. Ed. Roger Sherman Loomis. Oxford: Clarendon, 1959. 528–40. Rpt. in Howard and Zacher 3–23.

Luria, Maxwell and Richard Hoffman. *Middle English Lyrics*. New York: Norton, 1974.

Luttrell, Claude. "An Introduction to the Dream in *Pearl*." *Medium Aevum* 47 (1978): 274–91.

Mâle, Emil. *The Gothic Image*. Trans. Dora Nussey from the 3rd French ed. New York: Harper, 1958. Rpt. of *Religious Art in France of the Thirteenth Century*. New York: Dutton, 1913.

———. *Religious Art in France, The Twelfth Century: A Study of the Origins of Medieval Iconography*. Trans. Marthiel Mathews from the 1953 French ed. Princeton: Princeton University Press, 1978.

Mancinelli, Fabrizio. *Catacombs and Basilicas*. Florence: Scala, 1981.

Marie de France. *Les Lais de Marie de France*. Ed. Jean Rychner. Paris: Honoré Champion, 1978.

______. *The Lais of Marie de France*. Trans. Robert Hanning and Joan Ferrante. Durham, NC: Labyrinth, 1978.

Matter, E. Ann. *The Voice of My Beloved: The Song of Songs in Western Medieval Christianity*. Philadelphia: University of Pennsylvania Press, 1990.

Matthew of Vendôme. *Ars versificatoria. Les arts poétiques du xiie et du XIIe et due XIIIe siècle. Ed. Edmond Faral. Paris: Honoré Champion, 1958. 106–93.*

______. *The Art of Versification by Matthew of Vendôme*. Aubrey E. Galyon, trans. Ames: University of Iowa Press, 1980.

McGinn, Bernard. *Visions of the End: Apocalyptic Traditions in the Middle Ages*. Records of Civilization, Sources and Studies 96. New York: Columbia University Press, 1979.

______. "Revelation." Alter and Kermode. 523–41.

McKenzie, John L. *The Gospel according to Saint Matthew. The Jerome Biblical Commentary*. 2: 62–114.

Means, Michael. "The Homiletic Structure of Cleanness." *Studies in Medieval Culture* 5 (1975): 165–72.

Menner, Robert J., ed. *Purity, a Middle English Poem*. [Cleanness]. New Haven: Yale University Press, 1920; rpt. Hamden, CT: Archon, 1970.

Middle English Dictionary. Ed. Hans Kurath et al. Ann Arbor: University of Michigan Press, 1952- .

Miller, Joseph M., Michael H. Prosser, and Thomas W. Benson, eds. *Readings in Medieval Rhetoric*. Bloomington: Indiana University Press, 1973.

Minnis, A[lastair] J. *Medieval Theory of Authorship: Scholastic literary attitudes in the later Middle Ages*. 2nd ed. Philadelphia: University of Pennsylvania Press, 1984.

Moorman, Charles. *The Pearl-Poet*. New York: Twayne, 1968.

______, ed. *The Works of the Gawain-Poet*. Jackson: University Press of Mississippi, 1977.

Morey, Charles M. *Early Christian Art*. Princeton: Princeton University Press, 1942.

Morris, Richard, ed. *Early English Alliterative Poems in the West*

Midland dialect of the Fourteenth Century. EETS 1. London: Tbner, 1864; 1869. Rpt. London: Oxford University Press, 1965.

Morse, Charlotte C. *The Pattern of Judgment in the Queste and Cleanness*. Columbia: University of Missouri Press, 1978.

Murphy, James J. *Rhetoric in the Middle Ages*. Berkeley: University of California Press, 1974.

Muscatine, Charles. *Poetry and Crisis in the Age of Chaucer*. Notre Dame: University of Notre Dame Press, 1972.

Nelson, Cary. "*Pearl*: the circle as figural space." *The Incarnate Word: Literature as Verbal Space*. Urbana: University of Illinois Press, 1973.

Nelson, William. "From 'Listen, Lordings' to 'Dear Reader.' " *University of Toronto Quarterly* 46 (1976–77): 110–24.

New American Bible, The. Saint Joseph edition. Trans. Members of the Catholic Biblical Association of America. New York: Catholic Book, 1970.

New English Bible, The. Oxford: Oxford University Press and Cambridge University Press, 1970.

Nichols, Stephen G., Jr., ed. *The New Philology*. Special issue of *Speculum* 65 (1990).

———. *Romanesque Signs: Early Medieval Narrative and Iconography*. New Haven: Yale University Press, 1983.

Nolan, Barbara. *The Gothic Visionary Perspective*. Princeton: Princeton University Press, 1977.

Olson, Glending. "Deschamps' Art de Dictier and Chaucer's Literary Environment." *Speculum* 48 (1973): 714–23.

Osgood, Charles, ed. *The Pearl: A Middle English Poem*. Boston: Heath, 1906.

Patch, Howard R. *The Other World, according to Descriptions in Medieval Literature*. Cambridge: Harvard University Press, 1950.

Piehler, Paul. *The Visionary Landscape: A Study in Medieval Allegory*. Montreal: McGill-Queen's University Press, 1971.

Piers Plowman in Three Parallel Texts. Ed. Walter W. Skeat. 2 vols. London: Oxford University Press, 1886; 1969.

Planchenault, René. *L'Apocalypse d'Angers*. Paris: Caisse Nationale des Monuments Historiques et des Sites, 1966.

Prior, Sandra Pierson. "*Gomens* and *Hert-Huntyng*: The Role of the Hunt in *Sir Gawain and the Green Knight* and in *The Book of the Duchess*." Master's Thesis. Columbia University, 1977.

______. "Parodying Typology and the Mystery Plays in the Miller's Tale." *Journal of Medieval and Renaissance Studies* 16 (1986): 57–73.

______. "*Patience*—Beyond Apocalypse." *Modern Philology* 83 (1986): 337–48.

______. "Poet of the Word: Patterns and Images of the Apocalypse in the Works of the Pearl Poet." Diss. Columbia University, 1983.

Readings in Medieval Rhetoric. Ed. Joseph M. Miller, Michael H. Prosser, and Thomas W. Benson. Bloomington: University of Indiana Press, 1973.

Renoir, Alain. "Descriptive Techniques in *Sir Gawain and the Green Knight*." *Orbis Litterarum: International Review of Literary Studies* 13 (1958): 126–32.

______. "The Progressive Magnification: An Instance of Psychological Description in *Sir Gawain and the Green Knight*. Moderna Språk 54 (1960): 245–53.

Robertson, D. W., Jr. "*The Pearl* as a Symbol." *Modern Language Notes* 45 (1950): 155–61. Rpt. in Conley. 18–26.

Russell, David. *The Method and Message of Jewish Apocalyptic, 200 BC–AD 100*. Philadelphia: Westminster, 1964.

Russell, J. Stephen. *The English Dream Vision: Anatomy of a Form*. Columbus: Ohio State University Press, 1988.

Salter, Elizabeth. "Alliterative Revival I." *Modern Philology* 64 (1966–67): 146–50.

Savage, Henry L. *The Gawain-Poet: Studies in His Personality and Background*. Chapel Hill: University of North Carolina Press, 1956.

Sawles Warde. Early Middle English Verse and Prose. Ed. J. A. W. Bennett and G. V. Smithers. 2nd ed. Oxford: Clarendon Press, 1968. 246–61.

Schapiro, Meyer. *Romanesque Art*. New York: Braziller, 1977.

Scenes from the Life of Christ in English Manuscripts. Oxford: Bodleian Library, 1951.

Schless, Howard H. "*Pearl's* "Princes Paye" and the Law." *Chaucer Review* 24 (1989): 183–85.

Schleusner, Jay. "History and Action in *Patience*." *PMLA* 86 (1971): 959–65.

Schneidau, Herbert N. "The Word Against the Word: Derrida on Textuality." *Derrida and Biblical Studies*. 5–28.

Shoaf, R. A. *The Poem as Green Girdle: Commercium* in *Sir Gawain and the Green Knight*. University of Florida Monographs, Humanities 55. Gainesville: University Presses of Florida, 1984.

______. "The 'Syngne of Surfet' and the Surfeit of Signs in *Sir Gawain and the Green Knight*." Baswell and Sharpe. 152–69.

Silverstein, Theodore. *Sir Gawain and the Green Knight: A New Critical Edition*. Chicago: University of Chicago Press, 1984.

______. "Sir Gawain in a Dilemma, or Keeping Faith with Marcus Tullius Cicero." *Modern Philology* 75 (1977–78): 1–17.

Smalley, Beryl. *The Study of the Bible in the Middle Ages*. Notre Dame: The University of Notre Dame Press, 1964.

Spearing, A[nthony] C. *Medieval Dream-Poetry*. Cambridge: Cambridge University Press, 1976.

______. *The Gawain-Poet, a Critical Study*. Cambridge: Cambridge University Press, 1970.

Stanbury, Sarah. *Seeing the Gawain-Poet*. Philadephia: University of Pennsylvania Press, 1991.

Stevens, Martin. "Laughter and Game in *Sir Gawain and the Green Knight*. Speculum 47 (1972): 65–78.

Tajima, Matsuji. "Additional Syntactical Evidence against the Common Authorship of Ms. Cotton Nero A.x." *English Studies* 59 (1978): 193–98.

Tayler, Edward W. *Milton's Poetry: Its Development in Time*. Pittsburg: Duquesne University Press, 1979.

———. *Donne's Idea of a Woman: Structure and Meaning in The Anniversaries*. New York: Columbia University Press, 1991.

Tertullian. *On Monogamy*. Trans. S. Thelwell. In *The Writings of Tertullian*, vol. 3. Ed. Alexander Roberts and James Donaldson. Edinburgh: T. & T. Clark, 1870. 21–55.

Thiébaux, Marcelle. *The Stag of Love*. Ithaca: Cornell University Press, 1974.

———. "Sir Gawain, the Fox Hunt, and Henry of Lancaster." *Neuphilologische Mitteilungen* 71 (1970): 469–79.

———. "The Mediaeval Chase." *Speculum* 42 (1967): 260–74.

Tolkien, J. R. R. and E. V. Gordon, eds. *Sir Gawain and the Green Knight*. 2nd ed. rev. by Norman Davis. Oxford: Clarendon Press, 1967.

[*Trinity College Apocalypse*]. MS. R.16.2. Trinity College, Cambridge.

The Trinity College Apocalypse. 2 vols. Ed. Peter H. Brieger. London: Eugrammia, 1967.

The Trinity College Apocalypse. Ed. Montague Rhodes James. London: Roxburghe Club, 1909.

Turville-Petre, Thorlac. *The Alliterative Revival*. Totowa, NJ: Rowman and Littlefield, 1977.

van der Meer, Frederick. *Apocalypse: Visions from the Book of Revelation in Western Art*. London: Thames and Hudson, 1978.

Vance, Eugene. *Mervelous Signals: Poetics and Sign Theory in the Middle Ages*. Lincoln, Nebraska: University of Nebraska Press, 1986.

Vantuono, William. "*Patience*, *Cleanness*, *Pearl*, and *Gawain*: The Case for Common Authorship." *Annuale Medievale* 12 (1971): 37–69.

———. "The Structure and Sources of *Patience*." *Mediaeval Studies* 34 (1972): 401–21.

———. *The Pearl Poems: An Omnibus Edition*. 2 vols. The Renaissance Imagination 5 and 6. New York: Garland, 1984.

The Vatican Collections: The Papacy and Art. New York: Metropolitan Museum of Art; Harry N. Abrams, 1982.

Vincent of Beauvais. *Speculum historiale*. Graz, Austria: Akademische Druck, 1965. Vol. 4 of *Speculum quadruplex sive speculum maius*. 4 vols. Rpt. of 1624 ed.

Waldron, Ronald. A. "Oral-Formulaic Technique and Middle English Alliterative Poetry." *Speculum* 32 (1957): 792–804.

Williams, John. *Early Spanish Manuscript Illumination*. New York: Braziller, 1977.

Wilson, Edward. *The Gawain-Poet*. Leiden: Brill, 1976.

Wilson, R[ichard]. M. *The Lost Literature of Medieval England*. 2nd edition. London: Methuen, 1970.

Wood, Ann Douglas. "The Pearl-Dreamer and the 'Hyne' in the Vineyard Parable." *Philological Quarterly* 52 (1973): 9–19.

Zarnecki, George, Janet Holt, and Tristram Holland. *English Romanesque Art 1066–1200*. London: Arts Council of Great Britain, 1984.

INDEX